VIOLENCE

IN AMERICA
OPPOSING VIEWPOINTS®

Other Books of Related Interest in the Opposing Viewpoints Series:
America's Prisons
Chemical Dependency
Crime and Criminals
Criminal Justice
The Death Penalty
Drug Abuse

Additional Books in the Opposing Viewpoints Series:
Abortion
AIDS
American Foreign Policy
American Government
American Values
America's Elections
America's Future
Animal Rights
Biomedical Ethics
Censorship
Central America
China
Civil Liberties
Constructing a Life Philosophy
Death and Dying
Economics in America
The Elderly
The Environmental Crisis
Euthanasia
Genetic Engineering
The Health Crisis
The Homeless
Israel
Japan
Latin America and U.S. Foreign Policy
Male/Female Roles
The Mass Media
The Middle East
Nuclear War
The Political Spectrum
Poverty
Problems of Africa
Religion in America
Science & Religion
Sexual Values
Social Justice
The Soviet Union
The Superpowers: A New Detente
Teenage Sexuality
Terrorism
The Third World
The Vietnam War
War and Human Nature

VIOLENCE IN AMERICA
OPPOSING VIEWPOINTS®

David Bender & Bruno Leone, *Series Editors*

Janelle Rohr, *Book Editor*

OPPOSING VIEWPOINTS SERIES ®

Greenhaven Press, Inc.   PO Box 289009   San Diego, CA 92198-0009

Library of Congress Cataloging-in-Publication Data

Violence in America: opposing viewpoints / Janelle Rohr.
     p.   cm. — (Opposing viewpoints series)
   Includes bibliographical references.
   Summary: Various authors debate the causes of violence, the prevalence of family and teen violence, the motivation of serial killers, and ways to reduce violence.
   ISBN 0-89908-449-4 (lib. bdg.). — ISBN 0-89908-424-9 (pbk.)
   1. Violence—United States. 2. Family violence—United States. 3. Serial murders—United States. [1. Violence. 2. Critical thinking.]   I. Rohr, Janelle, 1963-   . II. Series.
HN90.V5V55   1990
303.6'0973—dc20
                                                        89-25943
                                                             CIP
                                                              AC

"Congress shall make no law...
abridging the freedom of speech,
or of the press."

First Amendment to the U.S. Constitution

The basic foundation of our democracy is the first amendment guarantee of freedom of expression. The *Opposing Viewpoints Series* is dedicated to the concept of this basic freedom and the idea that it is more important to practice it than to enshrine it.

Contents

Why Consider Opposing Viewpoints?

"It is better to debate a question without settling it than to settle a question without debating it."

Joseph Joubert (1754-1824)

The Importance of Examining Opposing Viewpoints

The purpose of the Opposing Viewpoints books, and this book in particular, is to present balanced, and often difficult to find, opposing points of view on complex and sensitive issues.

Probably the best way to become informed is to analyze the positions of those who are regarded as experts and well studied on issues. It is important to consider every variety of opinion in an attempt to determine the truth. Opinions from the mainstream of society should be examined. But also important are opinions that are considered radical, reactionary, or minority as well as those stigmatized by some other uncomplimentary label. An important lesson of history is the eventual acceptance of many unpopular and even despised opinions. The ideas of Socrates, Jesus, and Galileo are good examples of this.

Readers will approach this book with their own opinions on the issues debated within it. However, to have a good grasp of one's own viewpoint, it is necessary to understand the arguments of those with whom one disagrees. It can be said that those who do not completely understand their adversary's point of view do not fully understand their own.

A persuasive case for considering opposing viewpoints has been presented by John Stuart Mill in his work *On Liberty*. When examining controversial issues it may be helpful to reflect on this suggestion:

> The only way in which a human being can make some approach to knowing the whole of a subject, is by hearing what can be said about it by persons of every variety of opinion, and studying all modes in which it can be looked at by every character of mind. No wise man ever acquired his wisdom in any mode but this.

Analyzing Sources of Information

The Opposing Viewpoints books include diverse materials taken from magazines, journals, books, and newspapers, as well as statements and position papers from a wide range of individuals, organizations and governments. This broad spectrum of sources helps to develop patterns of thinking which are open to the consideration of a variety of opinions.

Pitfalls to Avoid

A pitfall to avoid in considering opposing points of view is that of regarding one's own opinion as being common sense and the most rational stance and the point of view of others as being only opinion and naturally wrong. It may be that another's opinion is correct and one's own is in error.

Another pitfall to avoid is that of closing one's mind to the opinions of those with whom one disagrees. The best way to approach a dialogue is to make one's primary purpose that of understanding the mind and arguments of the other person and not that of enlightening him or her with one's own solutions. More can be learned by listening than speaking.

It is my hope that after reading this book the reader will have a deeper understanding of the issues debated and will appreciate the complexity of even seemingly simple issues on which good and honest people disagree. This awareness is particularly important in a democratic society such as ours where people enter into public debate to determine the common good. Those with whom one disagrees should not necessarily be regarded as enemies, but perhaps simply as people who suggest different paths to a common goal.

Developing Basic Reading and Thinking Skills

In this book carefully edited opposing viewpoints are purposely placed back to back to create a running debate; each viewpoint is preceded by a short quotation that best expresses the author's main argument. This format instantly plunges the reader into the midst of a controversial issue and greatly aids that reader in mastering the basic skill of recognizing an author's point of view.

A number of basic skills for critical thinking are practiced in the activities that appear throughout the books in the series. Some of the skills are:

Evaluating Sources of Information   The ability to choose from among alternative sources the most reliable and accurate source in relation to a given subject.

Separating Fact from Opinion   The ability to make the basic distinction between factual statements (those that can be demonstrated or verified empirically) and statements of opinion (those that are beliefs or attitudes that cannot be proved).

Identifying Stereotypes   The ability to identify oversimplified, exaggerated descriptions (favorable or unfavorable) about people and insulting statements about racial, religious or national groups, based upon misinformation or lack of information.

Recognizing Ethnocentrism   The ability to recognize attitudes or opinions that express the view that one's own race, culture, or group is inherently superior, or those attitudes that judge another culture or group in terms of one's own.

It is important to consider opposing viewpoints and equally important to be able to critically analyze those viewpoints. The activities in this book are designed to help the reader master these thinking skills. Statements are taken from the book's viewpoints and the reader is asked to analyze them. This technique aids the reader in developing skills that not only can be applied to the viewpoints in this book, but also to situations where opinionated spokespersons comment on controversial issues. Although the activities are helpful to the solitary reader, they are most useful when the reader can benefit from the interaction of group discussion.

Using this book and others in the series should help readers develop basic reading and thinking skills. These skills should improve the readers' ability to understand what they read. Readers should be better able to separate fact from opinion, substance from rhetoric and become better consumers of information in our media-centered culture.

This volume of the Opposing Viewpoints books does not advocate a particular point of view. Quite the contrary! The very nature of the book leaves it to the reader to formulate the opinions he or she finds most suitable. My purpose as publisher is to see that this is made possible by offering a wide range of viewpoints which are fairly presented.

David L. Bender
Publisher

Introduction

"Violence is as American as cherry pie."

—Stokely Carmichael

While violence and crime have plagued the United States since its founding, skyrocketing violent crime rates in the 1960s sharpened public concern. Between 1960 and 1975, crime rose 232 percent and the murder rate increased from 4.7 per 100,000 people to 10.2 per 100,000 people. The public also learned that teenagers were implicated in violent crimes more often—the Office of Juvenile Justice and Delinquency Prevention linked youths eighteen years old and younger to almost one-fourth of the violent crimes committed. This violence raises questions that haunt sociologists, criminologists, and others. Do people act violently because of environmental factors or is violent behavior an innate characteristic?

Several experts contend that the seeds of violence are sown in childhood. They cite studies showing that 70 to 80 percent of the inmates in prisons were victims of child abuse. Researchers Joan Kaufman and Edward Zigler found that almost one-third of abused children grow up to abuse their children. And Los Angeles lawyer Paul Mones, who specializes in defending children who kill their parents, believes that over 90 percent of children who kill their parents suffered physical, sexual, and mental abuse. In addition to the abuse they suffer, Mones contends, "It's the violence they witness being done to people around them. It desensitizes them to violence."

Children who grow up in neighborhoods where drug dealing and crime are common also witness a great deal of violence, and many observers fear that these children too are more likely to grow up to be violent teens and adults. In a nationally televised speech on drug policy, President George Bush cited the case of Dooney Waters, a first grader in Washington, D.C., who lived in a crack house. Dooney's mother was a crack dealer and his thirteen-year-old brother had been arrested six times in two years for a variety of offenses. Random gunfire and fighting were common on Dooney's street. Dooney asked his teachers if he could sleep on the school's floor so he would not have to go home. "Drugs have wrecked my mother," he observed, "if I don't be careful, drugs

13

are going to wreck me too." He said, "I don't want to sell drugs, but I will probably have to." While most people do not experience the extent of violence that Dooney witnessed, a large percentage of violent criminals are born and raised in such environments.

Some authorities consider this an exaggerated and inaccurate view. These people believe individual choice plays a large role in violent behavior. A leading proponent of this perspective is Stanton E. Samenow, a psychologist who has counseled criminals for many years. Samenow points out that the majority of children who are abused do not grow up to be violent criminals. He states, "In nearly every case, when I interview a criminal from an oppressive social environment, I find that he has siblings and neighbors living under the same or perhaps worse conditions who are law-abiding citizens." According to Samenow, the delinquent "begins making a series of choices to live a life that he considers exciting, a life in which he is determined to do whatever he wants, a life in which he ignores restraint and eventually turns against his family and scoffs at those who live responsible lives." Thus Samenow concludes, "It is *not* the environment per se that is critical, but how people *choose* to respond to that environment."

Similarly, Jack Katz, a sociologist who has studied youth gangs, found that some teens choose the deviant and violent life-style of the gang because they want attention. In his book, *Seductions of Crime*, Katz quotes a teen who scoffs at the idea that "dudes is after the things straight people got. . . . People in the life ain't looking for no home and grass in the yard." Gang members choose a violent life-style, this teen maintains, because it satisfies their need to be "the show people. The glamour people. Come on the set with the finest car, the finest woman, the finest vines. Hear people talking about you. Hear the bar get quiet when you walk in the door." Samenow, Katz, and others believe that a certain amount of violence is inevitable, simply because some people will always choose to use violence to get what they want.

With one in four households victimized by theft or violent crime, the controversy over its causes inspires heated debate. *Violence in America: Opposing Viewpoints* probes the following questions: Is Violence in America a Serious Problem? How Can Drug-Related Violence Be Reduced? What Causes Family Violence? What Causes Teen Violence? What Motivates Serial Killers? What Policies Would Reduce Violence? No matter what the cause, violence remains a frightening and perplexing problem. What factors cause some of America's children to become violent criminals will remain a critical issue.

Is Violence in America a Serious Problem?

Chapter Preface

Catherine Genovese had only one hundred yards to walk to her Queens apartment building after she got off work and parked her car at 3:20 a.m. on March 13, 1964. As she walked toward the building, Winston Moseley attacked her with a knife. Genovese screamed for help and Moseley left briefly. When he returned, he stabbed her again and she screamed, "I'm dying, I'm dying." He left and she crawled indoors. Later he returned and found her in a staircase. He sexually assaulted her and stabbed her yet again. She screamed, then lost consciousness and died.

The horror of the crime was not the only thing that attracted attention: During the thirty-minute attack, thirty-eight people in the neighborhood were awake, heard Genovese's screams, and did nothing. No one intervened; no one called the police. Genovese could probably have been saved had someone called, according to A.M. Rosenthal, then a *New York Times* reporter who later wrote a book on the incident. The Genovese case and similar incidents raised questions about Americans' attitudes toward violence and their willingness to take action to fight violence. Some experts believe that the apparent indifference shown in the Genovese case is a widespread attitude that exacerbates the problem of violence in America.

The U.S. has the highest rate of violent crime among industrialized nations—every five seconds a violent crime is committed. Sociologists, historians, and others offer many different reasons as they try to determine why a wealthy, prosperous society like the U.S. suffers from so much alarming violence.

"Violent crime has risen substantially."

Violence Is Increasing

Elliott Currie

Amid fears of escalating anarchy after the shocking assassinations of Martin Luther King Jr. and Robert Kennedy, President Lyndon B. Johnson appointed the National Commission on the Causes and Prevention of Violence in 1968. The Commission warned that the U.S. was becoming a more violent society. In the following viewpoint, Elliott Currie argues that many of the Commission's worst predictions have come true: The rate of violent crime has escalated significantly. Currie was the assistant director of one of the Commission's task forces. He has written many books, and is a research associate at the Center for the Study of Law and Society at the University of California at Berkeley.

As you read, consider the following questions:

1. According to Currie, what was the Commission's prediction of how most Americans would react to increasing violence?
2. Why does the author discount the drop in crime rates in the early 1980s?
3. What does Currie believe is most troubling about the increasing rate of violence?

Elliott Currie, "Crimes of Violence and Public Policy: Changing Directions," in *American Violence and Public Policy*, edited by Lynn A. Curtis. Copyright © 1985 by Yale University Press. Reprinted by permission.

Writing in 1969, in a time of extraordinary social upheaval and frightening rises in the reported rate of violent crime, the Violence Commission offered a fearful scenario of what American cities might look like in "a few more years" in the absence of "effective public action."

Central business districts, surrounded by zones of "accelerating deterioration," would be reasonably protected even in the daytime only because large numbers of people would be working or shopping under the watchful protection of the police. Except for police patrols, the districts would be largely deserted at night. "Upper-middle and high-income populations" would huddle in "fortified cells"—high-rise apartments and residential compounds complete with elaborate security devices and private guards. Homes would be "fortified by an array of devices from window grilles to electronic surveillance equipment"; armed citizen patrols would supplement inadequate police in neighborhoods near the central city.

The more affluent would speed along heavily patrolled expressways which—in the Vietnam-era military language that often popped up, consciously or otherwise, in discussions of domestic social policy—would be "sanitized corridors" connecting "safe areas." Cars and taxis would be "routinely" equipped with unbreakable glass and even "light armor." Armed guards would ride "shotgun" on public transportation. Ghetto slums would be "places of terror" that might be entirely out of police control after dark. Schools and other public facilities would be patrolled by armed guards. Those who had business in or near the central city would have access to inside garages or valet parking.

When the commission's *Final Report* was released in late 1969, this scenario was one of the things that interested the media and the public most strongly. I can remember, in fact, thinking at the time that it was a usefully overwrought portrait—one that exaggerated the terrors before us considerably, but did so deliberately, in the wholly justifiable cause of spurring public action against the roots of urban violence.

The Scenario Came True

But the "few years" have passed, and what most strikes me today about the commission's scenario is that, with some exceptions, it came true to such an extent that we now simply take most of it for granted. There are a couple of false notes; the bit about "light armor" on the cars *was* overwrought, and though there have been some armed patrols in areas threatened by high crime, they haven't been a *common* response in the cities.

But much of the rest of the portrait has, by the 1980s, become simply the stuff of routine urban life. Not all cities fit the picture, but many do. I was struck by this during a recent foray into the newly "revitalized" downtown area of a large, high-crime western city that shall remain nameless. The high-rise buildings were there, all right. Most of them seemed, indeed, to be banks; they gleamed and glittered and fairly oozed urban prosperity. But the guards were there, too—inside the buildings, in the lobbies *and* in the elevators; outside the buildings, in the parking garages (imagine the commission, in 1969, thinking it worthy of note that downtown visitors would insist on protected parking!) and in the immaculate, if mainly deserted, plaza between the buildings.

Almost literally a stone's throw away is a towering new jail that, along with the banks, has been the *other* big architectural transformation downtown. Unlike the banks, the jail is built of gray stone with narrow slits for windows, not wide expanses of tinted glass and steel, but it is almost equally imposing.

A few blocks from downtown you can indeed find armed guards in school yards and in the housing projects and in some of the remaining neighborhood stores as well. In some of the better-heeled suburbs, you can indeed find electronic home security devices on a scale and sophistication reserved for military operations back in the sixties. Meanwhile this city's ghettos *are* "places of terror," though there are cities that are considerably worse in

Bill Garner. Reprinted by permission.

this regard. The "sanitized corridor" metaphor is probably a little strong for this city, but it is not for some others, where people do sometimes lose their lives because their cars stall in the wrong part of town. In a neighboring big city, the police department politely, but officially, tells tourists simply to avoid traveling through the ghetto areas nearest to downtown if at all possible and, if not, to keep windows rolled up, doors locked, and avoid stopping their cars at all costs.

The figures, of course, tell the same story. In 1968, when the commission began its deliberations, the national homicide rate as measured by the Uniform Crime Reports was 6.8 per 100,000. In 1981, there was much celebration in the media because the rate had fallen slightly—to 9.8—from 10.2 of the year before. The jump between 1968 and 1980 in this, the most reliable of indicators of criminal violence, amounted to exactly 50 percent.

Little Comfort

Overall rates of criminal violence have apparently fallen slightly from their peak in 1980, but the comfort we can take from this is small. So far, crime rates haven't fallen below their usual late-1970s' levels; they've only returned to a more typical course after the sudden upward surge at the close of the decade. More important, though the recent decline is certainly welcome, its sources are mysterious. We don't know why it happened nor whether any particular policy or set of policies can take any credit for it. It's sometimes said that the decline reflects the effect of community crime prevention programs, but it isn't clear that such programs are, nationally, more widespread or much better designed than they were in 1980, when violent crime apparently rose sharply. The recent decline is also sometimes attributed to tougher sentencing, and it's certainly true that we have locked more offenders up than ever before in recent years. But that trend began *well* before the fractional decline in violent crimes and it coincided with the opposite trend—sharply *rising* criminal violence—in the late 1970s.

Moreover, looked at more closely, the *pattern* of this decline is also somewhat mystifying. If we look at age-specific rates of homicide victimization, for example, from recent vital statistics data, we learn a puzzling fact about the slight decline in homicide between 1980 and 1981. That decline took place for some age groups but not others. It was sharpest among infants under one year, while homicide death rates *rose* slightly both for other children under fourteen and for adults aged thirty-five to forty-four, as well as for some older adults, including those sixty-five to seventy-four and over eighty-five (but *not* those aged seventy-five to eighty-four). What do we make of this? Someone may have an explanation, but I don't. What it suggests to me is that we know

20

very little about the meaning of either the recent decline or the only slightly less recent upward spurt in violent crime that preceded it.

Meanwhile, our more general situation is clearly, and painfully, apparent. Overall, violent crime has risen substantially since the Violence Commission's report. Even then, as the commission noted, with irony, the United States was the "clear leader" among otherwise comparable societies in its high levels of criminal violence. In many cases, those disparities have *risen* since the sixties. Even more than when the commission wrote, the United States more closely resembles some less developed countries of the Third World in this respect than it does any other advanced industrial society.

A Serious Problem

I need hardly persuade you that crime is a very serious and growing problem in the United States today. The evidence is everywhere. Every time you read a newspaper or watch news on TV, you see evidence of rampant violence, inhumanity and social chaos. We hear of robberies, rapes, muggings, vandalism and murder. We hear of gangland slayings, of escalating drug-related violence, of city neighborhoods being turned into war zones, and of modern vigilantes taking desperate and violent steps in efforts to rid themselves of gang violence.

Richard Whitney, *The People*, March 25, 1989.

What's especially troubling about our present situation is that it exists in the face of a decade and a half of extraordinarily intensive anticrime efforts. Indeed, the seventies and early eighties have been unique in the degree to which vast social and economic resources, as well as a good deal of human ingenuity, were poured—sometimes recklessly, sometimes with considerable care and creativity—into the fight against crime. Since the commission wrote, we have doubled the national incarceration rate, spent enormous sums on police hardware and software, instituted thousands of local crime prevention programs, "hardened" our "targets" through the extensive application of security measures to homes and businesses, and, not least, changed our daily routines in a multitude of ways to avoid victimization. All this, according to common sense and even to some criminological theory, *should* have helped the crime problem a great deal more than it did.

Instead, by the early eighties, we had reached what was widely regarded as a frustrating and depressing impasse. *Newsweek*'s cover story on crime in 1981 reflected the sentiment well, noting that the response to violent crime had become a "dispiriting malaise" and that we had lost the "old optimism proclaiming that we know what the problems are and that we have the solutions at hand." *Newsweek* concluded its gloomy review with the suggestion that we learn "not to expect too much," a quietism that was echoed by the Reagan administration's Task Force on Violent Crime, which opted out of even seriously *considering* the causes of crime as a possible subject for public policy, citing the "risks of assuming that the government can solve whatever problem it addresses."

Hope for the Future

Is this impasse inevitable? I don't think so. I think we know a great deal more about the causes of crime than much fashionable argument since the mid-1970s has suggested; and that we also know a great deal more about what, broadly, we might do about it. . . .

The criminology of the sixties often raised issues on the level of analysis only to drop them, for all practical purposes, on the level of policy. Some of the reasons no doubt have to do with the imperatives of politics; but others have to do with more fundamental conceptual questions—questions that, I think, must lie at the heart of a credible approach to criminal violence in the eighties.

Let me give a specific example. The Violence Commission pointed out at several places that the economic transformation of the rural South was intimately related to the problems of the cities and that, more generally, the rural-to-urban migrations of recent decades were deeply implicated in rising crime rates. Yet the commission's response to this crucial recognition was revealing: it described these problems as broad "demographic" ones. Despite some brief nods to the notion that such matters might become the focus of policy, the most common posture of both public and private authorities at the time was that these issues of regional, economic, and technological change were things about which no one felt responsible.

The economist Geoffrey Faux has described this phenomenon as he witnessed it among Washington policymakers during the sixties. Faux notes that the infusion of federal aid to agriculture from the 1940s to the 1960s created an enormous increase in agricultural mechanization, which, on one side of the social and economic ledger, raised farm productivity greatly, but on the other side, threw millions of tenant farmers and farm workers out of livelihoods and into the cities. "During that time," Faux writes,

> I attended a briefing at the Agriculture Department at which researchers predicted (accurately it turned out) the rough magnitude and destination of the large numbers of Southern farmworkers who would be forced out of the tobacco fields. When I asked what was being done to create jobs for them, the answer was that the Agriculture Department's job was to in-

crease farm productivity, not to alleviate urban poverty. Efforts to get other departments to address the problem were in vain; it wasn't their problem yet.

The social costs of this mentality, as Faux points out, were (and are) enormous. In terms of understanding America's violent crime problem in the sixties, seventies, and eighties, they are crucial. But we are no further today than we were in the sixties to accepting public responsibility for them. . . .

Bad Odds

The Department of Justice has published some unsettling prognostications about the future of crime in the United States. According to its figures, 83 percent of 12-year-old Americans will be victims or intended victims of violent crimes before they die. One out of 133 Americans will be murdered, 87 percent will be victimized by personal theft three times or more, and one out of 12 women will confront rape attempts.

The Washington Times, March 10, 1987.

As Faux also observes, "National economic policy remains the only significant organized human activity in America where planning ahead is considered irrational." But if we are to be serious about reconstructing—or constructing—the context of family and community life for the urban disadvantaged, we will have to bite the bullet and think directly about public planning for urban economic development. Without that focus, we can expect, at best, to recapitulate the default of the more progressive criminology of the sixties. With it, we may begin to achieve a major impact on violent crime in America—not tomorrow, not next year, but in the not-so-distant future. And we may begin, finally, to roll back the long-term deterioration in the quality of American life that the Violence Commission predicted, with such unfortunate foresight, at the close of the 1960s.

23

"Violent crime will decrease."

Violence Is Decreasing

Georgette Bennett

Georgette Bennett argues in the following viewpoint that people fear violence more than is warranted. In her 1989 book *Crimewarps*, Bennett predicts a drop in the rate of violent crime. The fear of violence is high, she writes, because the media exaggerate the crime problem and cover gruesome murder and assault cases that are atypical. For most Americans, she concludes, the chances of being victimized on the street are declining. Bennett is a former sociology professor at City University in New York and was an adviser to the New York City Police Department.

As you read, consider the following questions:

1. Why did the murder of Caroline Isenberg make Bennett sick?
2. What kind of crime does the author predict will increase in the future?
3. What factors will lead to a drop in the rate of violent crime, according to the author?

Crime. We fear it. We're fascinated by it. Our notions about crime—molded mostly by what we read and hear—are often distorted. Yet those perceptions determine our sense of safety at home and on the streets, in a store or in an office, in the investments we make and the air we breathe. Because we feel vulnerable on every front, we need to understand the state of crime today and what it tells us about the time to come. . . .

A Stereotypical Crime

Sunday, December 2, 1984. A quiet New York Street. A lone woman returning from the theater entered the elevator of her West End Avenue building. At 1:40 a.m., the stillness was shattered by her screams. Caroline Isenberg, a twenty-three-year-old Harvard graduate, had been forced to the roof at knife point. There, twenty-one-year-old Emmanuel Torres robbed her of twelve dollars, tried to rape her, and repeatedly stabbed her.

For days, the details of the crime exploded in the headlines: Caroline's dying words about the bitter price she paid for not giving in to the rape; the forty detectives who were assigned to the case; the grief of her mother and psychiatrist father; her prep school; her promising life; her nascent acting career. Then there was the killer: whom a prosecutor described as the irresponsible drifter son of the building's superintendent; his estranged parents; his inability to complete high school; Emmanuel's doctor-brother who made good; the remorseless confession in which Torres described the murder in all its horror.

And, a week after Caroline's death, the vigil. The neighbors and strangers—Hispanic, black, white—who lit candles and stood watch outside 929 West End Avenue, while one mourner intoned: "Yis gadal v'yiskadash sh'mei rabba," the life-affirming Jewish prayer for the dead.

That's how the life of an upscale, bright young white woman was extinguished by a reportedly unemployed, dope-smoking, black Hispanic on a crisp winter night in the season of goodwill. It was the stereotypical crime with the stereotypical cast of characters—the apotheosis of all our most primitive fears and prejudices about crime.

Crimes like this are the ones that fire the imaginations of press and public alike. Their luridness precludes a reasoned separation of fact and frenzy.

I'm a sociologist and criminologist. I'm also a journalist. So I work both sides of the street—fact and frenzy. I've spent most of my career dealing with criminals, victims, law enforcers, attorneys, prison officials, court personnel. I've taught thousands of college, graduate, and professional students; advised police commissioners; designed programs for federal, state, and city governments; counseled corporations. I've developed stories for "60 Minutes,"

"20/20," "MacNeil/Lehrer News-Hour"; worked crime beats for local news programs and covered the nation for NBC News. . . .

But this story made me sick—not only because of the heinousness of the act itself, but because it's so misleading. As a journalist, I know that stories like Isenberg's sell papers and boost ratings. As a social scientist, I know that this crime and others like it are anomalies today; *they'll be even more rare tomorrow.*

Normative Victims and Criminals

Today's normative victim and criminal share this profile: young, male, black or Hispanic, undereducated, unmarried, unemployed. Emmanuel Torres fits. Except for her age, Caroline Isenberg doesn't. She was a fluke. And so was the crime.

The prototypical street crime is not interracial. Blacks prey on blacks, whites on whites. Street punks usually victimize their own neighbors. Torres traveled a relatively long way to menace Caroline but, because of his father's job, he was no stranger to her apartment building. The majority of murders and assaults are committed by people who have some knowledge of their victims, even if only in passing. Among violent crimes, only robberies are committed mostly against strangers. (The data on rape are inconclusive.)

Caroline was an unlikely street crime victim. As a woman, her odds of being targeted were half those of a man. As a white, they were a little more than half those of a black. As an affluent person, they were half those of a poor person. Finally, her kind of tragedy is only an infinitesimal part of the total crime picture. Yet, it's the kind of crime that conditions our sense of safety.

The Lowest Level Since 1975

A fourth of the 93 million households in the United States were touched by a crime of violence or theft in 1988, the same proportion that were touched by crime during each of the previous 3 years. The estimate remained at the lowest level since 1975, the first year it was available, when a third of American households were touched by crime.

U.S. Department of Justice, *Bulletin: Households Touched by Crime, 1988.*

If you're like most people, you think of crime in terms of violence—rape, murder, assault. Your fear attaches not to just any crime, but specifically to a random attack by a stranger lurking in the street. Most people believe we're in the midst of an unprecedented crime wave. Maybe you're one and I don't blame you. You turn on your local "Action News" and 20 percent of the airtime is devoted to a body count.

26

My friend Joan watches too. She says her daily exposure to TV news makes her afraid to walk around her West Hollywood neighborhood at night. This middle-aged lawyer loves her home, her city, and her work, but her fear of crime makes her constantly uneasy. "With what I hear, I'm afraid to go out. I always lock my door when I'm driving. I always keep my eyes to the ground. I never make eye contact. I've always been careful—but now I'm careful and scared."

Like most people, Joan has never been a street crime victim. The odds are she never will be, because she's white, female, and no longer in the crime-prone fourteen- to twenty-four-year-old age group. But media-manufactured myths about crime have robbed her of her sense of safety. . . .

Robert Nascimben, a twenty-seven-year-old technician for Texas Instruments, . . . made a nice salary and was living the good life in Houston with his wife. Finding a house was his major preoccupation, and crime was very far from his mind. Then it happened. Not at the hands of a mugger or a burglar as you might expect, but through the manipulations of a swindler.

Timothy Leighton, thirty-nine, a mobile-home salesman, had used a stolen computer terminal provided by a confederate to access Nascimben's credit information. Investigators say he used the data to open accounts with Visa, MasterCard, and First City National Bank of Dallas. Bank losses of $10,000 were incurred in Nascimben's name. His credit rating could have been destroyed, and his sense of privacy was profoundly violated.

White-Collar Crimes Will Increase

Nascimben's experience is typical of the kind of crime that will bedevil us in the future: a white-collar offense taking place in the Sunbelt, involving an older victim and criminal, abetted by a computer, detected by new investigation techniques, and deeply impacting our right to privacy.

Nascimben's victimization stands in stark contrast to the street crimes that are normative today. The case of Michael "Meathead" McReynolds, a nineteen-year-old black Atlantan, illustrates a kind of crime that is on the wane. Early in 1983, McReynolds was shooting baskets with his friends when he was shot by his neighbor, eighteen-year-old Bobby Lester, also black. Two months before, Lester's brother had burglarized McReynolds' home and stolen his father's .38. Thinking that his former victim was out to get even, Lester launched a preemptive strike: five bullets in the back on a Love Street basketball court. Lester pleaded guilty to aggravated assault.

Had McReynolds died of his wounds, the crime with which Lester could have been charged is murder, a felony whose rate plummeted during most of the 1980s. But he survived. In the

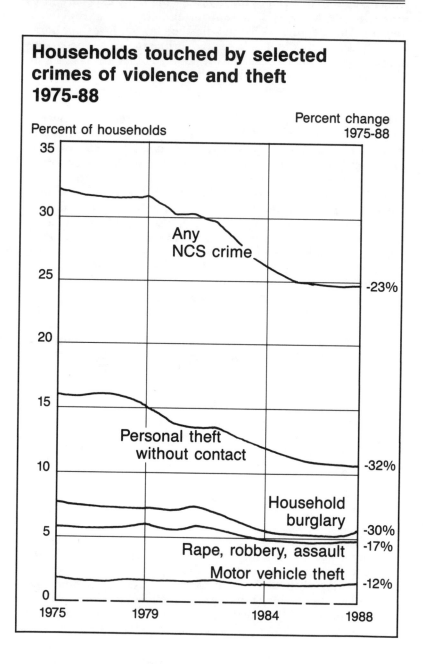

Households touched by selected crimes of violence and theft 1975-88

Percent of households

Percent change 1975-88

35

30

Any NCS crime

25

−23%

20

15

Personal theft without contact

10

−32%

Household burglary

5

−30%

Rape, robbery, assault

−17%

Motor vehicle theft

−12%

0

1975   1979   1984   1988

Source: U.S. Department of Justice.

future, his odds of being a street crime victim will be greatly reduced. Crimes like the ones his family suffered—burglary and aggravated assault—have declined, as have all crimes (except for minor ones like stealing a bicycle or throwing your best friend a light punch). The decrease in crime is no longer a blip on a graph. . . .

Less Chance of Being a Street Victim

The good news: *The chances of being a street crime victim are getting smaller and will continue to shrink for the next several decades.* Today, each household has 2.5 chances in 10 of being touched by crime. That's a drop of 22 percent in victimization by personal and household crimes since 1975. If the odds keep decreasing at that rate, the year 2000 will see the risk drop to less than 2 in 10.

When you look at individuals instead of households, the drop in crime rates is even more dramatic: more than 20 percent just since 1981, when violent crimes peaked. The largest declines— over 30 percent each—took place in robbery and rape, the crimes that scare us the most.

One reason crime will continue to ebb is the aging of our population. Most street criminals are young, with ages fourteen to twenty-four being the most dangerous years. By the time they reach their twenty-fifth birthday, most of the hell-raising is over. Come the year 2000, two thirds of the population will have cleared the crime-prone age barrier. Today only 60 percent have crossed that threshold. The median age, which is now thirty, will creep steadily to nearly forty-two by the year 2050. *The rate of conventional crime will drop as the median age rises.*

Now the bad news.

In the future, when crime strikes, it could well be less violent, less personal, more tricky, and more profitable. *The criminal will be older, more sophisticated. And so will the victim.* As the population ages, we can expect more crimes like the credit fraud that ensnared Robert Nascimben and several Houston banks. White-collar crimes are usually committed by older, "respectable" criminals against older, more affluent victims. Reliable baselines don't exist, but since this part of the population is growing, we can expect the rate of white-collar crime to grow too. . . .

Although rapes, robberies, assaults and contact thefts dropped more than 20 percent in the 1980s, in the latter part of the decade the declines began to slow down as a rise in drug-related killings started to make itself felt.

Violence Will Decrease

While violent crime will decrease, it won't disappear.

The murders, rapes, robberies, and thefts that make us shudder are generally the province of young criminals and young victims, who are disproportionately black and Hispanic. Here the new demographics contain a time bomb: Census Bureau projections indicate that by the year 2050, there will be a 7 percent smaller proportion of whites in this country. Blacks and Hispanics will make up about one quarter of the population, compared to less than one fifth today.

More Fear, Less Violence

Perhaps more remarkable than the number of crimes is the evidence about the public's perception of crime. Public fear of crime has increased or held steady during a period when the number of crimes seems to have declined. For example, the number of victimizations for 1984, great as it was, was approximately 14 percent lower than the 1981 peak of 41.5 million. The number of households touched by crime was down from the peak of 32 percent measured in 1975.

Edwin Meese III, in *Crime and Punishment in Modern America*, 1986.

According to Lawrence Sherman, former research director for the Police Foundation, high-crime-risk minorities have suffered "destruction of the family and increasing illegitimacy. That has to have an effect." The effects will be felt, asserts Sherman, in more domestic violence. It will also be felt in more thefts. Because future job creation will take place in the crime-prone service industries that hire minorities, "theft will go off the wall!" according to Sherman.

This may be so. But Marvin Wolfgang, one of the nation's leading criminologists, feels it won't be due to greater numbers of criminals. He asserts that *the volume of juvenile offenders is shrinking, but the crimes committed by the remaining ones are growing in number and violence.* To this I would add that the "remaining ones" won't be sufficient to bring us back to the sky-high crime levels of the 1960s and 1970s.

"Violence has been a companion of Americans since Europeans planted the first seeds of civilized order in the New World."

America's History Contributes to Violence

Richard C. Wade

The U.S. has the highest rate of violent crime of any industrialized country. Some people, including author Richard C. Wade, believe America's history explains this situation. According to Wade, violence in the U.S. was very high in the nineteenth century, both as an outgrowth of the settling of the frontier and the rapid increase in urban populations. In addition, prejudice against immigrants, native Americans, and blacks led to further violence, he argues. Wade has been Distinguished Professor of History at the City University of New York since 1971. He has written and edited many books on American history, including *The Urban Frontier*.

As you read, consider the following questions:

1. Why does the author contend that the founding of the U.S. contributed to its violent heritage?
2. Why were nineteenth-century city police forces ineffective in stopping violence, in the author's view?
3. Why do people think there is more violence today than ever before, according to Wade?

Richard C. Wade, "The Sources of Violence in American History." Reprinted by permission of Westchester County Department of Community Mental Health from *Mental Health and Violence* copyright 1985.

I will address the historical dimension of violence in the conventional sense of the word—the use of physical force against other people—and confine my observations to American society in peacetime, treating the question of organized, official violence when it impinges on domestic events. After all, the Republic was born of a violent revolution which lasted for over eight years; it engaged unofficially in a war with France between 1798 and 1800, won a "Second War for Independence" against the British in 1812 and grabbed a large part of the southwest by an unprovoked war with Mexico in 1845. Moreover, the Republic itself was kept united only after immense bloodshed. Our own century has been accompanied, for all its "progress," with unprecedented violence. And, of course, we are the first generation with the capacity for the most violent act of all—the extinction of civilization, of the human race itself.

As American as Cherry Pie

Stokely Carmichael astonished the American public in the 1960's by saying that "violence is as American as cherry pie." This discordant note did not sit well with white society, but, as an historian (especially of American cities) I could only reply that at least he didn't say "apple pie." For violence has, in fact, been a companion, to be sure an unwanted one, of Americans since the beginning of the Republic. Its roots are many and some very persistent. . . .

Yet this country was born at a time when the perfection of man was assumed and that "a peaceable kingdom" would be developed in the New World. However, the circumstances of the Europeans dictated a collision with native Americans, with the bloodshed and injustice that we all know. Frederick Jackson Turner, the most influential of American historians, called this a struggle of "civilization against barbarism;" meanwhile a dozen governors around the country are inheriting the consequences of the "best Indian is a dead Indian" attitude which dominated America for two centuries, and are trying to make amends for an indefensible past.

After the birth of the Republic, the establishment of governmental authority occasioned violence. Putting down Shays' rebellion in Massachusetts had the support of even Sam Adams, whose activities had been so much a part of the Boston violent resistance to the British in 1776. President Washington had to order troops to the Pittsburgh area in 1794 to put down the popular resistance against a federal tax on whiskey. Andrew Jackson forcibly removed Indians in the 1820's from the South to Oklahoma where, incidentally, he put them down on the richest oil area in the country; they would be, again forcibly, removed to other areas in the West. Finally, it took a Civil War to establish the supremacy of the federal government over any regime or state.

The sources of violence in America's development are not obscure.

The nation was ultimately occupied by people from different countries, different religions, different languages who carried with them old hostilities to other groups from their homelands. Many were received grudgingly by their American hosts whose roots were in the soil of the mother country (Britain).

Excessive Frontier Violence

Violence in America west of the Mississippi during what we so romantically recall as the "frontier years" was marked by shootings and hangings. American literature in the past and television in the present offer this violence as a badge of entertainment and even nostalgia.

A certain amount of lawlessness and crime is almost inevitable in the settlement of a new country, but the amount which characterized the American western frontier probably surpasses any measure of reasonableness.

Irving J. Sloan, *Our Violent Past: An American Chronicle*, 1970.

Ethnic and religious conflict constituted a source of intermittent conflict which sometimes spilled over into visible violence. Protestant resistance to Irish immigration mounted throughout the 1830's and included the sacking and burning of a convent in Boston in 1834. It also established the lineaments of a national political party in the next two decades, culminating in the anti-Catholic Know-Nothing movement in the 1850's. Locally, this immigrant hostility led to rioting, bloodshed and deaths. In Louisville the anti-German riots in the 1850's left behind burned down neighborhoods, deaths and bitterness. Yet within a decade Louisville had a German police chief and later a German mayor. In Chicago an attempt to control the closing hours of taverns led to the "beer riots"—with mass protest and some deaths.

Jews suffered more than others since their large numbers came late and they were mostly poor. Rampant discrimination often turned violent, and the Frank lynching in Atlanta became a symbol of the precarious position of Jews in urban America. In the 1920's members of the Ku Klux Klan were as much anti-semitic as anti-black. Indeed, attacks on Jews were persistent enough, and ubiquitous enough, to prompt Jewish leaders to establish an organization solely for protective purposes.

In short, one source of violence in this country was ethnically oriented. The newcomers not involved in violence or crime resented the indiscriminate connection of all immigrants to crime. Even so, the Irish and Germans ran up crime rates. (When con-

33

fronted with high Irish crime, George Bernard Shaw replied, "Of course, crime takes imagination.") As time went on, however, the newcomers were grudgingly accepted. . . .

Another source of violence is the "endemic disorder" which accompanied the rapid urbanization of the country. We began as a Republic less than 5 percent urban and saw our metropolitan areas grow until the 1920 census revealed that over half of all Americans lived in cities; by 1980 well over three quarters did so. The nineteenth century was especially chaotic. These young and growing cities did not have traditions, nor habits of deference to authority. Indeed, it took a long time to agree on what constituted proper authority to create laws and sustain order. In the first urban explosion between 1830 and 1860 every city witnessed riots, lawlessness and sporadic violence.

The 1850's have been dubbed by one historian the "violent decade" because of the constant violence that afflicted every large city not only in vigilante-prone San Francisco but in Philadelphia, Baltimore, Cincinnati and others.

Nineteenth-Century Police Forces

Cities were policed by whomever civil authorities anointed. Every time there was a change in city hall, the blue uniforms were placed on another who was given a manual, gun and club and sent forth to protect the peace of the community. In the 1860's New York City had two police forces—one appointed by the mayor and the other by the governor. They spent most of this time fighting each other.

Moreover, in most cities, there were places where the police simply did not go, and what passed for order was kept by local gangs, or, occasionally, vigilante groups. In St. Louis a police commissioner admitted that his rule of thumb for deploying police in the notorious crime infested Second Ward was "Two if by day; platoons if by night."

In some places citizens were not too happy seeing the police around anyway because of the ubiquitous collusion between the police and criminal elements. It was so pervasive in Chicago that there is the story, probably apocryphal, that children played a game called "cops and cops." The cry for reform usually came when someone with a fancy name walked into one of these neighborhoods and didn't come out.

The professionalization of policing is a twentieth-century phenomenon. Until then we did not have police academies, few career police, or even the slightest semblance of non-partisan politics. The Knapp Commission reports in the 1970's demonstrate how painfully slow the progress has been and the recent furor over "police brutality" resulted in an inquiry by a committee of Congress. Politicians who run on law and order platforms are simply modern manifestations of the century-old refrain for city reforms.

What is, however, different today is the ubiquity of crime and violence, once sheltered in the corners of urban society. Now crime and violence know no boundaries. Aggravated crimes, the FBI figures tell us, are going up much more rapidly in the suburbs than in the cities. . . .

However, there is probably less violence in America now than 100 years ago. It is simply more visible, more ubiquitous, and our tolerance is less because our expectations are higher. In addition, we now attempt to measure it with percentages going up and down, when previously no serious data existed at all. Also, we have a media system that records the violence, wherever it might occur, in our living room each night, magnifying its importance relative to other events and almost always at the expense of analysis. Moreover, we have become more sensitively aware of violence, which used to be defined in a public sense, now to include family violence and inward violence. The historian is constrained to say that if we had data on such matters for 1900, we would conclude that American society is much less violent today than, say, in 1900.

The Settlers' Fears

The United States, and the 13 colonies that preceded it, was a land of immigrants whose living conditions fostered more lethal violence than England had or any of the other countries from which they had come. . . .

The settlers feared the native Indians, and they especially feared the African slaves whom they imported, primarily in the South. Also evoking fear were the thousand or more British convicts sentenced each year during the colonial era to transportation to America. To recoup the cost of passage the sea captains were authorized to sell the convicts as indentured servants for a term of labor, but many of these ex-convicts then escaped and fled into the wilderness. The successive influx of new immigrant groups, as well as ethnic group migration within the country, has repeatedly aroused in American communities fear of people who seemed different, and violence against them.

Daniel Glaser, in *Violence in the Home*, 1986.

Labor disputes, or some might call them class conflicts, also occasioned widescale disorder. At the turn of the century, Winston Churchill, already a keen student of American affairs, observed that the United States had the most violent industrial relations of any western country. Most of this rioting started with a confrontation of labor and management over the right to organize, wages and hours, or working conditions. Unlike the other disorders, these were often nationwide in scope—occurring at widely scattered points. Yet the violence was seldom uniform or confined to the strikers. As in the railroad strike in 1877 it flared in Chicago and Pittsburgh: yet St. Louis remained quiescent. But in many instances the damage to life and property was extensive. In the Homestead lock out alone, 35 died and property damage ran into the millions. In the 1930's the organizing of steel, auto and rubber unions brought an ugly recrudescence of this earlier industrial violence.

Of all the sources of civil disorder, however, none has been more persistent than race. Whether North or South, whether nineteenth or twentieth century, this question has been at the root of more physical violence than any other. In 1822, with the most flimsy proof, Charleston, South Carolina officials hanged 37 blacks and deported many more. Seven years later in Cincinnati, whites invaded "Little Africa" and burned and killed and ultimately drove half the blacks, all free, from the city. In New York in 1863 the draft riots took an ugly twist before they subsided. Over 75 ultimately died and property damage was assessed in the millions.

Emancipation freed the blacks from bondage, but did not grant them either equality or immunity from white aggression. From the New Orleans riot of 1866, through a long list of racial disorders to the end of World War II with datelines running through Atlanta, Springfield, East St. Louis, Washington, Mobile, Beaumont, Chicago, Detroit and Harlem, something of the depth of the crisis and the vulnerability of American cities to racial disorders is revealed. These riots were on a large scale, involved many deaths, extraordinary property damage, and left behind scars which have never been fully erased. . . .

A Companion of Americans

Violence has been a companion of Americans since Europeans planted the first seeds of civilized order in the New World. In 1721 Cotton Mather, pillar of Boston society, could utter the timeless lament of a parent about his "miserable, miserable, miserable, son Increase. The wretch has brought himself under public infamy by bearing a part in a Night-riot in town." In 1742 Philadelphia hoped to substitute ballots for riotous activity and this resulted in one of the country's "bloody elections." Bostonians embarrassed Benjamin Franklin in London when they rioted against the Stamp Tax which he had supported. Aaron Burr killed Alexander Hamilton in a duel and Abraham Lincoln witnessed the public whipping of a slave. Theodore Roosevelt, as Police Commissioner of New York, ordered his men, in case of strikes, to "shoot" and "not above their heads."

"Criminals repeatedly slip through our 'criminal justice' system and victimize innocent citizens time and time again."

The Criminal Justice System Contributes to Violence

Allan Brownfeld

Allan Brownfeld is a syndicated columnist whose editorials appear frequently in such conservative publications as the *Washington Inquirer* and the *Conservative Chronicle*. In the following viewpoint, he argues that violence remains a serious problem in the U.S. because the justice system does not effectively deal with criminals. Under plea bargaining arrangements, parole, and legal technicalities, many criminals are set free who then murder, rape, or rob again, Brownfeld believes.

As you read, consider the following questions:

1. What point does the author make by citing the cases of Wayne Lamar Harvey, Frank DeCherico, and Larry Singleton?
2. In Brownfeld's opinion, what factors prevent the sure and swift punishment of violent crime?
3. Why do few criminals spend time in prison, according to Brownfeld?

Allan Brownfeld, "Repeat Offenders Belong in Prison," *Washington Inquirer*, September 1, 1989. Reprinted by permission of *Washington Inquirer*, P.O. Box 28526, Washington, D.C. 20005.

Violent crimes reported nationwide in 1988 increased 5.5 percent from 1987 to a new high, with murders rising 2.9 percent to 20,695, the FBI [Federal Bureau of Investigation] declared in a report which was recently released.

Washington, D.C. led the nation in the rate of murders and non-negligent homicides, with 59.5 per 100,000. The FBI report said that 369 people were killed in the nation's capital in 1988. The rate is much higher for the first six months of 1989.

One reason for the unprecedented number of violent crimes, argues John Ray, a member of the Washington, D.C. City Council and a candidate for mayor, is that the same individuals are apprehended time and again—and released to commit additional crimes. Mr. Ray reports that in a police action, "Operation Clean Sweep," there were 48,000 arrests made, but there were only 7,000 people arrested. The same criminals repeatedly slip through our "criminal justice" system and victimize innocent citizens time and time again.

Releasing Killers

Throughout the country, many of the most celebrated murder cases involve killers who were once in the hands of the law, once in prison, but were released and put back onto the streets.

Consider the case of Wayne Lamar Harvey, which is all too typical. Harvey participated in the brutal shotgun killing of two people in a Detroit bar in December 1975. A plea-bargain reduced his two first-degree murder charges to second degree, and he was given a 20-40-year prison sentence. On the day he entered prison, he was automatically granted nine and a half years of "good-time" credits, which he was allowed to keep despite 24 major prison rule violations during his incarceration. His minimum sentence was further reduced by two years under Michigan's "Prison Overcrowding Emergency Powers Act."

Harvey was paroled to a halfway house in July 1984 after serving eight and a half years of his original minimum sentence. On October 25, 1984, Harvey and a female halfway-house escapee killed a 41-year-old East Lansing police officer and father of 6, then proceeded to a nearby home where Harvey shot and killed a 33-year-old woman as she opened the door.

In a September 1988 New York case, artist Judith Wrappe died so that her killer could get high on a vial of crack. Her murderer, Frank DeCherico, was a paroled convicted killer with a string of arrests. His previous arrest had also been for murder, and he had been out on parole less than two years when he killed Wrappe.

In July 1988, Connecticut Valley Hospital, a state-run mental institution, released one of its inmates on a day-pass. He had been sentenced to 15-years confinement in 1988, having been charged with assault and burglary and found not guilty by reason of insanity. While on his day-pass, this inmate went to a sporting goods store, bought a hunting knife and approached 9-year-old Jessica Short on the main street of Middletown, Connecticut. Then he stabbed her to death. A few days after this incident, while administrators were still trying to clarify why this murderer had been given a pass, another inmate with a history of violent behavior simply walked out of the same institution. . . .

The Singleton Case

Our society seems unwilling to punish violent crime and protect innocent citizens from such brutal attacks. In 1987, California authorities released Larry Singleton on parole after serving eight years of a 14-year sentence for raping 15-year-old Mary Bell Vincent, chopping off her arms with an ax, and leaving her to die in a ditch.

A Bureau of Justice study of prison entrants in 1979 found that, at the time of their admission, 28 percent would still have been in prison if they had served their maximum prior sentence. The study found that these "average recidivists" accounted for approximately 20 percent of the violent crimes committed by all those sent to prison that year as well as 28 percent of the burglaries and auto thefts, and 31 percent of the stolen property offenses.

In Texas, in 1987, the average inmate was released after serving less than one-quarter of his sentence; by comparison, in 1982,

Copyright © 1989 Joel Pett, Lexington Herald-Leader.

inmates were released after serving over half of their sentences. It is now possible to be released on parole after serving three months of a two-year term, 7.6 months of a five-year term, and 15.2 months of a 10-year sentence.

A Crime Wave

We are now in the midst of a crime wave and the same criminals are perpetrating crimes for which they are never properly punished. A violent crime is committed every 5 seconds. The U.S. Bureau of Justice Statistics estimates that 83 percent of children now 12 years old will become victims of actual or attempted violence if crime continues at current rates. Punishment for criminals is neither sure nor swift. Nationwide, the police are able to solve only 1 in five major crimes. When the police do manage to arrest a suspect, it may take more than a year in crowded urban court systems to dispose of the case. In the meantime, about 1 in 6 defendants who are free on bail is arrested for new crimes. Up to 9 cases in 10 end in plea bargains that reduce the charges against criminals.

Sadly only 1 case in 6 leads to a prison term, and the average time in custody remains short. Most "life" terms for our most violent criminals end before ten years are spent behind bars. In Los Angeles County, inmates serve only one day for every 30 days stated in the sentence.

Richard B. Abell, assistant attorney general in charge of the Office of Justice Programs, states that, "If the threat of prison is to discourage persons from becoming criminals, it must be a credible threat. It must be backed up with actual prison terms . . . when chances of imprisonment were high."

A Pathologically Soft Society

What kind of society permits violent criminals to roam its streets in search of additional victims? Professor Stanley C. Brubaker of Colgate University states: "There is a point in the history of society when it becomes so pathologically soft and tender that among other things it sides with those who harm it, criminals, and does this quite seriously and honestly. Punishing somehow seems unfair to it."

Making certain that crime is punished swiftly and severely should be the highest priority of local, state and federal officials. Rather than wringing our hands about the escalating rate of violence, let us finally act to put it to an end.

"Violence by minorities can be an attempt . . . to take back that which has been denied—a poor minority male's form of income redistribution."

Economic and Racial Injustice Contributes to Violence

Lynn A. Curtis

Minorities commit a disproportionate amount of the violent crime in the U.S. and are also more likely to be victims of violence. In the following viewpoint, Lynn A. Curtis writes that poor young minorities are more likely to commit crimes because they have less to lose and more to gain than middle-class people. If they are successful, they may gain money or status from committing the crime. Violence will continue, he concludes, as long as poverty and racial injustice persist. Curtis has been a member of presidential commissions on violence, has served as an adviser to the Department of Housing and Urban Development, and is president of the Milton S. Eisenhower Foundation in Washington, D.C.

As you read, consider the following questions:

1. Why does Curtis argue that violence may be a minority's attempt to even the scales?
2. Why have many blacks been unable to succeed in the U.S. economy, while immigrants have been able to, according to Curtis?

[Blacks are] inferior to whites in the endowments both of body and mind.

—Thomas Jefferson

The nation's inner cities can be reclaimed. Argus, created by ghetto residents, staffed by them, managed by them, with help from the outside, teaches children how to heal their pain, reach for a broader world and live in it. Their achievement can be a reference point for efforts on a larger scale.

—Elizabeth Sturz

Sturz is right and Jefferson was wrong. We will show that this is so by briefly profiling the extent and character of violent crime in America. . . .

Based on both crimes reported to the police and on U.S. Census Bureau victimization surveys of household samples, we can reasonably conclude that rates of serious violent crime—murder, assault, rape, and robbery—have increased since the late 1960s. Today, the chance of becoming a victim of violent crime is greater than the chance of divorce, the risk of being in an automobile accident, or the probability of dying from cancer.

The level of violent crime in the United States remains astronomical—much higher than in other industrialized democratic nations.

Considerably more than half of all murders, assaults, and rapes continue to be committed by minorities on minorities. In robbery, offenders are disproportionately minority, though nationally victims are about as likely to be white as minority.

Both victims and offenders are disproportionately young in serious violence, with the exception of robbery where the distribution between younger and older victims is more equal.

Deprivation and Crime

The evidence from decades of research shows an almost linear relationship between economic deprivation and serious crime. But social class and income level do not account for all the disparity between minorities and whites in rates of committing serious violent crime and delinquency. For example, when Marvin E. Wolfgang et al. compared different groups in their Philadelphia cohort study of boys born in 1945, no other variables emerged quite so clearly as did race as a determinant of contrast. Poor boys were involved in more reported delinquencies than were middle- or upper-class boys; but even within the lower class, nonwhite boys were involved in significantly more delinquencies than white boys. A later Philadelphia cohort study, of boys born in 1958, found that the racial imbalance remained pervasive and startling and that the second cohort was significantly more violent than was the first.

Overall, the most typical murder or assault is committed for an ostensibly trivial motive by a young, poor, inner-city, minority male against someone with the same characteristics. Murder is the number one cause of death in the United States for young black men. The murder and assault victim-offender patterns hold for forcible rape, except, of course, for the gender of the victim. In robbery, there are two dominant patterns—young, poor, inner-city, minority males who victimize persons with similar characteristics and also victimize older whites. A very large proportion of all violent crime is committed by a very small proportion of the offending population. . . .

Children in Poverty

The gangs, the drugs, the senseless violence are attractive only because children of the black community—and children of poverty, regardless of race—have been made to feel like nothing, like worthless objects, like dirt staked on top of other generations of dirt.

The society at large, and particularly those blacks who have somehow escaped the terrible feeling of insignificance and invisibleness, should be ashamed of the pain that is allowed to visit upon the children. The pain stalks black children living in the midst of hopeless welfare; it stalks white children living under the burden of alcoholism; it stalks Hispanic children with no support and no love; it stalks them all who were born into unfortunate situations.

Herb Cawthorne, *San Diego Tribune*, November 3, 1988.

In the late 1960s, the National Commission on the Causes and Prevention of Violence (hereinafter referred to as the Violence Commission), concurring with the findings of the National Advisory Commission on Civil Disorders 1968 (hereinafter referred to as the Kerner Commission), concluded that:

> To be a young, poor male; to be undereducated and without means of escape from an oppressive urban environment; to want what the society claims is available (but mostly to others); to see around oneself illegitimate and often violent methods being used to achieve material success; and to observe others using these means with impunity—all this is to be burdened with an enormous set of influences that pull many toward crime and delinquency. To be also a Black, Mexican or Puerto Rican American and subject to discrimination adds considerably to the pull.

Violent crime is too complex for any brief statement to be entirely accurate in explaining disproportionate minority involvement in violent and related crimes. But no explanations since the Violence and Kerner Commissions better explain the available statistics on levels of violence, trends in violence, the role of relative economic deprivation, and the independent determinant of race. . . .

Acquisitive violence by minorities can be an attempt, however illusory or symbolic, to take back that which has been denied—a poor minority male's form of income redistribution. Assaultive behavior by young men, even if inflicted predominantly by minorities on other minorities, can reflect an acceptance of violence in everyday life as an available means of expressing anger, frustration, and masculinity. A lethal outcome is all the more likely, given the easy availability of handguns in the United States and traditions of weapons carrying as further proof of masculinity among poor minority youth. In some parallel ways, motherhood is a means by which some teen minorities perceive that they can express their womanhood in a society with opportunities blocked to them. . . .

C.E. Silberman pointed out that this is not the first time in the history of American ethnic groups that it has become necessary to dispute those who see no relation between crime, relative poverty, and discrimination. In the last part of the nineteenth century and the first part of the twentieth, many of the people most responsible for street crime were Irish-, German-, Italian-, and Polish-Americans. During each period there were academic "experts" who were certain that reducing poverty would have little effect on crime because the poor, they said, actually preferred their crime-ridden way of life. Yet each of these groups moved out of crime as they moved into the middle class. . . .

The Underclass

But why can't poor blacks, in particular, climb up into [the] material consumption role as did all of Silberman's other ethnic groups in American history? As James P. Comer eloquently noted, unlike other immigrant groups that were allowed to use kinship and family as a source of security and basis for development, West African culture was "broken in the enslavement process and replaced by the powerlessness and degradation of the slave culture." The fashionable contemporary (yet also very Jeffersonian) version of the slave culture is called the underclass—those who were unable to rise to the middle class during the last two decades. Underlying so much modern commentary on the urban underclass, like the work of Nicholas Lemann and Charles Murray, are the assumptions that poor minorities created it, are responsible for perpetuating it, and would not change if the economic and racial inequalities causing it were dissolved. . . .

The modern underclass was, in truth, created by whites through slavery, and perpetuated by whites through continued class and racial inequities. Although there were many failures, the programs of the 1960s and 1970s did provide opportunities for some to escape and suggested how future programs might be constructed to facilitate further progress. Yet, at the national public sector level, at least, many of the successful or partially successful programs (for example, the Job Corps) were eliminated or reduced; their replacements (for example, the Job Training Partnership Act) have not been directed at those in most need; promising new private sector initiatives (for example, the Competing Competencies Program and JobStart) have not been adapted as public policy on a broad scale; and destructive old policies (for example, federal welfare regulations) have been maintained. . . .

The Poverty Cycle Must Be Broken

When economic opportunities for blacks began to open up in the 1960's, their rate of death from homicide declined—by about 30 percent between 1970 and 1983. Since then, the resurgence of inner-city poverty and the onset of deadly drug wars have arrested the decline. . . .

The poverty cycle must be broken. Economic opportunities and discipline must be created for the alienated, poorly educated young people at the lower margins of black society—who still suffer from the persistent consequences of historical segregation—and of white society.

Ted Robert Gurr, *The New York Times*, April 13, 1989.

Some researchers and social commentators have asserted that poverty and race could not have been responsible for the increase in violent crime in the 1960s and 1970s because blacks had made "great advances." There were, indeed, some gains. Perhaps most publicized was the increase in the number of blacks and other minorities in managerial and professional jobs. By the 1980s, over 1.5 million blacks held such jobs—a doubling in one decade. These changes appear to have resulted primarily from federal education, employment, and affirmative-action programs targeted at minorities. Yet the gains were limited, and economic deprivation continued or increased for those in the group who were disproportionately involved in violent crime—young, poor, inner-city, minority males. The National Urban League's estimates of unemployment among this group during the 1970s were in the range of 50% to 60%; and this rate increased over many of the same years when the crime rate increased. . . .

To an intelligent young man who has a substandard education, few legal-market heroes, and an address in a public housing project with an 80% youth unemployment rate, it is often "rational"—that is, consistent with his values and experiences—to pick up one or more of the illegal options. Both the written literature and personal interviews with incarcerated youth to whom this writer has had access suggest this kind of reasoning: If I'm successful with the crime, I win; if I'm killed, I don't have to worry about tomorrow; and if I'm caught, I'll have food, shelter and continuing (illegal labor-market) education in prison. . . .

To reduce violence in inner cities through remedial education, employment, and extended family programs, we are advocating a very targeted policy—at the "ships in the mud." But the "rising tide" philosophy to lift all ships is relevant in that we need a macro-economic framework that ensures sufficient employment opportunities. This means the kind of demand-side economic policy of the early 1960s that produced 4% unemployment and low inflation. It does not mean the supply-side economics of the 1980s that has fostered further segmentation of America into two societies— one rich and prospering and one becoming poorer. . . .

The Need for Vision

In a speech in Houston the night before he was assassinated, President Kennedy quoted Proverbs: "Where there is no vision, the people perish." Our times await that vision with renewed anticipation. The political will to deal with the American Dilemma and the causes of violence has been dormant. But the dream has not perished. We are undiminished in our capacity to empower the minority poor with youthful vigor and noble purpose.

Distinguishing Between Fact and Opinion

This activity is designed to help develop the basic reading and thinking skill of distinguishing between fact and opinion. Consider the following statement: "Seventy-five percent of the violent crime victims in 1989 were young black men." This is a factual statement because it can be checked by looking at the FBI's 1989 *Uniform Crime Reports*, which contain national statistics on crime. But the statement "Young black men provoke attackers and invite the crimes that are committed on them" is an opinion. Someone who believes innocent black men are being victimized would disagree that they provoke criminal attacks, and many people would object to blaming victims for criminals' behavior.

When investigating controversial issues it is important that one be able to distinguish between statements of fact and statements of opinion. It is also important to recognize that not all statements of fact are true. They may appear to be true, but some are based on inaccurate or false information. For this activity, however, we are concerned with understanding the difference between those statements which appear to be factual and those which appear to be based primarily on opinion.

Most of the following statements are taken from the viewpoints in this chapter. Consider each statement carefully. *Mark O for any statement you believe is an opinion or interpretation of facts. Mark F for any statement you believe is a fact. Mark I for any statement you believe is impossible to judge.*

If you are doing this activity as a member of a class or group, compare your answers with those of other class or group members. Be able to defend your answers. You may discover that others come to different conclusions than you do. Listening to the reasons others present for their answers may give you valuable insights in distinguishing between fact and opinion.

O = *opinion*
F = *fact*
I = *impossible to judge*

1. Assaultive behavior by young men reflects an acceptance of violence in everyday life as a means of expressing anger.

2. The modern underclass was, in truth, created by whites through slavery.

3. Violent crimes reported nationwide in 1988 increased 5.5 percent from 1987.

4. The same criminals repeatedly slip through our "criminal justice" system and victimize innocent citizens time and time again.

5. A violent crime is committed every 5 seconds.

6. Murder is the number one cause of death in the United States for young black men.

7. One source of violence in this country was ethnically oriented. The Irish and Germans ran up crime rates.

8. Nineteenth-century cities did not have traditions, nor habits of deference to authority.

9. The 1950s have been dubbed by one historian "the violent decade."

10. The chances of being a street crime victim are getting smaller and will continue to shrink for the next several decades.

11. At the turn of the century, Winston Churchill, already a keen student of American affairs, observed that the United States had the most violent industrial relations of any western country.

12. While violent crime will decrease in the future, it won't disappear.

13. What's especially troubling about our present crime situation is that is exists in the face of a decade and a half of intensive anticrime efforts.

14. Today's normative victim and criminal share this profile: young, male, black or Hispanic, undereducated, unmarried, unemployed.

15. *Newsweek's* cover story on crime in 1981 reflected the frustrating and depressing impasse our nation had reached.

16. Media-manufactured myths about crime have robbed women of their sense of safety.

Periodical Bibliography

The following articles have been selected to supplement the diverse views presented in this chapter.

Vanessa Baird	"Blow by Blow," *New Internationalist,* September 1988.
Robert James Bidinotto	"The Law Criminals Love," *Reader's Digest,* September 1989.
Robert L. Bonn	"The Lived Experience of Crime," *The World & I,* March 1989.
Tony Bouza	"Pandering to Popular Fear Won't Stop Crime," *In These Times,* October 18-24, 1989.
Patrick M. Buchanan	"Crime and Race," *Conservative Digest,* July/August 1989.
Harold Evans	"When the Guilty Go Free," *U.S. News & World Report,* May 22, 1989.
Dianne Feinstein	"Law-Ordered Release of Vicious Felons Is a Crime," *Los Angeles Times,* May 4, 1987.
Andrew Hacker	"Black Crime, White Racism," *The New York Review of Books,* March 3, 1988.
Albert L. Huebner	"The Pleasure Principle," *East/West,* May 1989.
Alex Kotlowitz	"Urban Wastelands: In Some Small Cities, Poverty, Crime Top Metropolitan Levels," *The Wall Street Journal,* June 22, 1988.
Gerald F. Kreyche	"A Nation Afraid," *USA Today,* May 1989.
Thomas Moore	"The Black-on-Black Crime Plague," *U.S. News & World Report,* August 22, 1988.
National Review	"Calling Lyndon Johnson," May 5, 1989.
Jim Naughton	"The Mothers' Crusade in Murder City," *The Washington Post National Weekly Edition,* July 6, 1987.
Boyce Rensberger	"New Findings on the Crime Rate of Urban Black Youth," *The Washington Post National Weekly Edition,* September 4, 1988.
Jean C. Weiss	"Prejudice, Conflict, and Ethnoviolence: A National Dilemma," *USA Today,* May 1989.

How Can Drug-Related Violence Be Reduced?

Chapter Preface

*We're tolerating more. . . . The height of it was about three months
ago when I saw a man dead with a bullet wound in his head. I
remember how I used to feel if I saw a dead animal in the road or
something. I couldn't eat. But this just sort of struck me as routine,
like I almost expected to see it.*
   —Tedd Miller, resident of a Washington, D.C.,
      neighborhood plagued by drug dealers

In 1988, Washington, D.C. was dubbed the nation's murder
capital when its homicide rate became the highest among U.S.
cities. Almost sixty out of one-hundred thousand people were
murdered there that year. The District of Columbia's Office of
Criminal Justice estimated that the motive in 80 percent of the
murders was drug-related. Far from being an anomaly, Washington
is part of a national trend of drug-related violence. Detroit, Miami,
Chicago, Baltimore, Houston, Los Angeles, and several other large
cities also suffer from scores of drug-related killings.
   In several cities, the violence is committed by members of drug-
dealing gangs. Los Angeles gangs are the most numerous. That
city is estimated to have between five and six hundred different
gangs with memberships totaling fifty to seventy thousand people,
mainly teenagers. For many, the incentive to join drug-dealing
gangs is immense. Reporter William Shawcross points out that
"Dealers can buy a kilo of cocaine for about $12,000 and sell it
in little packets on the streets for about $250,000." The drug trade
offers jobs to children of all ages, Shawcross notes. "Nine-year-
olds employed as lookouts may be paid $100 a day. Slightly older
kids who 'run' the stuff from place to place will get $300." It is
not surprising then that drug dealing and gangs are most prevalent
in America's inner cities, places where jobs are scarce and drug
money is highly attractive.
   The drug-related crime that affects many of America's neighborhoods is a central concern of the authors in the following
chapter.

51

*"Some parts of our cities are being destroyed
by gangs competing for the right to destroy
lives by selling drugs. Those gangs have to be
defeated."*

More Law Enforcement Can Reduce Drug Violence

James Q. Wilson and John J. DiIulio Jr.

James Q. Wilson, the co-author of *Crime and Human Nature*, is the
Collins Professor of Management and Public Policy at the University of California in Los Angeles. John J. DiIulio Jr., the author
of *Governing Prisons*, teaches political science at Princeton University in Princeton, New Jersey. In the following viewpoint, Wilson
and DiIulio argue that the damage drug abuse inflicts on users
also hurts society as a whole. They support arresting and imprisoning drug dealers as a way to reduce drug-related violence.

As you read, consider the following questions:

1. What effects has crack had on inner city neighborhoods,
   according to Wilson and DiIulio?
2. What do the authors mean by the phrase, "revolving door
   criminal justice system"? How can this system be made
   more effective, in their opinion?
3. How do the authors hope communities will respond to
   increased law enforcement?

James Q. Wilson and John J. DiIulio Jr., "Crackdown," *The New Republic*, July 10, 1989.
Reprinted by permission of THE NEW REPUBLIC, © 1989, The New Republic, Inc.

According to the projections, crime was supposed to be under control by now. The postwar baby-boom generation, which moved into its crime-prone years during the early 1960s, has grown up, yielding its place to the (proportionately) less numerous baby-bust generation. With relatively fewer 18-year-olds around, we should all be walking safer streets.

And in fact for most people crime *has* gone down. The Census Bureau's victimization surveys tell us that between 1980 and 1987 the burglary rate declined by 27 percent, the robbery rate by 21 percent. Despite what we hear, 3,000 fewer murders were committed in 1987 than in 1980. Even in some big cities that are in the news for the frequency with which their residents kill each other, the homicide rate has decreased. Take Los Angeles: despite freeway shootings and gang warfare, there were 261 fewer murders in 1987 than in 1980, a drop of more than 20 percent.

Enclaves of Violence

But in specific enclaves the horror stories are all too true. In south central Los Angeles, in much of Newark, in and around the housing projects of Chicago, in the South Bronx and Bedford-Stuyvesant sections of New York, and in parts of Washington, D.C., conditions are not much better than they are in Beirut on a bad day. Drugs, especially crack, are sold openly on street corners; rival gangs shoot at each other from moving automobiles; automatic weapons are carried by teenagers onto school playgrounds; innocent people hide behind double-locked doors and shuttered windows. In Los Angeles there is at least one gang murder every day, Sundays included. A ten-foot-high concrete wall is being built around the junior high school one of us attended, in order, the principal explained, to keep stray bullets from hitting children on the playground.

The problem is drugs and the brutal struggles among competing gangs for control of the lucrative drug markets. The drug of choice is crack (except in Washington, where it is PCP). The crack craze has led to conditions far worse than were found in these same neighborhoods a decade or so ago, when heroin was the preferred drug. The reasons for the change are not reassuring.

Crack is a stimulant; heroin is a sedative. Crack produces exceptional euphoria; heroin produces, after a quick "rush," oblivion. Crack (and PCP) addicts are often stimulated to acts of violence and daring that make them dangerous to themselves as well as to others; heroin addicts are rarely violent when high— the drug even depresses the sexual drive.

Crack is marketed by competitive distribution systems, some of whose members are fighting—literally—to establish monopoly control. Heroin (at least on the East Coast) was marketed in a criminal environment dominated by established monopolies that were well equipped, in muscle and in political connections, to protect their market shares with a minimum of random violence.

Crack users have no attractive chemical alternative. The drug is far more rewarding than any substitute. Heroin users who had progressed to the point where they wanted nothing but relief from the pains of withdrawal and the diseases caused by intravenous injection could take oral methadone. The heroin substitute, though addictive, required no injections, prevented withdrawal pains, and (in the correct dosages) produced little or no "high."

In short, certain neighborhoods of our larger cities are being ravaged by a drug that consumers find more alluring than heroin, that stimulates rather than sedates its users, that suppliers must use violence to sell, and that therapists are at a loss to manage by chemical means.

Costs and Drug Policy

Attempting to suppress the use of drugs is very costly. Some people therefore conclude that we must eliminate all the costs of law enforcement by repealing the laws that are being enforced. The result would be less crime, fewer and weaker gangs, and an opportunity to address the public health problems in a straightforward manner.

But legalizing drugs would also entail costs. Those costs are hard to measure, in part because they are to a large degree moral and in part because we have so little experience with legalized drugs.

Jail Time

A full frontal assault should be waged against the drug user. Those arrested for possession or use should be prosecuted to the fullest extent of the law. A minimum sentence for those convicted on misdemeanor drug counts should be two or three days in local jail. No exception should be made for first-time offenders (the rationale being that the shock of jail will deter them from future use). Mandatory jail sentences on misdemeanor counts should become progressively stiffer with repeated offenses. Eventually, a message will be sent to users that anyone arrested for drugs—no matter how small the quantity—will serve at least a few days in jail.

Joseph Perkins, *The Wall Street Journal*, May 26, 1988.

There is an obvious moral reason for attempting to discourage drug use: the heavy consumption of certain drugs ravages human character. These drugs—principally heroin, cocaine, and crack—are for many people powerfully reinforcing. The pleasure or oblivion they produce leads many users to devote their lives to seeking pleasure or oblivion, and to do so regardless of the cost in ordinary human virtues, such as temperance, duty, and sympathy.

The dignity, autonomy, and productivity of users is at best impaired, at worst destroyed. . . .

We believe that the moral and welfare costs of heavy drug use are so large that society should continue to enforce the laws against its use for the sake of keeping the number of users as small as possible. But we recognize that by adopting this position, we are placing a heavy burden on those poor communities where drug use is endemic. We are allowing these neighborhoods to be more violent than they would be if the drug were legal. Since we do not live in such communities, we must ask ourselves whether our preferences can be justified to people who do.

The answer to that question is given by the testimony of those who live in the midst of the problem. They want drugs kept illegal. They say so and their representatives in Congress say so. We hope that our libertarian critics will not accuse the people of Watts, Anacostia, and the South Bronx of suffering from false consciousness on this matter. These people know what drug use is and they don't like it.

Protecting Inner Cities

But if drugs are to be kept illegal, we have a special responsibility to prevent the streets of inner-city neighborhoods from being controlled by those who seek to profit from the trade. We have not done a very good job of this.

In some places there may not be enough police. In others the cops are just badly used, as when the focus is on making a case against "Mr. Big," the local drug kingpin. There are two things wrong with this. First, nothing is easier than replacing Mr. Big; indeed, often the police get evidence on him from tips supplied by his would-be replacement. Meanwhile the distribution of drugs goes on unabated. Second, arresting Mr. Big does nothing to improve the lives of the decent people in the neighborhood who want the drug dealers off the street.

Arrest Dealers

Many cities, notably New York, have recognized this and are concentrating on street-level dealers. The NYPD [New York Police Department] has wrested control from the drug dealers in parts of the Lower East Side, all of Washington Square Park, much of West 107th Street, and other places. But they have done so at a cost, what Aric Press of *Newsweek* calls the criminal justice equivalent of bulimia. The police go on an arrest binge, and then, "overwhelmed and overfed, the rest of the system—prosecutors, defenders, judges, and jailers—has spent its days in an endless purge, desperately trying to find ways to move its population before it gets hit with another wave tomorrow." The purgatives included granting early release to some inmates and trying to shift other city prisoners to state penitentiaries; pressuring the governor to authorize the appointment of more judges while encouraging faster plea bargaining to clear the crowded dockets; and building "temporary" holding facilities for new arrestees.

The District of Columbia has begun to enter the bulimia phase. The number of people going through the criminal justice system on drug charges has exploded. Between 1983 and 1987 drug arrests increased by 45 percent, drug prosecutions by over 500 percent, drug convictions by over 700 percent. Clearly judges and prosecutors were starting to get tough. But until very recently, the toughness stopped at the jailhouse door. As recently as 1986, only seven percent of the adults arrested on drug charges—and only 20 percent of those convicted on such charges—were sent to the city's principal correctional facility at Lorton. Then, suddenly, the system lurched into overdrive. Between 1986 and 1987 the number of drug incarcerations more than doubled, so that by the end of the year an adult arrested on a drug charge had a one-in-five chance of going to jail, and one convicted on such a charge had a one-in-two chance of winding up at Lorton.

Upgrade the System

The General Accounting Office reports that in New York City individuals arrested for drug trafficking spend an average of less than 18 hours in the criminal justice system, from arrest to release. Fewer than five percent spend more than 30 days in jail. Not surprisingly, law enforcement officials complain bitterly that even repeat drug offenders often receive virtually no punishment. Police frustration with this situation may well account for the surprisingly low proportion of local police officers assigned to narcotics work. According to a survey by the International Association of Chiefs of Police, full-time narcotics personnel in local police departments constitute only one to five percent of the total force.

In short, the state and local criminal justice system is buckling under the weight of the drug war. If drug users are to be deterred, and dealers punished, it will be necessary to upgrade substantially every aspect of that system, from police to prisons.

Jeffrey A. Eisenach, The Heritage Foundation *State Backgrounder*, July 7, 1989.

This means that, until very recently, the price of drug dealing in Washington has been quite low. Those who say that "law enforcement has failed" should remember that until 1987 it was barely tried. Police Chief Isaac Fulwood says that the same dealer may be arrested eight or nine times in the space of a few weeks. The city has been operating a revolving-door criminal justice system.

One reason for the speed with which the door revolves is that in Washington, as in most parts of the country, the prisons are jammed full. Another factor is that professional drug dealers know they can get a favorable plea bargain if they threaten to make the system give them a full trial, replete with every conceivable motion. The mere threat of such a demand is ordinarily enough to ensure that an attractive bargain is offered.

More Prisons

How can an overtaxed system help protect people in the drug-ridden neighborhoods? Building more conventional prisons is part of the answer, but that takes a lot of time, and no one wants them in their back yard. The goal is to take drug dealers off the streets for a longer period than the time it takes to be booked and released. One step is to ensure that no good arrest is washed out for want of prosecution because of a shortage of judges, prosecutors, and public defenders. These are not cheap, but candidates for these posts are more readily available than vacant lots on which to build jails.

Nevertheless, prisons are still needed and can be had, provided we are willing to think of alternatives to conventional holding tanks. One is to reserve regular prison space for major traffickers and to use parts of present (or all of former) military camps as boot camps for lower-level dealers. At these minimum-security camps, inmates would receive physical training, military discipline, and drug-abuse treatment, all under the direction of military personnel and with the aim of preparing them for a life that would combine, to the extent possible, the requirement of regular drug tests and the opportunity for gainful employment.

Meanwhile, the chances of released inmates rejoining old gangs can perhaps be reduced by enforcing a law, such as the one passed in California, that makes mere membership in certain gangs illegal and attaches civil or criminal penalties to parents who knowingly allow their children to join them.

Critics of punishment object that (1) incarceration is not a deterrent, either because young drug dealers are not "rational" or because drug trafficking is so lucrative as to make short stays behind a fence worth it; and that (2) the only true solution to the drug problem is to reduce the demand for drugs by education and treatment. We are tempted to respond to these views by pointing out that, insofar as we can tell, each is wrong in whole or in substantial part. Instead, let's assume that these views are entirely correct. They are also irrelevant.

Roust the Bad Guys

At this stage, we are not trying to deter drug sales or reduce drug use. All we wish to do is to reassert lawful public control over public spaces. Everything else we may wish to achieve—reducing the demand for drugs, curing the users of drugs, deterring the sale of drugs—can only be done after the public and the police, not the dealers and the gangs, are in charge of the neighborhoods. In the short run, this can be done by repeatedly arresting every suspected dealer and user and sending them through the revolving door. If we cannot increase the severity of the penalties they face, we can at least increase the frequency with which they bear them. In police terms, we want to roust the bad guys.

After the bad guys find they are making repeated trips to the same prison camps, the decent people of the neighborhood must form organizations willing and able to work with the police to keep the bad guys from regaining control of the streets. The Kenilworth-Parkside area of Washington shows what can be done. This neighborhood, the site of a public housing project, was an open-air drug market that spawned all manner of crime. In 1982 a tenants' committee led by Kimi Gray formed a corporation and assumed control of the housing project. Though the residents were primarily unwed mothers living on welfare, over the next five years their association collected the rents, ran the buildings, enforced school attendance on the children, and got rid of the addicts. In 1988 the association signed a contract to purchase the project from the government. . . .

Much is made these days of "community-oriented" policing. Both of us have written favorably about it and the problem-solving, police-neighborhood collaboration that lies at its heart. But the success stories are always in communities in which the people are willing to step forward and the police are willing to meet them halfway. Where open-air drug markets operate every night, where Uzi-toting thugs shoot rivals and bystanders alike, it is a brave or foolhardy resident who will even testify against a criminal, much less lead an anticrime crusade. But once the police have shown that they can control the streets, even if the dealers they have chased off spend only brief (albeit frequent) periods in prison camp, there is an opportunity to build new partnerships. . . .

Saving Cities

The facts are these: some parts of our cities are being destroyed by gangs competing for the right to destroy lives by selling drugs. Those gangs have to be defeated, even if it means hiring more judges and building more correctional faciliters. After that we can help communities reorganize themselves so that the good people control the streets and the teachers, doctors, and scientists have a chance to find out what will prevent another addictive epidemic from breaking out when some chemist discovers a drug that is even cheaper and more euphoria-inducing than crack. And that last event, we can be certain, will happen.

"We cannot prosecute our way out of the drug problem."

More Law Enforcement Cannot Reduce Drug Violence

Kurt L. Schmoke

Baltimore's mayor Kurt L. Schmoke received national attention in April 1988 when he made a speech at a mayor's conference advocating the legalization of drugs. A former state's attorney who prosecuted drug dealers, Schmoke contends that the criminal justice system has been deluged with drug cases. Spending more money to catch drug dealers is useless, he writes, because the over-burdened criminal justice system cannot prosecute all the dealers, and overcrowded prisons cannot house convicted offenders. Simply arresting dealers and drug users would do nothing to reduce violence, he concludes.

As you read, consider the following questions:

1. Why does Schmoke argue that decriminalization is a means to a desired end?
2. According to the author, how does prosecuting drug offenders actually harm the criminal justice system?

Kurt L. Schmoke, prepared testimony before the U.S. House Select Committee on Narcotics Abuse and Control, September 29, 1988.

"The addict is denied the medical care he urgently needs, open and above-board sources . . . are closed to him, and he is driven to the under-world where he can get his drug, but of course surreptitiously and in violation of the law." (from *American Medicine,* 1915)

The foregoing observation was made on the heels of the passage of the Harrison Narcotics Act. It hasn't aged a day. As the writer was quick to recognize, the effectiveness of the Harrison Narcotics Act—the federal government's first attempt to stamp out the use of narcotics (and other drugs incorrectly labeled narcotics)—is hampered by two inescapable facts. First, addiction is a disease and, whether we want to admit it or not, addicts need medical care. And second, in the absence of access to legitimate sources of drugs for medical care, a criminal underworld will quickly step into the breach and sell the addict the drugs that he or she cannot otherwise obtain.

A Failed Policy

Since the Harrison Narcotics Act was first passed, the United States has made herculean efforts to try to get around the reality that drug prohibition increases crime without doing away with addiction. Nevertheless, that reality remains as true today as ever. We have spent years and untold billions of dollars trying to square the circle, and inevitably we have failed.

That is not to say that there have been no drug-related changes since 1914. There are now more kinds of drugs (crack and PCP, to name two) and more potent drugs. There are more addicts (heroin addiction has doubled since 1914), and as is apparent to anyone living in a major city, there is more crime. Much more. The only thing there is less of now than in 1914 is hope—hope that law enforcement can bring an end to this long national nightmare.

It is sometimes said that the United States has no drug policy. That is both true and untrue. We *do* have a drug policy, and it can be stated with almost child-like simplicity. Our policy is zero use of all illicit drugs all the time. Among Schedule I drugs, few distinctions are made as to physical harm or psychological effects. It's a policy that is both unambiguous and unimaginative. It is also unattainable. And in that sense, zero use, or zero tolerance as it is sometimes called, is not a policy at all—it's a fantasy.

There is, however, an alternative to a drug policy based primarily on law enforcement, and it is an alternative that has worked before. The repeal of alcohol Prohibition helped rather than hurt this country, and a measured and carefully implemented program of drug decriminalization would do the same.

The case for decriminalization is overwhelming. But that is not to say that it is without risk. Providing legal access to currently illicit substances carries with it the chance—although by no means the certainty—that the number of people using and abusing drugs will increase. But addiction, for all of its attendant medical, social and moral problems is but one evil associated with drugs. Moreover, the criminalization of narcotics, cocaine and marijuana has not solved the problem of their use. Twelve million Americans used cocaine at least once in 1985. And marijuana use is estimated to be at least twice that number. According to the General Accounting Office, Americans in 1987 bought 178 tons of cocaine, 12 tons of heroin and 600,000 tons of marijuana. Overall, millions of Americans are regularly using illegal drugs. Their reasons may vary, as do their race, income level and ability to quit. Nevertheless, in asking the criminal justice system to put an end to this tragic reality of American life, we have, quite simply, asked it to do the impossible.

While some may disagree, I believe the unwelcome honor of the worst drug-related evil goes to crime and the disintegration and demoralization of our cities—an evil that only the decriminalization of drugs has any chance of solving.

Except for libertarians—which I am not—advocates of decriminalization do not base their position on a belief that people have an inherent right to use drugs. On the contrary, advocates of decriminalization simply view it as preferable to our present policy.

Ed Gamble. Reprinted by permission.

Decriminalization is a means to a much desired end: getting the criminal justice system out of the business of trying to control the health problem of drug abuse and putting that responsibility where it belongs—in the hands of our public health system. This is by no means a new idea.

In 1936, August Vollmer, who in the course of his career served as a police chief, professor of police administration and president of the International Association of Chiefs of Police, wrote:

> Drug addiction, like prostitution and liquor, is not a police problem; it never has been and never can be solved by policemen. It is first and last a medical problem, and if there is a solution it will be discovered not by policemen, but by scientific and competently trained medical experts whose sole objective will be the reduction and possible eradication of this devastating appetite.

August Vollmer was right in 1936 and he's still right. . . .

Our current drug policy is destined to fail and ought to be changed for precisely the reasons suggested by *American Medicine* in 1915.

Addiction Is a Disease

To begin with, addiction *is* a disease. In the words of the American Medical Association, "It is clear that addiction is not simply the product of a failure of individual will power. . . . It is properly viewed as a disease, and one that physicians can help many individuals control and overcome."

The nature of addiction is very important to the argument in favor of decriminalization. We cannot hope to solve addiction through punishment. As pointed out in the 1972 *Consumer Union's Report* on drugs, even after prolonged periods of incarceration, during which they have no access to heroin, most addicts are still defeated by their physical dependence and return to drugs. Moreover, the results are pretty much the same when addicts leave a therapeutic treatment setting such as Synanon. The sad truth is that heroin and morphine addiction is, for most users, a lifetime affliction that is impervious to any punishment that the criminal justice system could reasonably mete out.

Given the nature of addiction—whether to narcotics or cocaine—and the very large number of Americans using drugs (The National Institute on Drug Abuse estimates that one in six working Americans has a substance abuse problem), laws restricting their possession and sale have had predictable consequences— most of them bad. What follows is a summary of just some of those consequences.

Addicts commit crimes in order to pay for their drug habits. According to the Justice Department, 90% of those who voluntarily seek treatment are turned away. In other words, on any given day, nine out of every ten addicts have no legal way to satisfy their addiction. And failing to secure help, an untreated addict will commit a crime every other day to maintain his habit.

Whether one relies on studies—such as the analysis of 573 narcotics users in Miami, who during a 12-month period were shown to have committed "6000 robberies and assaults, almost 6700 burglaries . . . and more than 46,000 other events of larceny and fraud"—or simple observation, it is indisputable that drug users are committing vast amounts of crime and non-drug using Americans are frequently the silent victims of those crimes. Baltimore, the city with which I am most familiar, is no exception to this problem. According to James A. Inciardi, of the Division of Criminal Justice at the University of Delaware, a 1983 study of addicts in Baltimore showed that ". . .there were high rates of criminality among heroin users during those periods that they were addicted and markedly lower rates during times of nonaddiction." The study also showed that addicts committed crimes on a persistent day-to-day basis and over a long period of time. And the trends are getting worse. Thus while the total number of arrests in Baltimore remained almost unchanged between 1983 and 1987, there was an approximately 40% increase in the number of drug-related arrests. This increase, which is no doubt due in part to the increase in cocaine distribution and use, was taking place at the same time the federal government was increasing its enforcement and interdiction efforts.

The Costs of Prohibition

Every dollar spent to punish a drug user or seller is a dollar that cannot be spent collecting restitution from a robber. Every hour spent investigating a drug user or seller is an hour that could have been used to find a missing child. Every trial held to prosecute a drug user or seller is court time that could be used to prosecute a rapist in a case that might otherwise have been plea bargained. These and countless other expenditures are the "opportunity costs" of drug prohibition.

Randy E. Barnett, in *Dealing with Drugs*, 1987.

On the other hand, statistics compiled by the Maryland Drug and Alcohol Abuse Administration indicate that crime rates go down among addicts when treatment is available. Thus, for example, of the 6,910 Baltimore residents admitted to drug abuse treatment in fiscal year 1987, 4,386 or 63% had been arrested one or more times in the 24-month period prior to admission to treatment. Whereas, of the 6,698 Baltimore City residents who were discharged from drug treatment in fiscal year 1987, 6,152 or 91.8% were not arrested during the time of their treatment. These statistics tend to support the view that one way to greatly reduce drug-related crime is to assure addicts access to methadone or other drugs without having to resort to the black market. As Professor Ethan Nadelmann points out, "If the drugs to which addicts are addicted were significantly cheaper—which would be the case if they were legalized—the number of crimes committed by drug addicts to pay for their habits would, in all likelihood, decline dramatically.". . .

Overload of the Criminal Justice System

We cannot prosecute our way out of the drug problem. There are several reasons for this, but the most basic reason is that the criminal justice system cannot—without sacrificing our civil liberties—handle the sheer volume of drug-related cases.

Nationwide in 1987, over 750,000 people were arrested for violating drug laws. Most of these arrests were for possession. In Baltimore, there were 13,037 drug-related arrests in 1987. Between January 1, 1988 and July 1, 1988, there were 7,981 drug-related arrests. Those numbers are large, but they hardly reflect the annual total number of drug violations committed in Baltimore. Should we therefore try to arrest still more? Yes—as long as the laws are on the books. But as a practical matter, we don't have any place to put the drug offenders we're arresting now. The population in the Baltimore City Jail is currently 2,900 inmates. *The capacity of the Baltimore City Jail is only 2,700 inmates.* This shortage of prison space has led to severe overcrowding, and the City is now under court order to reduce its jail population.

The extent to which drug crimes consume prison space can be seen in Baltimore City. Of the total Baltimore City Jail population, 700 persons, or about 25%, are incarcerated for possession and/or possession with intent to distribute. However, it is estimated that 80% of the Baltimore City Jail population is incarcerated for drug-related crimes.

In jurisdictions outside of Baltimore, the numbers are just as bad, or worse. In New York City, for example, drug-law violations accounted for 40% of all felony indictments, and in Washington, D.C., the number was 50%.

Our federal prison system has similar problems. It was built to house 28,000 prisoners and now has 44,000, one-third of whom are there on drug charges. Fifteen years from now, it is expected that half of the 100,000 to 150,000 federal prisoners will be incarcerated for drug violations.

Will more prisons help? Not in any significant way. We simply can't build enough of them to hold all of America's drug offenders—which number in the millions. And even if we could, the cost would far exceed what American taxpayers would be willing to pay.

Decriminalization is the single most effective step we could take to reduce prison overcrowding. And with less crowded prisons, there will be less pressure on prosecutors to plea bargain and far greater chance that non-drug criminals will go to jail—and stay in jail.

Already Swamped

Since the courts and jails are already swamped beyond capacity by the arrests that are routinely made (44,000 drug dealers and users over a two-year period in Washington alone, for instance) and since those arrests barely skim the top of the pond, arguing that stricter enforcement is the answer begs a larger question: Who is going to pay the billions of dollars required to build the prisons, hire the judges, train the policemen and employ the prosecutors needed for the load already on hand, let alone the huge one yet to come if we ever get serious about arresting dealers and users?

Hodding Carter III, *The Wall Street Journal*, July 13, 1989.

And then there is this related question: How many predatory crimes of violence are going uninvestigated, unprosecuted and un-punished because of the enormous effort being put into the war on drugs? We may never know. But, regardless of whether the number is large or small, it is the individual citizen and our com-munities that are paying the price of that neglect.

The unvarnished truth is that in our effort to prosecute and im-prison our way out of the war on drugs, we have allowed the drug criminals to put us exactly where they want us: wasting enormous resources—both in money and personnel—attacking the fringes of the problem (the users and small time pushers), while the heart of the problem—the traffickers and their profits—goes unsolved.

In a nutshell, we're only arresting, prosecuting and incarcerating the tip of the iceberg; nevertheless, that tip is far larger than we have the capacity to handle. . . .

Harmful Policies

If the drug laws of the United States simply didn't achieve their intent, perhaps there would be insufficient reason to get rid of them. But our drug laws are doing more than not working—they are violating Hippocrates' famous admonition: first do not harm.

The legal prohibition of narcotics, cocaine and marijuana demonstrably increases the price of those drugs. For example, an importer can purchase a kilogram of heroin for $10,000. By the time that kilogram passes through the hands of several middlemen (wholesalers, retailers and purchasers), its street value can reach $1,000,000. Those kinds of profits can't help but attract major criminal enterprises willing to take any risk to keep their product coming to the American market. . . .

As we learned during alcohol Prohibition, when the government bans a substance that millions of people are determined to use— either out of foolishness, addiction or both—violent criminal syndicates will conspire to manufacture and sell that substance. And they'll do so for one simple reason: enormous black market profits. Punishment won't deter the trade and neither will internecine conflicts (including murder) among the traffickers. Such conflicts are just a way of reducing the competition. Drugs are a multi-billion dollar business, and as long as that's the case, willing buyers will always be able to find willing sellers. . . .

A Soldier in the War on Drugs

As a person now publicly identified with the movement to reform our drug laws through the use of some form of decriminalization, I consider it very important to say that I am not soft on either drug use or drug dealers. I'm a soldier in the war against drugs. I spent years prosecuting and jailing drug traffickers, and had one of the highest rates of incarceration for drug convictions in the country. And if I were still State's Attorney, I would be enforcing the law as vigorously as ever. My experience as a prosecutor did not in any way alter my passionate dislike for drug dealers, it simply convinced me that the present system doesn't work and can't be made to work.

As State's Attorney, I was confronted daily with the victims of our drug crimes, who for the most part are ignored by the opponents of drug decriminalization. One of my most painful duties as State's Attorney was prosecuting drug dealers who injured and sometimes killed police officers. In Baltimore, as in so many other cities, our police officers and undercover agents serve with distinction and uncommon bravery. Their work is dangerous and needs to be highly commended. But that is no reason to ignore common sense. The end-game in the war on drugs is not less supply or more jails, or even the death penalty. It's less profit and less demand— and that will only come about through increased efforts at treatment and prevention.

During the Revolutionary War, the British insisted on wearing red coats and marching in formation. They looked very pretty. They also lost. A good general does not pursue a strategy in the face of overwhelming evidence of failure. Instead, a good general changes from a losing strategy to one that exploits his enemy's weaknesses while exposing his own troops to only as much danger as is required to win. The drug traffickers can be beaten and the public health of the United States can be improved if we're willing to substitute common sense for rhetoric, myth and blind persistence.

"Drug abuse and drug traffickers are responsible for much of the violent crime in our nation."

Upholding Drug Laws Can Reduce Drug Violence

Edward I. Koch

Edward I. Koch served as the mayor of New York City from 1978 to 1990. He has also been a member of the U.S. House of Representatives. A well-known spokesman on the drug issue, Koch argues in the following viewpoint that drug abuse causes violent crime. He cites several studies which show that the majority of people arrested for committing crimes tested positive for drug use. Koch advocates more funding for the war on drugs in order to reduce drug-related violence. This viewpoint is excerpted from testimony Koch presented before the House Select Committee on Narcotics Abuse and Control.

As you read, consider the following questions:

1. Why does Koch argue that providing drugs to addicts is illogical?
2. In the author's opinion, what does the British experience with drug legalization prove?
3. How does Koch propose funding an intensive war on drug abuse?

Edward I. Koch, prepared statement before the U.S. House Select Committee on Narcotics Abuse and Control, September 29, 1988.

Given the devastation that drugs have wrought on our communities and nation, particularly over the last few years, I find it astounding that I am here to discuss a notion that seems to me to be the equivalent of extinguishing a raging fire with napalm—a fire that at this very moment is frying the brains of thousands of Americans.

This committee, along with the very active support of the vast majority of America's mayors, has made valiant efforts in the past few years to devise ways to combat the drug scourge that continues to tear at our nation. Today, a small, small number in these ranks are unwittingly impeding our progress by suggesting that we wave the white flag in the war on drugs and succumb to the enemy. Is their vision for the future of this country nothing better than one of its becoming a banana republic?! I hope not, but surely that is where their proposition would lead us.

I am far from alone in feeling this way. The September 15, 1988 *New York Times* reported that an ABC News poll found that more than 90% of the American public *reject* decriminalizing all illicit drugs. They also believe, by a 2 to 1 ratio, that the legalization of drugs would lead to an increase in crime.

And yet, in part because of the frustration some have had with the difficult task of addressing the drug problem, the idea of legalization has been elevated, undeservedly, to a place within the realm of debatable, if not potential, policy alternatives. Now that it is there, it may in fact be necessary to put the question of legalization on the table, but only to put it to rest, so that we can move forward with the strategies that *will* have an impact.

The Impact of Drugs

Before I continue, let me cite some statistics which reveal the dimension and impact of the drug problem.

There are over 500,000 heroin abusers in this country and six million people who have a serious cocaine or crack abuse problem. Even more troubling is the increasing numbers of our youth who are abusing certain drugs. Although no one knows for certain the number of juveniles using drugs, surveys of high school students have shown dramatic increases in their use of cocaine since 1978.

The devastating effects of drug abuse and the drug trafficking that supplies the abusers with their poison are quite clear. Reliable studies have concluded that drug abuse and drug traffickers are responsible for much of the violent crime in our nation.

These assertions are supported by data from the National Institute of Justice's drug forecasting survey which showed that in New York City, 79% of the surveyed arrestees tested positive for at least one drug (including marijuana), 63% tested positive for cocaine, including crack, and 25% tested positive for heroin.

Indeed, the New York City Police Department has arrested almost 150,000 people for drug related crime between 1986 and 1988—up 17% from 1986 to 1987 and 11% in the first five months of 1988. These data clearly underscore the relationship between drug abuse and crime.

It is undeniable that, if we do not reduce drug abuse, its resulting crime and other destructive physiological consequences will continue to escalate and will result in a national tragedy of much greater proportions than it is today.

A Shocking Suggestion

The suggestion that we should legalize drugs is therefore all the more shocking. How would legalization reduce drug abuse and its resulting devastation and crime? Let's analyze the legalization arguments.

To start with, some would have us believe that the laws against drug use and drug trafficking are prohibitions against a manner of personal conduct or style and that they are the imposition of society's moral values on the individual. This is just not the case. Rather, they are laws that prohibit conduct which destroys not only the individual users, but their families, the innocent victims of their crimes and the very foundation of a productive society.

No Surrender

The war against drugs has been a difficult one. But I cannot believe that we, as a society, are really ready to say: "It's too much trouble to protect our young people from drugs. The use of the military would cause some difficulties—more law enforcement would mean spending more—sound education is too much of a burden—it's just too much trouble for us adults to fulfill our basic responsibilities. So let's open it up, and let our kids take their chances." I cannot believe any society dedicated to the nurture and protection of its children could embrace such reasoning. I don't believe our nation will. So we need not surrender and we need not despair; we can win the war against drugs.

William J. Bennett, Speech at the Second Annual Conference on Drug Free Schools, May 24, 1988.

The proponents of legalization are weak on the specifics of the implementation of a policy of "drugs for all." Some suggest that government should play a "big brother" role, providing fixed doses to addicts, and thereby limiting drug use. Their lack of understanding of drug abuse is startling, since there is no such thing as a fixed dose that will satisfy a drug addict's appetite for greater and greater quantities. Accordingly, the black market that legalizers say will be eliminated, would, of necessity, exist to provide an additional avenue of obtaining that which is not available from "legitimate" sources.

Piggy-backing on the assertion that legalization will eliminate the high profit margins on drug sales and therefore the black market, proponents say that crime associated with drug trafficking will diminish once drugs become an acceptable commodity. They ignore history and the facts.

Britain's Experience

Cheap drugs won't reduce crime and they never have.

In fact, given England's desperate failure to relieve its heroin addiction problem through heroin distribution programs during the 1960s and 1970s, the opposite is closer to the truth.

Until 1970, heroin was freely prescribed in Britain by private doctors. But over-prescription led to a doubling of the addicted population between 1970 and 1980. Then it took off.

Cheap heroin from Pakistan, which sold for $5 a fix on the street, began flooding the black market. Not only was it super cheap, it was more potent than what the government was handing out and came without bureaucratic restrictions. Cheap, potent and hassle free, the new street heroin *quadrupled the number of addicts in five years*. By 1986 the British Home Office estimated that there were 50,000 to 60,000 heroin addicts in the country. Some unofficial estimates were three times greater.

How was crime in Britain affected by legalization? In one 1978 study, 50% of the addicts in government programs were convicted of crimes in their first year of participation. Unemployment among addicts remained chronic too, as did other kinds of drug use—84% of the addicts registered with the government were found to use other illicit drugs as well. All told, the government program was a disaster.

Behavioral Effects

Another facet of the crime problem associated with drugs that is frequently overlooked is that a number of drugs, and crack in particular, have been shown to have behavioral effects that result in violent criminal conduct, not limited to theft, to obtain money to purchase drugs. I don't think that we would be too far from the mark by assuming that the emerging "designer" drugs would have similar effects as the drug sellers search for a product that gives quicker and more intense highs. Should the government distribute or condone these crime-inducing drugs too?

Permitting drug use and encouraging even greater drug use by legalization would perpetuate and *expand* the devastating effects of drug abuse and its resulting crime.

Another erroneous argument for legalization is based on the economic rationale that it would be cheaper to provide drugs to addicts than it is to enforce the laws and pursue anti-drug strategies. It would not be cheaper. As the drug using population increases, the costs to society for the crime and other detrimental health effects of drug abuse would be far greater than they are now. We would still require the police, courts, prosecutors and jails to deal with drug related crime. We would need to dramatically increase treatment programs for those who, once on drugs, want to get off. And we would still have the economic impact on business, not only in terms of lost productivity, but in terms of increased health care insurance, worker safety and unemployment benefits.

Percentage of male arrestees testing positive for any drug, including marijuana (June–November 1987)

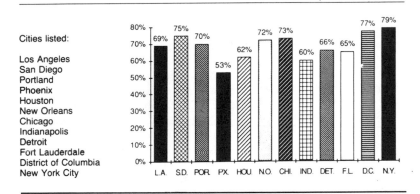

Percentage of male arrestees testing positive for cocaine (June–November 1987)

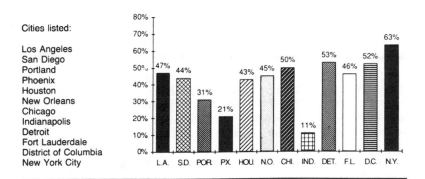

Source: United States Government Printing Office.

Even if it is more expensive to do what we are doing to eradicate this problem, can government's obligation to protect the public safety be abdicated because it is expensive? Clearly not.

In September 1988 on a nationwide television broadcast on this same topic, it was suggested that anti-drug law enforcement efforts, now estimated at $8 billion nationwide, could be cut to $2 billion if drugs were legalized. How can we say that $8 billion is too much to spend? How much is too much? I read in the *Washington Post* that leaders of the infamous Medellin drug cartel offered to pay off Colombia's estimated $15 *billion* national debt in return for immunity from prosecution and the scrapping of the country's extradition treaty with the U.S. This handful of individuals were willing to spend almost twice as much to stay in the game than we, at 240 million strong, are to keep them out. I think that it is all too painfully obvious that $8 billion is not nearly enough and we need to commit more—in the right places.

Part of our problem has been a lack of national commitment— not on the part of the average American, but by those who are representing them. The tough choices that have to be made are not being made. . . .

On a number of occasions I have suggested a three year federal income tax surcharge dedicated *solely* to eliminating the drug problem. I believe that the American public would support such a tax if it were proposed in this context. However, everyone in Washington is loathe to mention that "T" word for any purpose. I believe that that is terribly shortsighted.

Now I'm not throwing the entire burden in the lap of the federal government, but whether it's Los Angeles, New York, Utica or Topeka, on its own, a city can't win the war on drugs. Washington must do its job too.

The cities are already doing their part. New York City, in particular, is dedicated to do whatever it can in terms of fighting the drug war. With 1,400 officers dedicated solely to narcotics interdiction, we are spending *nearly half a billion dollars* in city money to address all aspects of drug control. . . .

Wave the Battle Flag

What it comes down to is this. When people say that we should legalize drugs because law enforcement efforts have failed, they ignore the fact that a truly effective war has yet to be launched against drugs. What we really need to do is more, not less. A real war on drugs must include interdiction of illicit drugs by the armed forces at the borders, in the air and on the high seas. It must include more federal funding for education and treatment on demand. It must include "federalization" of drug prosecution and incarceration. . . .

It is time to raise the battle flag, not wave the white one.

"Most, if not all, 'drug-related murders' are the result of drug prohibition."

Repealing Drug Laws Can Reduce Drug Violence

James Ostrowski

Some people have begun advocating a new approach to reduce drug-related violence—legalizing drugs. James Ostrowski argues in the following viewpoint that legalizing drugs would take the profits out of the drug trade. By legalizing drugs, the government could control the dispensing of drugs and thus eliminate the violence associated with illegal drug deals, he maintains. A Buffalo, New York attorney, Ostrowski has written on drug laws for the Cato Institute, a libertarian research organization in Washington, D.C.

As you read, consider the following questions:

1. Why does the author relabel "drug-related violence" as "prohibition-related violence"?
2. How does the enforcement of drug laws affect the criminal justice system, in the author's opinion?
3. What does the author believe the British experience with drug legalization proves?

James Ostrowski, "Thinking About Drug Legalization," *Cato Institute Policy Analysis*, May 25, 1989, no. 121. Reprinted by permission of the Cato Institute.

On Thursday, March 17, 1988, at 10:45 p.m., in the Bronx, Vernia Brown was killed by stray bullets fired in a dispute over illegal drugs. The 19-year-old mother of one was not involved in the dispute, yet her death was a direct consequence of the "war on drugs."

By now, there can be little doubt that most, if not all, "drug-related murders" are the result of drug prohibition. The same type of violence came with the Eighteenth Amendment's ban of alcohol in 1920. The murder rate rose with the start of Prohibition, remained high during Prohibition, and then declined for *11 consecutive years* when Prohibition ended. The rate of assaults with a firearm rose with Prohibition and declined for *10 consecutive years* after Prohibition. In the last year of Prohibition—1933—there were 12,124 homicides and 7,863 assaults with firearms; by 1941 these figures had declined to 8,048 and 4,525, respectively. . . .

The Crisis of Drug Prohibition

Several events have dramatized the failures and costly side effects of the war on drugs: A woman sitting in her kitchen in Washington, D.C., is killed by a stray bullet from a drug dealers' shootout. A policeman guarding a witness in a drug case is brutally executed in Queens. In Los Angeles, drug-related gang warfare breaks out. General Manuel Noriega engineers a coup d'etat in Panama after he is accused of being one of history's great drug dealers. Colombia's courts refuse to extradite major drug dealers to the United States, and its attorney general is brazenly murdered by the Colombian drug cartel. An update of the Kerner Report concludes that the economic status of blacks relative to whites has not improved in 20 years—in part because many blacks are trapped in drug-crime-infested inner cities, where economic progress is slow.

In spite of the greatest anti-drug enforcement effort in U.S. history, the drug problem is worse than ever. What should be done now? Get tougher in the war on drugs? Imprison middle-class drug users? Use the military? Impose the death penalty for drug dealing? Shoot down unmarked planes entering the United States?

The status quo is intolerable—everyone agrees on that. But there are only two alternatives: further escalate the war on drugs, or legalize them. Once the public grasps the consequences of escalation, legalization may win out by default. . . .

Drug laws greatly increase the price of illegal drugs, often forcing users to steal to get the money to obtain them. Although difficult to estimate, the black market prices of heroin and cocaine appear to be about 100 times greater than their pharmaceutical prices. For example, a hospital-dispensed dose of morphine (a drug from which heroin is relatively easily derived) costs only pennies; legal cocaine costs about $20 per ounce. It is frequently estimated that at least 40 percent of all property crime in the United States is committed by drug users so that they can maintain their habits. That amounts to about four million crimes per year and $7.5 billion in stolen property.

Supporters of prohibition have traditionally used drug-related crime as a simplistic argument for enforcement: Stop drug use to stop drug-related crime. They have even exaggerated the amount of such crime in the hopes of demonstrating a need for larger budgets and greater powers. But the more astute prohibitionists have noticed that drug-related crime is in fact drug-*law*-related. Thus, in many cases they have begun to argue that even if drugs were legal and thus relatively inexpensive, drug users would still commit crimes simply because they are criminals at heart.

The fact is, while some researchers have questioned the causal connection between illegal drugs and street crime, many studies over a long period have confirmed what every inner-city dweller already knows: Drug users steal to get the money to buy expensive illegal drugs. . . .

Prohibition also causes what the media and police misname "drug-related violence." This *prohibition*-related violence includes all the random shootings and murders associated with black market drug transactions: ripoffs, eliminating the competition, killing informers, and killing suspected informers.

Competition

Legalization would bring competition to the drug industry, removing the extraordinary profits to be made in the illicit drug trade.

Faced with the thin margins of a real competitive enterprise, the violent drug lords would retreat to other enterprises. Just as the repeal of Prohibition marked the diminution of gangsters, so would the legalization of drugs lessen the violent drug wars on our urban streets.

Richard Dennis, *The Drug Policy Letter*, March/April 1989.

Those who doubt that prohibition is responsible for this violence need only note the absence of violence in the legal drug market. For example, there is no violence associated with the production, distribution, and sale of alcohol. Such violence was ended by the repeal of Prohibition.

The President's Commission on Organized Crime estimates a total of about 70 drug-market murders yearly in Miami alone. Based on that figure and FBI [Federal Bureau of Investigation] data, a reasonable nationwide estimate would be at least 750 such murders each year. Estimates from New York and Washington would suggest an even higher figure.

About 10 law enforcement officers are killed enforcing drug laws each year. In New York City, 5 officers were killed in 1988. These men—Robert Venable, Edward Byrne, John F. McKormick, Christopher Hoban, and Michael Buczek—were also victims of drug prohibition.

Do Drugs Cause Crime?

It is often thought that illegal drugs cause crime through their biochemical effects on the mind. In fact, marijuana laws were originally justified on that basis. Today, the notion that marijuana causes crime "is no longer taken seriously by even the most ardent [anti-]marijuana propagandists," [according to Erich Goode]. Regarding heroin [Arnold Trebach writes]:

> There is no doubt that heroin use in and of itself . . . is a neutral act in terms of its potential criminogenic effect upon an individual's behavior. . . . There is nothing in the pharmacology, or physical or psychological impact, of the drug that propels a user to crime. . . .

When the New York City Police Department announced that 38 percent of murders in the city in 1987 were "drug-related," Deputy Chief Raymond W. Kelly explained:

> When we say drug-related, we're essentially talking about territorial disputes or disputes over possession. . . . We're not talking about where somebody is deranged because they're on a drug. It's very difficult to measure that. . . .

Each dollar spent enforcing drug laws and fighting the violent crime these laws stimulate is a dollar that cannot be spent fighting other violent crime. The one law enforcement technique that definitely works is the specific deterrence of incarceration. Put a violent career criminal in prison for five years and that person simply will not commit his usual quota of over 100 serious crimes per year.

But right now, there are not enough judges and prosecutors to try cases or enough prison spaces to house convicts. In 1987, the federal prison system had 44,000 inmates, including 16,000 drug offenders, while official capacity was only 28,000. About 40 statewide prison systems are operating under court orders due to overcrowding or poor conditions.

Because of the sheer lack of prison space, violent criminals frequently are given deals, probation, or shorter terms than they deserve. Then they are back on the streets, and often back to serious crime. For example, in 1987 in New York City, a man who had been released after serving 5 years of a 15-year term for robbery was arrested again for auto theft, released on bail, and finally arrested once more and indicted for rape and robbery at knifepoint.

In a world of scarce prison resources, sending a drug offender to prison for one year is equivalent to freeing a violent criminal to commit 40 robberies, 7 assaults, 110 burglaries, and 25 auto thefts. . . .

Drug prohibition has had devastating effects on inner-city minority communities. A poorly educated young person in the inner city now has three choices: welfare, a low-wage job, or the glamorous and high-profit drug business. It is no wonder that large numbers of ghetto youth have gone into drug dealing, some of them as young as 10 years old. When the most successful people in a community are those engaged in illegal activities, the natural order of the community is destroyed. A *New York Times* article reported that "the underground drug economy . . . puts more power in the hands of teen-agers" and makes the entire community more violent. How can a mother maintain authority over a 16-year-old son who pays the rent out of his petty cash? How can a teacher persuade students to study hard, when dropouts drive BMWs? The profits from prohibition make a mockery of the work ethic and of family authority.

A Healthy, Safe Society

We law reformers want to see our children grow up drug free in a healthy, democratic, and safe society. We want all Americans to be able to walk the streets without worrying about harm from violent criminals. We want the freedom and privacy of all Americans to be preserved and protected by the government. We want the twin scourges of AIDS and drug abuse to be controlled and its victims treated effectively and compassionately by medical authorities and society. We want uncorrupted police institutions capable of providing the intelligent assistance that a democratic people expect of their law enforcement agencies.

We oppose the drug war because it does not bring us these important goals which are vital to a free society with an expanding economy. Indeed, the drug war creates conditions that prevent proper controls on drug abuse, on crime, on corruption, and on invasions of privacy.

Arnold S. Trebach, Testimony before the House Select Committee on Narcotics Abuse and Control, September 29, 1988.

A related problem is that prohibition also forces drug users to come into contact with people of real criminal intent. For all the harm that alcohol and tobacco do, one does not have to deal with criminals to use those drugs. Prohibition drags the drug user into a criminal culture. . . .

As a general rule, legal drug use is less dangerous than illegal drug use and is influenced by the mores of society. Legal drug use involves nonlethal doses, nonpoisoned drugs, clean needles, and warning labels. The night basketball star Len Bias died from a cocaine overdose, his friends, fearing the police, waited until after his third seizure before calling an ambulance. Illegal drug users have been arrested at hospitals after seeking medical attention. Legalization would put an end to this kind of nonsense. Users would be free to seek medical attention or counseling, if needed, and would not be alienated from family and friends as many are now. . . .

Since the goal of reform is to eliminate the black market and its attendant problems, the only valid test for judging the success or failure of reform is whether that goal has been accomplished. However, opponents of decriminalization or legalization sometimes proffer different criteria for evaluating the results of reform. The prime example is embodied in their ubiquitous claim that "the British system failed," pointing to the fact that overall heroin use in England rose substantially during the 1960s, when doctors were allowed to prescribe heroin on a long-term basis. However, their evaluation of the old British system cannot withstand scrutiny.

In the 1920s, the British elected to follow the "medical model" of drug control (while the United States adopted the "criminal model"). Private physicians were allowed discretion in prescribing heroin and other controlled drugs for their patients. By most accounts, the system worked fairly well for the next 40 years: The number of users remained low, they received quality-controlled drugs under medical supervision, and no substantial black market developed.

New Heroin Users

However, in the 1960s the number of heroin users increased substantially, especially among the young. These new users received heroin from illegal imports and from "gray market" sellers, users who received large amounts of prescribed heroin from a few cooperative physicians.

In response to this situation, the system was altered in the late 1960s. The right of individual physicians to prescribe heroin was revoked, and Drug Treatment Centers (DTCs) were set up to treat users. While heroin could still be prescribed at DTCs, the emphasis shifted to "curing" users instead of maintaining them on a long-term basis. As a result, prescription of heroin in England today has slowed to a trickle.

To argue that the system *caused* the increased use of heroin in England in the sixties is to confuse correlation with causation. If the system caused increased drug use in the sixties, why did it not do the same during the preceding four decades it was in effect? And if the system caused increased drug use in Britain, what caused the similar increase in the United States during the same period? It should be noted that drug use in England continued to rise even under the new British system. . . .

Given that neither the old British nor the American system stopped drug use, which minimized the social harmfulness of drug use? The obvious answer is the old British system, under which there was virtually no black market or organized crime and little drug-related crime or violence. The users were better off too, since they received quality-controlled drugs and medical treatment and were not branded as criminals and social outcasts. . . .

Hope for the Future

It is clear that most of the serious problems the public associates with illegal drug use are, in reality, caused directly or indirectly by drug prohibition.

Let's assume the war on drugs was given up as the misguided enterprise that it is. What would happen? The day after legalization went into effect, the streets of America would be safer. The drug dealers would be gone. The shootouts between drug dealers would end. Innocent bystanders would not be murdered anymore. Hundreds of thousands of drug "addicts" would no longer roam the streets, shoplifting, mugging, breaking into homes in the middle of the night to steal, and dealing violently with those who happened to wake up. One year after prohibition was repealed, 1,600 innocent people who would otherwise have been dead at the hands of drug criminals would be alive.

Within days of prohibition repeal, thousands of judges, prosecutors, and police would be freed up to catch, try, and imprison violent career criminals—criminals who commit 50 to 100 serious crimes per year when on the loose, including robbery, rape, and murder. For the first time in years, our overcrowded prisons would have room for them. Ultimately, repeal of prohibition would open up 75,000 jail cells.

The day after repeal, organized crime would get a big pay cut—$80 billion a year.

How about those slick young drug dealers who are the new role models for the youth of the inner cities, with their designer clothes and Mercedes convertibles, always wearing a broad, smug smile that says crime pays? They snicker at the honest kids going to school or to work at the minimum wage. The day after repeal, the honest kids will have the last laugh. The dealers will be out of a job, unemployed.

"Because of the drug trade, civility and civilized life itself are rapidly vanishing from black communities."

A War on Drugs Can Reduce Violence in Black Neighborhoods

Playthell Benjamin

Playthell Benjamin's articles on politics and urban affairs appear regularly in the *Village Voice*, and his music, theater, and literary criticism has been published in *Freedomways*, *Views on Black American Music*, and *The New York Times Book Review*, among other publications. He was recommended for a Pulitzer Prize in 1988 and in 1989 won the Association of Black Journalists' Griot Award. In the following viewpoint, he advocates waging war on drug dealers by whatever means necessary. Without such a war, Benjamin writes, the black community will be destroyed by the violence perpetrated by drug dealers and addicts.

As you read, consider the following questions:

1. What is Benjamin's response to George Bush's war on drugs?
2. How would the author eliminate the importation of illicit drugs?
3. What is Benjamin's opinion of proposals to legalize drugs?

I live in Washington Heights, smack dab in the middle of the hub of the crack/cocaine trade in the rotten Apple. I live in the center of a war zone. Hence, my views on the drug plague have been forged under fire. My basic view of the matter is simple: I hate crack! It is robbing our children of their future and, perhaps, even their dreams. I am in favor of suppressing and eradicating the violent criminal element associated with the drug trade by any means necessary. I am indifferent to the moral issues surrounding the consumption of drugs. For me it is a question of the survival of my family and my community. From where I sit there is no question of declaring a war on drugs, because the war already exists. The war is between the narco-terrorists and law-abiding, hardworking families, American citizens enduring a reign of terror and sustaining mounting casualties. And right now, we feel abandoned by our government.

I believe there is no alternative to winning this war. A defeat will sound the death knell for the African-American community. Because of the drug trade, civility and civilized life itself are rapidly vanishing from black communities all over the country. In order to reverse this trend I am prepared to resort to mass executions by firing squads and concentration camps in the Arizona desert. In formulating my battle plan to deal a death blow to the narco-terrorists now wreaking havoc on the black community, I would give no quarter. While I treasure civil liberties as much as anyone, in a war, everyone must sacrifice.

My War Is for Real

How does the war on drugs declared in September 1989 by President Bush measure up to my standards of combat? Succinctly stated: too little, too late. He is using war as a metaphor—my war is for real. With great fanfare, the president proposes to "make our streets and neighborhoods safe" by doubling federal assistance to state and local police and allocating an extra billion-and-a-half dollars for courts and prisons. The dollar amounts and the sense of urgency in Bush's voice impressed many Americans. But neither I nor anyone I talked to in my community believe the police can be trusted to honestly enforce the drug laws. We see too much evidence of police collusion with the drug merchants.

Only three days after the presidential proclamation, [a] *Newsday* . . . story revealed that two housing police officers, Dominick Davanzo and Alfred Talavera, had been arrested on August 16, 1989. According to *Newsday*, it is alleged that these two officers conspired with other policemen to rob dealers of drugs and money, then sell the drugs to other dealers and act as enforcers for those dealers. It is also alleged that these officers were acting on information supplied by sources inside the Organized Crime Control Bureau's Narcotics Division, the agency responsible for conducting surveillance and raids on drug locations. So this could be just the tip of the iceberg regarding this kind of police corruption. All of us have heard stories of police dealing drugs in this area—for years I have been told by street sources that "the police got all the best dope." In my community the belief that the police are shamelessly lining their pockets with dope money is so widespread that many people are reluctant to even report illegal activity.

Federal Troops

After talking the problem over with several of my neighbors, I have devised a counterplan to the Bush proposal. First we would create a procedure whereby a beleaguered community could declare a state of emergency and request the deployment of federal troops. For this purpose a committee for the defense of the community would be formed. It would consist of the congressperson, state and local elected officials who represent the area, and members of the area planning board, plus heads of established community organizations who would be elected like school board members. This committee would have the power to call a referendum in which all registered voters could participate. If the community voted for a state of emergency, martial law would be declared and federal troops dispatched to the area.

Turning to Dope

We have watched many of our young kids turn to dope to cope because they are without hope. Young Black children who have the capacity to become doctors and lawyers and engineers and scientists have given up working at summer jobs of flipping burgers and ringing cash registers in exchange for the street corner hustling of cocaine and crack and marijuana. From welfare mothers sitting at home with nothing to do to kids from good homes and good neighborhoods to our growing class of young professionals, Black America has watched and wept as many lives have become twisted and have been snuffed out by the powerful lure of drug addiction.

Charles B. Rangel, Prepared statement before the House Select Committee on Narcotics Abuse and Control, September 16, 1988.

Upon arrival, the military commander would consult with the committee in planning all strategy. To minimize the possibility of racist abuses, the commanding officers would be of the same race as the dominant population of the occupied community. An intelligence-gathering unit would be set up in a secret location outside the community so that residents could supply information on drug traffic in a confidential manner, thereby removing the fear of reprisals from narco-terrorists. After acquiring the proper search warrants from a special narcotics court, the soldiers would conduct search-and-seizure raids armed with state-of-the-art military weapons. Since the prisons are already overloaded—there were 90,000 drug-related arrests in New York City in 1988, although the capacity of the entire state and local penal system is under 60,000—special arrangements would have to be made for incarceration of those arrested. All bail would be suspended for persons caught with whatever quantities and types of drugs are specified by the committee. The construction of prisons is a costly and time-consuming endeavor, so penal colonies would be established and maintained by the military in rural areas. If soldiers fighting for the country can sleep in foxholes, tents would be more than adequate accommodations for the narco-terrorists. After a proper trial, those convicted of felony murders in connection with drugs would be publicly shot. The same fate would be meted out to chronic or large-scale offenders in drug sales. The state of emergency would last as long as the committee deemed fit.

Drugs and Foreign Policy

Simultaneous with the domestic crackdown would be an all-out, no-holds-barred effort to stop the flow of illicit drugs to the U.S. Here is what President Bush had to say on the matter: "Our strategy allocates more than a quarter of a billion dollars in military and law enforcement assistance for the three Andean nations of Colombia, Bolivia, and Peru. This will be the first part of a five-year, $2 billion program to counter the producers, the traffickers and the smugglers." It should be obvious to anyone with a casual knowledge of American foreign policy in this hemisphere that this plan is obscurantist jive. American policy toward the nations of the Caribbean and Latin America has been one of brazen big-power chauvinism and shameless imperialism. The uninvited interventions in the internal affairs of these nations would require volumes to discuss in depth. Often armed invasions have been launched for the flimsiest of reasons. Neither the 1965 invasion of the Dominican Republic nor the shameful 1983 assault on Grenada addressed real threats to the security of the U.S. In contrast, the cocaine traffic from Peru, Colombia, and Bolivia threatens to bring the nation to its knees. . . .

Bomb the Coca Fields

The drug problem exposes the true nature of American foreign policy, guided by a narrow anticommunism that defines the national interest in terms of the business requirements of America's financial oligarchy. It is our so-called friends who are exporting cocaine to our shores. Does anyone believe that this situation would be tolerated for a day if the cocaine was being produced in Cuba or Nicaragua? Bush insults our intelligence when he tells us we must wait for an invitation from the governments of the

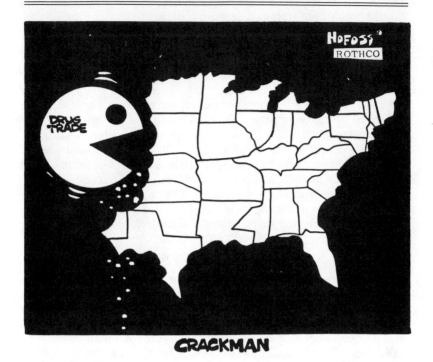

CRACKMAN

cocaine-producing nations before taking military action. I cry three tears in a bucket, if they don't give the word—after due warning to the hapless residents, let's carpet-bomb the coca fields with napalm.

It requires approximately 2000 pounds of coca leaves to make one kilo of cocaine. So what we are talking about here is gargantuan plantations. The CIA [Central Intelligence Agency] could pinpoint these plantations as easily as Michael Jordan could throw a grape through a hula hoop. The real deal is that each of the cocaine-producing nations is presently confronted with a leftist insurgency that seeks to overthrow the traditional oligarchies that monopolize land ownership, which is the basis of wealth in an agrarian society. Under the guise of suppressing cocaine producers, a secondary goal at best, the Bush administration is modernizing the armies in those countries. This strategy is just what we should expect from the former director of the CIA. In fact, it makes perfect sense if we consider the proposition that the election of George Bush amounted to a bloodless coup for the national security apparatus. This is the same power clique that collaborated with the contra leaders many intelligence experts and journalists believe were drug smugglers. In these people's view, socialist insurgencies in Latin America pose a greater danger to American security than streets flooded with drugs. It seems clear that they struck a Faustian bargain with anticommunist drug runners and now the devil must be paid. For the soul of America is being lost to the drug plague.

Common Sense

Above all, what is needed in the war on drug addiction is a strategy based on good common sense. History tells us that Germany lost World War II by trying to fight on too many fronts at once. We need a realistic policy that attacks the most serious problems. Insofar as it makes no distinction between narcotics and marijuana, Bush's proposal to severely penalize casual drug users will, I believe, prove unenforceable. I agree with Baltimore mayor Kurt Schmoke, a former drug prosecutor, that most drugs should be legalized with certain controls, including both marijuana and heroin. But crack, like angel dust and methamphetamine, can induce violent psychotic reactions in the user. It would be folly to make these drugs available upon demand. And for those readers who will no doubt think my prescription for suppressing crack is too severe, I can only invite you to hang out in my neighborhood for a while.

For people who live in idyllic places like Sundance, Utah, and Brooklyn Heights, the drug war in the city streets is a statistical abstraction. But in Washington Heights the gruesome body count mounts daily. The casualties in my own building constitute a striking case in point—and I live in a good building, too. Over [a period of] 90 days, one 20-year-old man was arrested for assault with a deadly weapon, his 16-year-old brother committed a homicide, and a 23-year-old, gainfully employed father of two was murdered in a mistaken-identity hit. But worst of all was an assassination of a 15-year-old boy right down the hall from my apartment. My children, both eight years old, happy and bright, were standing in the hall waiting for their mother to come up on the elevator. Twenty minutes later three gunmen forced their way into my neighbor's apartment and shot her 15-year-old son repeatedly through the head while the mother and two younger siblings watched. She later told me they asked him, "Do you have our money?" "No," said he, and they opened fire.

Death to Crack Dealers

That was when I concluded that the black community must adopt a triage ethic. Either we rid ourselves of these new jack nihilists, as Barry Cooper has aptly named them, or they will take us all down. That's why I cry power to the people, death to all crack dealers!

"Anybody who wants you to get behind the rulers' war on drugs is trying to get you to put the noose around your own neck and give it a sharp tug."

A War on Drugs Cannot Reduce Violence in Black Neighborhoods

Carl Dix

Carl Dix is a national spokesperson for the Revolutionary Communist Party, a political party that advocates a communist revolution. The following viewpoint is an excerpt from a speech Dix made at a July 1989 conference on the war on drugs. He contends that while advocates of the war on drugs claim it is justified as a way of reducing violence in black communities, it is actually being used to oppress blacks. The war on drugs gives more power to racist police who violate the civil liberties of blacks and imprison youths. Dix argues that black Americans must oppose the war on drugs.

As you read, consider the following questions:

1. What factors are leading U.S. rulers to intensify the war on drugs, in the author's opinion?
2. Why does the author believe that a socialist revolution would end the problem of drug addiction?

Carl Dix, "War on Drugs Is a War on the People," September 4, 1989, *Revolutionary Worker*, the weekly newspaper of the Revolutionary Communist Party, U.S.A.

We've got to be clear that the War on Drugs has nothing to do with stopping drugs. How could it—when the U.S. government itself is directly and indirectly responsible for the flood of drugs that sweeps the country? They and their system create and enforce the conditions that leave millions of oppressed youth facing a future of hopelessness and despair.

Black teen unemployment over 40 percent. Many of the jobs that are out there are minimum wage and dead-end. Youth are facing a future of being locked up in their jails, locked up in their welfare system, locked down in their projects, or being blown away. That kind of situation drives youth to want to "beam me on up, Scotty," or shoot something in their arms, or up their noses or wherever. And it leaves many with no other economic outlet but to deal with drugs. So the rulers are responsible for the crime of drugs in that way.

And then on top of that you've got the fact that it's the rulers and their international thugs and hitmen that supply the drugs to the inner city. The inner-city youth get busted and killed for getting caught up in it. You've got Oliver North hooked up with running drugs on the back end of the Contra supply network. You've got the U.S.-backed Afghan so-called freedom fighters who are the main suppliers of heroin to Europe and the United States. Even the two men who were the top hitmen for the Medellín drug cartel in Colombia—these are people who were in the past high-level CIA [Central Intelligence Agency] operatives over in Vietnam in the '60s. Then on the local level you've got police departments up to their necks in drug dealing. The cops lean on the youth, force them to deal the drugs, cut the profits off of it, and then try to rub the youth out when they are afraid they're going to talk.

The Real Purpose of the War on Drugs

This war on drugs ain't about stopping drugs, it is about clamping down. It's about the men who run this country, trying to get into a better position to ride out what is for them an increasingly dangerous and desperate global situation. They know that the conditions that they enforce in the ghettos and barrios across the U.S. are breeding much potential for explosion. And they're scared about having to face outbreaks of rebellion and protest here in the belly of the beast—in the midst of a world situation that presents them with challenge after challenge to their global holdings. . . .

The men who run this country remember the experience of the 1960s when it was the combination of the Vietnamese people's liberation struggle and the widespread resistance right here in the U.S.—and especially the struggle of Black people—that rocked their system back on its heels and shook it to its foundation. And they know that today they've got much more at stake than in the 1960s. It ain't just a small part of their empire that's on the line, that they stand to lose, but their whole global position. That's why they're lashing out in the ways they are.

Through their war on drugs, they are terrorizing the most oppressed people while also stretching their entire oppressive apparatus—creating political justification for these vicious attacks. And they want to influence middle-class people to go along with it—to accept the restrictions that they're putting down and the draconian laws that they're putting out in the name of trying to deal with drugs. What you've got is a situation comparable to Nazi Germany in the 1930s or Palestine and South Africa today in terms of the kinds of tactics that the rulers put down.

Oppose the Fascist Crackdown

So in light of all this, how are we going to deal with this war on drugs? And how are we going to deal with the wave of drugs that's flooding the United States and literally strangling large numbers of especially oppressed youth? Because that's part of this problem too. When we in the Revolutionary Communist Party said, "The fascist crackdown is worse than crack," some people said—"Well, you all must not know what the situation is out there with drugs. You all must not know the impact it's having." And we had to tell them, uh uh, we're clear on that, we know how that's coming down. We know that there are many, many youth who are strung out on drugs, and many more swept up in the turf wars over drugs and in the situation of being caught in a crossfire between rival drug dealers and the cops, and facing the future of being shot down or spending their lives in jail behind all this.

Black America Under Martial Law

Under the guise of a "war on drugs," they're trying to run America's inner cities like a police state. SWAT teams sweep through housing projects daily, paramilitary "task forces" carry out mass evictions of "drug suspects" and their families. Increasingly, calls are heard for deploying the National Guard and federal troops to patrol ghetto "war zones.". . . Ultimately, it's a plan to put black America under martial law.

Workers Vanguard, June 9, 1989.

But the other thing we know—and we're really clear on—is who are the criminals responsible for this crime of drugs? It's the U.S. rulers, the same people who want you to be suckers for their war on drugs. So how are we going to get out of this?

Let me briefly talk about how we *ain't* going to get out of this.

The way we *ain't* going to get out of this is buying into their war on drugs—whether this poison is being sold to you by George Bush, drug czar William Bennett, or even by Jesse Jackson. Anybody who wants you to get behind the rulers' war on drugs is trying to get you to put the noose around your own neck and give it a sharp tug, because that's what it comes down to. . . .

[Jesse Jackson] was campaigning in Los Angeles when the LAPD [Los Angeles Police Department] launched Operation Hammer, a supposedly antigang and antidrug sweep in which every weekend they'd arrest hundreds of Black and Latino youth on B.S. charges like littering, loitering, or resisting arrest. What did Jesse say in response to this brutal attack? He said not only did he endorse it, but he said he'd hit harder if he were elected president. Now, they weren't going to elect him president, but they did want to have him out front, fronting for this war on drugs so that people couldn't claim it was racist, so that maybe Black people would get suckered into it.

Revolution

So, what is the solution coming down to deal with this problem? We say that the solution to dealing with the problem of the war on drugs and the problem of drugs—and the whole situation that gives rise to it—is revolution. We're talking about millions of oppressed people—led by the revolutionary vanguard—rising up and overthrowing the bloodsuckers who run this country and oppress over half the world. And we're talking about going on to deal with everything foul this dog-eat-dog system spawns—whether that's whites lording it over non-whites, men dominating and suppressing women, or one nation lording it over much of the globe. Only this can stop the attacks that they hit us with from all sides. Only in this way can we put ourselves in the position to create a new society that can give hope back to those who see no hope today, for any kind of future.

Revolution is the hope of the hopeless. Look at how different things would be on this question of drugs and the war on drugs. First and foremost, a revolutionary society would be led by people who had *no interest* in drugging millions of people to get them to go along with the dead-end situation and the oppression and brutality that people are faced with under this system. This would make it possible for the masses who rise up and make revolution to target the biggest drug dealers and their thugs and hitmen and eliminate them.

Ending Addiction

As for those who today are addicted to drugs—when presented with a real chance to fight for a new and different future, many are going to be able to shake off this sickness, get this monkey off their back, and become staunch revolutionaries who can con-

Gary Huck. Reprinted by permission of *People's Daily World*.

tribute to making the revolutionary changes that we need. This is something that we saw in our own experience back in the 1960s through the work of leaders like Malcolm X or the Black Panther Party. They drew brothers and sisters out of heroin and into the revolutionary movement. Many others will be inspired by the new revolutionary society—and how different it is from the madness of today—to get the monkey of drugs off their back. And for those who aren't strong enough to handle it like that, the new revolutionary government will provide them with the help that they need over time to shake off their sickness—and *not* use that sickness as a way to criminalize them, vamp on them, or brutalize them. . . .

This has been done in the world before. Remember China. They used to talk about the situation in China where the streets of Shanghai and other major cities were filled with people who were strung out on opium. When the revolution won victory in China, they had 70 million drug addicts. That's a drug problem. Yet, in two years drug addiction as a social problem had been virtually wiped out. They didn't do this by lining the drug dealers up against the wall. But what they did actually changed the situation in China. Where there had been a government that was hooked into the drug trade and had its interest in drugging the people, the revolutionary government didn't have that interest and was able to target that trade and the big drug dealers. Through the revolutionary movement and the victory of the revolution, they were able to inspire people who had lost hope to throw drugs off on their own. And for those who couldn't, they provided the assistance and the treatment that was required for that to happen. I'm talking history here, not idle dreams.

Some say, "Okay, this would be nice, but let's be real, it can't happen. The rulers are too strong, the people are too divided for us to be really talking about revolution, so let's talk about something real." This is real. The rulers certainly fear that it's real, that it could happen. That's why they're lashing out the way that they are. But that's the rulers' game plan. There's another side to all this. There's millions of people who've got no stake in this system. Black people, for whom the American dream has been one long, never-ending nightmare. Immigrants from many different lands, driven here by the U.S. rape of their homeland. People who would leap at the chance to rise up and do this system in, if they thought they had a real shot at winning. And there are many others who are angered by the attacks that the system is launching out on many fronts. People who are horrified by the clampdown in Black and Latin communities, the attacks on immigrants, the attack on women's right to determine what happens to their own bodies. People who are feeling themselves forced by the reactionary atmosphere and climate that the rulers are putting down to adopt a more and more antigovernment stand. And people who can be swung over to all-out opposition to this system. . . .

Two Possible Futures

There are two alternate views of the immediate future here. Here's one view of what the future can be like: Black people locked down in housing projects and terrorized by sweeps through their communities. Black youth tagged as criminals who deserve every foul thing that the system does to them. Throughout society, people accepting restrictions on themselves in the name of the war on drugs and sharp divisions created between potential allies. That's one way that the immediate future can look like on this front.

But here's another way it can look. The attacks that the rulers are launching being met with determined and widespread resistance. They evict a family in the morning, and by nightfall people have rallied and put them back in. They surround a housing project or a community to sweep through and arrest youth and terrorize people, but before they can really get on to it activist lawyers, video crews, and others are there to catch them in the act and expose it widely to let people know what's going down. People who are horrified by the vicious clampdown that's coming down in the name of the war on drugs become emboldened to speak out. Prominent people add their voices to the resistance. Unity between people of many different backgrounds and different nationalities gets forged in the course of struggle.

Hope for Young People

The explosion of drug use and the growth of drug-related crime has taken place at a time when inequality has been on the increase in our society. . . .

We need a political and economic system that will engender hope among young people by providing a world free of nuclear weapons and a system which gives every person a right to quality education, a clean environment, a comprehensive health care system (including adequate treatment facilities for those who have been victimized by the disease of substance abuse), adequate housing, a decent paying job and a life free from racist and sexist discrimination.

Rudy Fichtenbaum, *People's Daily World*, March 10, 1989.

Now, I know that people have got many different perspectives and political approaches to things, but I'm sure that we can agree that the view of the future that we want is the second one. But the trick is, we've got to create it. Through creating such a situation, we can put ourselves in a much better position to carry the struggle forward in the future.

Youth's Role

I want to say something to the youth. I know you all get tired of the old folks up here talking about you. Let me say something *to* you. We know that the dogs who run this country have targeted you. They force you to stare into a future of joblessness and being locked up—either in their jail or their housing projects or their welfare system—or being killed. They put dope out there as the only economic outlet for many of you, then they bust you and terrorize you and the entire community when some use drugs and distribute them. They do this because they fear your angry stance. . . . They even fear your music. Public Enemy puts out a jam "Fight the Power" and the power is coming after them. Most of all, what they fear is your potential to explode in righteous rebellion against them and their rotten setup.

Let me be blunt, your rage is fully justified. We stand with you in that. . . .

Throwing down on each other, blowing away people who happen to be in the crossfire, dogging women and all kind of mess like that—we've got to break with that. That stuff ain't about nothing. That's doing the work of the system and adopting its outlook. We've got to be getting ourselves ready to do what's needed and that is—getting ready to take this whole system down. I ain't here to be your savior because you don't need one. I'm here to unite with you in a movement for self-emancipation. That's what it's got to be about.

Nobody can *save* oppressed people. Oppressed people have got to rise up, band together, and emancipate themselves through taking down this dog-eat-dog system. So we've got to go through some changes to do what's needed. But it's change that's worth going through because we've got something really worth fighting for, really worth living for, really worth dying for. We know that many of you all ain't afraid of nothing, you ain't even afraid to die. Well, let's put it on the line for bringing something new into being.

Let's put it on the line to take down this rotten dog-eat-dog system once and for all and bring into being a new future, a different future through revolution. And through our efforts to do that, let's create the kind of movement that can bring into being a political atmosphere where many of your peers, many of your brothers and sisters, are able to throw off the monkey of drugs from their back and begin to make their contribution to bringing this new future into being.

Recognizing Statements That Are Provable

From various sources of information we are constantly confronted with statements and generalizations about social and moral problems. In order to think clearly about these problems, it is useful to be able to make a basic distinction between statements for which evidence can be found and other statements which cannot be verified or proved because evidence is not available or the issue is too controversial.

Readers should be aware that magazines, newspapers, and other sources often contain statements of a controversial or questionable nature. The following activity is designed to allow experimentation with statements that are provable and those that are not.

Most of the following statements are taken from the viewpoints in this chapter. Consider each statement carefully. *Mark P for any statement you believe is provable. Mark U for any statement you feel is unprovable because of the lack of evidence. Mark C for statements you think are too controversial to be proved to everyone's satisfaction.*

If you are doing this activity as a member of a class or group, compare your answers with those of other class or group members. Be able to defend your answers. You may discover that others will come to different conclusions than you. Listening to the reasons others present for their answers may give you valuable insights in recognizing statements that are provable.

If you are reading this book alone, ask others if they agree with your answers. You will find this interaction valuable.

P = *provable*
U = *unprovable*
C = *too controversial*

1. Most drug-related murders are the result of drug prohibition.

2. In Los Angeles there is at least one gang murder every day.

3. Most people who are arrested for serious crimes are drug users.

4. Repeal of drug prohibition would open up 75,000 jail cells now being used to house convicted drug users and dealers.

5. More prisons are needed to hold drug dealers and punish them for their crimes.

6. Between 1983 and 1987 drug arrests in the District of Columbia increased by 45 percent, drug prosecutions by over 500 percent, drug convictions by over 700 percent.

7. Britain's experiment with heroin legalization proved that repealing drug laws would be harmful.

8. Legal drug use is less dangerous than illegal drug use and is influenced by the mores of society.

9. We cannot hope to solve addiction by punishing addicts.

10. The repeal of alcohol prohibition helped this country reduce organized crime.

11. Americans in 1987 bought 178 tons of cocaine, 12 tons of heroin, and 600,000 tons of marijuana.

12. Perhaps the biggest victims of our drug laws are children.

13. Crime rates go down among addicts when medical treatment is available.

14. The National Institute on Drug Abuse estimates that one in six working Americans has a substance abuse problem.

15. We cannot prosecute our way out of the drug problem.

16. It requires approximately two thousand pounds of coca leaves to make one kilo of cocaine.

17. The day after drug legalization went into effect, the streets of America would be safer.

18. There were 90,000 drug-related arrests in New York City in 1988, although the capacity of the entire state and local penal system is under 60,000.

Periodical Bibliography

The following articles have been selected to supplement the diverse views presented in this chapter.

William J. Bennett — "Restoring Authority," *New Perspectives Quarterly*, Summer 1989.

George Bush — "National Drug Control Strategy," *Vital Speeches of the Day*, October 1, 1989.

Philip C. Clarke — "The Monkey We Can't Shake," *American Legion Magazine*, September 1989.

Rachel Flick — "Why We're Losing the War on Drugs," *Reader's Digest*, October 1989.

Joel Garreau — "Washington's Underworld Entrepreneurs," *The Washington Post National Weekly Edition*, April 10-16, 1989.

Victor Gold — "The Year They Legalized Drugs," *The American Spectator*, November 1989.

Harper's Magazine — "When You're a Crip (or a Blood)," March 1989.

Michael Massing — "Crack's Destructive Sprint Across America," *The New York Times Magazine*, October 1, 1989.

Thomas Moore — "Dead Zones," *U.S. News & World Report*, April 10, 1989.

Tom Morganthau — "Children of the Underclass," *Newsweek*, September 11, 1989.

Salim Muwakkil — "Drugs as a Life(style) and Death Issue," *In These Times*, September 27-October 3, 1989.

Ethan A. Nadelmann — "Shooting Up," *The New Republic*, June 13, 1988.

Reason — "America After Prohibition," October 1988.

Mike Tidwell — "Murder Capital," *The Progressive*, July 1989.

Maxine Waters — "Drugs, Democrats, and Priorities," *The Nation*, July 24-31, 1989.

Mortimer B. Zuckerman — "The Enemy Within," *U.S. News & World Report*, September 11, 1989.

What Causes Family Violence?

Chapter Preface

No discussion of violence is complete without considering the problem of family violence. According to the Federal Bureau of Investigation, at least one-fifth of the murders in the U.S. are committed within families or intimate relationships. The FBI also found that 40 percent of the women killed in the U.S. are killed by family members. Former New York District Attorney and former member of Congress Elizabeth Holtzman writes that every eighteen seconds, a woman is beaten by a family member and two thousand to four thousand women are beaten to death each year.

Children are frequently victimized within families as well. While there is disagreement over exactly how many children are abused and what types of abuse are most prevalent, several commentators point to figures from the American Humane Association when trying to assess the problem. According to the Association, in 1986, 2.1 million children were suspected victims of abuse and neglect. David Finkelhor, a nationally known expert on the subject, estimates 5 to 16 percent of adult women were sexually abused as children. Daniel Sexton, the director of a child welfare organization, Childhelp USA, believes the problem may be worse: He maintains that one in three girls and one in eight boys are sexually abused before the age of eighteen.

Unfortunately, for every grim statistic there are thousands of physically and emotionally wounded people. Some of these people will use violence themselves, creating a sad and enduring cycle. As Los Angeles Police Officer Gloria Vargas argues, "Kids grow up seeing their father get away with beating up mom. So what happens? They grow up and beat up their wife or resort to other violence." One study reported by writer Marilyn Sherman found that 80 percent of the prisoners at San Quentin had been abused or neglected as children.

Why violence occurs in America's families is the subject debated in the following chapter.

"In our society, a person's earliest experiences
with violence comes in the home."

Traditional Values
Support Family Violence

Richard J. Gelles and Murray A. Straus

Richard J. Gelles and Murray A. Straus believe violence occurs
in American families because most people consider violence an
acceptable way to solve family problems. In conducting research,
they found that most people believe parents should use force to
discipline their children. In examining media reports of domestic
violence, they discovered that people tend to stereotype violent
families as different—poor, black, or mentally unbalanced. By
doing this, the authors conclude, Americans deny that family
violence occurs in all kinds of homes. Gelles, an anthropology and
sociology professor, is Dean of the College of Arts and Sciences
at the University of Rhode Island in Kingston. Straus, a sociology
professor, directs the Family Research Laboratory at the University of New Hampshire in Durham.

As you read, consider the following questions:

1. What do the authors believe is unrealistic about many
   people's fear of crime?
2. How does the inequality of women and children in society
   exacerbate the problem of domestic violence, in the
   authors' opinion?
3. Why are poor families more likely to be considered violent
   than are middle-class families, according to Gelles and
   Straus?

From the time we are children we are taught that danger lurks in the streets at the hands of strangers. Walking to school or in the school yard we are supposed to be wary of the stereotypical stranger in the old raincoat offering candy or a ride. As we grow older, we are warned not to run with the wrong crowd (presumably people our parents do not know). Dark alleys, strange cities, and the night are full of danger, ready to leap upon an innocent, unsuspecting victim. Women are taught a special brand of danger. Bars, dark alleys, hitchhiking, and strange men hold the threat of rape.

Today, the fear of danger on the street at the hands of strangers is as strong as ever. Milk cartons and shopping bags carry pictures of missing children who have been snatched by strangers. Stories of abducted children spread like fire across a parched field of grass. . . .

Today, parents selecting a day-care center or a summer camp not only have to consider the quality of the staff and the cleanliness of the facility; they also have to wrestle with the fear that a teacher or counselor is also a molester. . . .

A Cruel Irony

As real as the fear of violent crime is, so is the amount of crime. There is a very real danger in the streets. According to the United States Department of Justice, three Americans in a hundred are victims of violent crimes each year—this represents six million victims annually. But the cruel irony of staying home because one fears violence in the streets is that the real danger of personal attack *is in the home.* Offenders are not strangers climbing through windows, but loved ones, family members.

You are more likely to be physically assaulted, beaten, and killed in your own home at the hands of a loved one than anyplace else, or by anyone else in our society. Despite all the pictures of missing children on shopping bags and milk cartons, children are more likely to be kidnapped by their own parents than by strangers. Although the Federal Bureau of Investigation claims that there are 1.5 million children abducted each year, the agency actually investigated only sixty-seven cases of abduction in 1984. Experts outside the FBI say that there may be only six or seven hundred children abducted by strangers each year. On the other hand, hundreds of thousands of children are snatched by parents embroiled in custody disputes.

A somewhat grisly incident underscores the point that while the public is drawn to and fears instances of children being abducted or harmed by strangers, the real danger is in the home. In May 1985 a thirteen-year-old girl disappeared from her home in Minnesota. Seven weeks of searching failed to turn up any sign of her. As a result of the disappearance, the community organized a group to help find missing children. The missing thirteen-year-old's father was chosen leader of the group. In the course of advancing the cause of the group that sought to search and find missing children, the father testified on a panel with Minnesota state attorney general Hubert H. Humphrey III. A week after the testimony, while police questioned him to aid in their investigation, the father broke down and admitted that he had killed his daughter. The father admitted that he had been sexually abusing his daughter for years. He admitted that when his daughter fought his sexual advances he had stabbed her to death. He hid her body for a few days and then buried it in a field. . . .

A Rule We Live By

Violence in the home, we have found, is not altogether unpredictable or unexpected. In our society, a person's earliest experiences with violence comes in the home—spankings and physical punishments from parents. We learn that there is always going to be a certain amount of violence that accompanies intimacy. Moreover, we learn that children "deserve" to be hit. That "sparing the rod spoils the child." We grow to accept violence as a way of solving problems. Violence is also considered an appropriate means of expressing oneself. Violence in the home is not the exception we fear; it is all too often the rule we live by. . . .

Patriarchal Padlocks

For centuries men have owned women and children and enjoyed the legal right to use violence against them. . . . Today in most Western countries, women and children are no longer the legal property of men and many women are wage earners. But you only have to look at the steady increase in incest, rape and battering to know that attitudes are fundamentally unchanged. Patriarchy is still alive—and kicking with all its might

Vanessa Baird, *New Internationalist*, September 1988.

Early in our research, we concluded that the level of violence in historical and contemporary families was sufficiently great to justify our calling the marriage license a hitting license. Numerous surveys have discovered that a large number of people believe that under certain circumstances, it is perfectly appropriate for a husband to hit his wife. Approval of using violence to raise and train children is practically universal.

The U.S. Commission on the Causes and Prevention of Violence conducted a national survey on violence in the United States during the late 1960s. The survey focused not just on public violence, but on attitudes toward private violence. Among the findings of the commission were that:

• One quarter of adult men and one in six adult women said they could think of circumstances in which it would be all right for a husband to hit his wife or the wife to hit her husband.

• Eighty-six percent of those polled said that young people needed "strong" discipline.

• Seven out of ten thought it was important for a boy to have a few fistfights while he was growing up. . . .

Children "Need to Be Hit"

Parent-to-child violence is so common and so widely approved that one needs few case studies to make the point. In general, the large majority of Americans believes that good parenting requires some physical punishment. Over and over again, when we interview parents about hitting their children, we are told that kids "deserve to be hit" or "need to be hit." Among the thousands of people we have interviewed, it was *absence* of physical punishment that was thought to be deviant, not the hitting of children.

Even if violence is considered inappropriate by an individual, a group, or even by the society, the fact that violence is between family members means that most people will not want to intervene. One of our first research projects involved interviewing violent couples and their neighbors. Quite by chance we learned that the neighbors knew about the violence occurring next door. While neighbors might call the police, they almost never tried to get involved personally. Some feared for their own safety, but most simply said, "That's a family matter." Police officers, prosecutors, and judges have been known to say the same thing when confronted with domestic violence. When it comes to violence toward children, very few people try to intervene when a parent spanks or slaps a child in a supermarket or department store. While again, people might be hesitant because of fear for their own safety, by and large, even if one detests seeing a child hit, one tends to view it as the parent's own business.

Television also plays a role in perpetuating the support of private violence. Millions laughed (and still laugh) when Jackie Gleason rants, "Alice, you're going to the moon!" or "One of these days, pow, right in the kisser!" while shaking his fist at his television wife on the popular program, "The Honeymooners."

For those who think that it is *just* television that portrays and supports family violence, a quick examination of fairy tales, folklore, and nursery rhymes will graphically illustrate that a variety of media has for many years supported intimate violence, abuse, and neglect. Mother Goose's "Old Woman Who Lived in a Shoe" beat her children soundly when she sent them to bed. "Humpty Dumpty" is a thinly disguised metaphor of the fragility of children, and "Rock-a-Bye, Baby" is not even thinly disguised, with the baby and cradle falling from the tree. Wicked stepmothers

102

abound in children's fairy tales. Snow White's stepmother had Snow White taken out into the woods to be beheaded by the huntsman. Hansel and Gretel's parents left them to starve in the woods because money was scarce.

Changing Child-Raising Roles

Nonpunitive, nurturing child-raising techniques will be critical to any effort to make our families a peaceful place in which to live. Our data suggest that fathers' roles in both the batterers and battered women's homes were reportedly strict, punitive, and overly critical, even when they were rarely present. Boys need role models of men who can support and protect them so that they do not grow up to believe that this is a woman's role.

Lenore E. Walker, in *Family Abuse and Its Consequences*,1988.

A final means of making the marriage license a hitting license is to deny that the behavior is violent. Parents who hit children are not considered violent; they are thought to be properly disciplining their children. We have countless euphemisms such as "family matter" or "domestic disturbance" to serve as smokescreens for behaviors that would be considered assaults if committed by strangers. Denial also occurs when we create stereotyped images of what so-called "real violence" is. Stereotypical violence tortures, maims, or kills. For wife abuse, this has been labeled "burning bed" violence after the case of Francine Hughes, the Michigan housewife who endured years of violence before finally killing her husband by setting his bed on fire. In the case of child abuse, the stereotypical abuse is the 220-pound father punching his defenseless five-month-old son. There is little public support for these acts. Defining them as acts of "real violence" hides the more common forms of intimate violence, such as slaps, pushes, shoves, and occasional punches, behind closed doors. . . .

Social attitudes set the stage for violence as an acceptable means of solving problems and self-expression, and privacy shields the family from social control in cirumstances when the violence may not be considered normative. The socially structured inequality of the family further reduces the costs to violent partners, parents, and even children. Sexual and generational inequality take on many forms. First and most obvious, are the physical size differences. Husbands are typically larger and stronger than their wives. Parents are almost always bigger and stronger than their young children. Such physical size differences are important. We learned in one of our early analyses of mothers' use of violence toward their children, that mothers of teenage children are less likely to hit their children than are mothers of younger children. When we talk to the mothers we learned that the reason for this was not that there were less conflicts between mothers and teenagers than between mothers and preadolescents; actually there are more. Rather, the mothers said they were afraid that their teenagers would hit back. These sentiments were expressed by a forty-seven-year-old mother of a teenaged son and daughter:

> I used to spank my two kids until they got to be about four-
> teen or fifteen. . . . I still wanted to hit them but, you see, they
> got to be so big that I just was too afraid to hit them anymore.
> Why, if they even pushed me now they could really hurt me.

There is more to inequality than size. Men typically enjoy more social and economic status than do women. Because of their economic and social power, men can hit their wives without fear that their wives can extract a social or economic cost. By the same token, parents control the social and economic resources of their children.

Over and over again, the victims of family violence whom we have come to know say the same thing: The black and blue marks go away, the violence is only occasional, and they are willing to accept pain against the costs of trying to survive outside of the home with little money, credit, or experience.

Women and Children as Property

The inequality we describe is part of a centuries-old legacy in which women are men's property and children are the property of their parents. . . .

The legacy of women and children as property was carried forth with laws that allowed, under certain circumstances, the chastisement and physical punishment of women and children. The expression "rule of thumb" is said to come from old English common law which stated that a husband could beat his wife with a rod no thicker than his thumb. Colonial "stubborn child laws" gave Puritan parents the right to put unruly children to death, although there is little historical evidence that such a drastic punishment was ever meted out.

The sociologist Dair Gillespie points out that before the Civil War, American wives had many duties and few rights. Wives were not permitted to own property, even if they had inherited it. Husbands could collect and use their wives' wages, choose the education and religion of their children, and punish their wives if they displeased them. Husbands could even will children (born or unborn) to other guardians. If a divorce was granted, it was the husband who would decide who would have custody of the children. Husbands, according to Gillespie, were their wives' companions, superiors, and masters.

The victims of violence in the home are disproportionately the smaller, the weaker, and the less powerful. Part of their weakness comes from hundreds of years of subordination and being treated as property. Part of the weakness is due to the current social organization of society which offers few places to which victims can flee and live life safely with adequate social resources. The stigma of being a runaway child or a single parent serves to imprison many victims of violence in their homes. In few, perhaps no other, social settings are the cards so stacked against victims of personal violence. Few victims of public violence have to think about trading off the rewards of a home, hearth, and relationship against the costs of being physically assaulted. If you patronize a bar where you get beat up every fourth time you go there, you can freely stop going or change bars. Such options are not typically available to victims of intimate violence. . . .

Cruelty in Child-Rearing

The reason why parents mistreat their children has less to do with character and temperament than with the fact that they were mistreated themselves and were not permitted to defend themselves. There are countless people who are kind, gentle, and highly sensitive and yet inflict cruelty on their children every day, calling it child-rearing. As long as child beating was considered necessary and useful, they could justify this form of cruelty. Today such people suffer when their "hand slips," when an incomprehensible compulsion or despair induces them to shout at, humiliate, or beat their children and see their tears, yet they cannot help themselves and will do the same thing again next time. This will inevitably continue to happen as long as they persist in idealizing their own childhood.

Alice Miller, *For Your Own Good: Hidden Cruelty in Child-Rearing and the Roots of Violence,* 1983.

If people are violent because they can be, and if the modern family and system of social control is organized in such a way as to provide minimal social control over family behavior, does this mean that all families are violent? The answer is yes and no. Yes, there probably is some hitting in almost every household at some time. Almost all children are hit by their parents. Virtually all brothers and sisters hit each other. Perhaps half of all husbands and wives will physically fight at some point in the marriage. And many children, young and old, strike their parents, young and old. The answer is no if one confines the definition of violence to the outrageous acts of abuse that we hear about in the news each day. Abuse is not a common act, probably because enough social control is exerted over most individuals and most households to keep minor hitting from escalating into major abuse. Where abuse occurs, more often than not it is because a combination of factors exist—low social control, perhaps due to social isolation, high stress and frustration, and attitudes that hitting and even violence that causes injury are appropriate ways to raise children and control wives. . . .

All the research we have conducted, and the majority of the other clinical and survey investigations, find that intimate violence is more likely to occur in lower income or minority households. Official reports of child abuse and neglect include an overwhelming overrepresentation of the poor among reported abusers. Violence and abuse, however, *are not confined* to the poor or blacks. Middle- and upper-class parents and partners are violent. Japan's former Prime Minister Sato, a winner of the Nobel Peace Prize, was accused publicly of beating his wife. Aristotle Onassis, considered one the richest men in the world while he was alive, was accused of beating his mistress until he was forced to quit from exhaustion. The actor David Soul was profiled in *People* magazine as a former wife beater. The list of prominent wife beaters is quite long, yet not long enough to convince people that intimate violence occurs in all social groups.

Bias in Reporting Abuse

We mentioned that the poor are overrepresented in official statistics on child abuse. In part, this is due to their greater likelihood of being violent. However, it is also due to the fact that the poor run the greatest risk of being accurately and inaccurately labeled "abusers." An injured child with poor parents is more likely to be labeled "abused" than a middle-class child with the same injuries. The sociologists Patrick Turbett and Richard O'Toole conducted an experiment with physicians and nurses. Each group was divided in half. One-half received a medical file that described a child, the child's injuries, and facts about the parents. Unbeknownst to the participants in the experiment, the files were systematically varied. For one-half of the subjects, the child's father was described as being a teacher, while the other half read that the father was a janitor. Even though the injury to the child was identical, the son of the janitor was more likely to be described as a victim of abuse than the son of the teacher. Turbett and O'Toole next kept the occupation and injury the same but varied the race of the child. Half of the subjects read that the child was black, while the other half had a file that described the child as white. The black children were more likely to be labeled as "abused."

Here we see evidence that people want to see abuse as occurring in families "other than theirs." Seeing abuse as confined to poor or black families is yet another way people construct the acts of others as deviant and their own behavior as normal.

106

"Child abuse and other forms of family violence are fostered by 'major sociocultural changes that have seriously weakened the moral standards' governing American life."

Non-Traditional Values Support Family Violence

Bryce J. Christensen

Bryce J. Christensen directs the Rockford Institute's Center on the Family in America and edits its monthly newsletter. A conservative organization, the Center supports traditional Christian values. In the following viewpoint, Christensen argues that family violence, particularly child abuse, is exaggerated. The media support the myth that violence can occur in any home, Christensen believes, because they want to divert attention from the real cause of cases of abuse—the breakdown of traditional families.

As you read, consider the following questions:

1. What does the author maintain is misleading about statistics on child abuse and neglect?
2. What kinds of families are most likely to experience violence in the home, according to Christensen?
3. What groups encourage a distorted view of the child abuse problem, according to the author? What is their motive?

Bryce J. Christensen, "The Child Abuse 'Crisis': Forgotten Facts and Hidden Agendas," *The Family in America*, February 1989. Reprinted by permission of THE FAMILY IN AMERICA, a publication of the Rockford Institute in Rockford, Illinois.

Child abuse stirs the national passions as one of the most heinous offenses of our time, a horrible crime against innocent and defenseless victims. In recent years, state and Federal governments have launched new programs to combat the problem—with provisions requiring health and school officials to report every suspicion of child abuse to state officials, permitting anonymous reports from nonprofessionals, and mandating preventative instruction in the public schools. Most journalists have hailed these new measures as necessary responses to a widespread problem and have urged their readers to support them.

While it is hardly possible to overstate the horror of many particular instances—children mutilated, scalded, beaten, and murdered—the evidence suggests that child abuse does not occur nearly so often as the media and government officials have recently claimed. Close scrutiny of the issue also raises doubts about the frequency and protocol for state intervention. Even more fundamental questions arise when examining the motives of many of those calling for further expanding the state's power to intervene in family life.

Serious Abuse Is Not Widespread

In the first place, serious child abuse does *not* occur in hundreds of thousands of American homes each year. Of the 2.1 million children who were reported to state authorities in 1986 as abused or neglected, only about 30 percent had been physically abused and only about 10 percent of these children (3 percent of the total) had suffered an injury serious enough to require professional attention. According to Douglas Besharov, former director of The National Center on Child Abuse and Neglect, "nine-tenths of the cases labeled 'physical abuse' are really situations of excessive or unreasonable corporal punishment that, although a legitimate matter of government concern, are unlikely to escalate into a dangerous assault against a child." Besharov further emphasizes that almost 85 percent of all cases of "child maltreatment" are "really forms of emotional or developmental harm to children that pose no real physical danger."

Far more numerous than the instances of serious child abuse are the false allegations of child abuse. Nationwide, approximately 65 percent of all reports of child abuse and neglect are dismissed as "unfounded" after official investigation. Even if exonerated, those falsely accused of child abuse must submit to an intrusive and potentially traumatic investigation. Investigators routinely strip-search the children involved and question parents at length about their private conduct. Neighbors, teachers, and relatives are often told of the investigation into possible child abuse and questioned about any peculiarities they may have noted in the children's behavior. In many cases, children are removed from the home for a time and only returned after investigators conclude that the accusation against their parents was false. And in many states, accusations of child abuse remain on official files even after they have been investigated and disproved. . . .

Respect for Women

Violence between partners and child abuse—sexual as well as physical—all are far more prevalent in families where the divorced, or never-married, mom has a live-in boyfriend (which is increasingly the case).

Boys reared in households without a permanent male member who is committed to the family, rarely see loving interaction between the sexes and lack healthy role models. From the conduct of companions toward their mothers, many learn to view women as objects of exploitation.

Don Feder, *Conservative Chronicle*, July 12, 1989.

Amid the furor caused by inflated numbers and false accusations, few can think clearly about the root causes of child abuse. Often, indeed, activists and journalists describe child abuse as a ubiquitous evil, occurring in all sorts of American households. A typical article in *Glamour* declares that "child abuse is *not* the problem of any particular social group or part of the country. It cuts across all socioeconomic and geographic lines." Middle-class readers need to be ready to call the child protection agencies when they see any child in their suburban neighborhoods who is "withdrawn or clinging," who "looks unkempt," or who has "missing permanent teeth." Likewise, *Ladies' Home Journal* urges its middle-class readers to "watch out for all children" and to call police or social agencies when they suspect child abuse. "Child abuse has been allowed to remain the hidden tragedy of too many middle-class families," argues the *LHJ* writer. In a second article on the same subject, *LHJ* informed its readers that "child abuse occurs in every social and economic class, in every neighborhood. It could be happening to the three children who live in the lovely Tudor house down the block or the strange little girl who shares the luxury apartment next door with her divorced mother." John Crewdson, a senior writer for the *Chicago Tribune*, promotes the same view in his investigation of sexual abuse: "Child abusers look and act pretty much like everybody else. Many of them are men and women with jobs and families, liked by their co-workers and neighbors and respected in their communities. . . . Child abusers can be rich or poor, smart or stupid, boorish or charming, failed or successful, black or white." Predictably, analysis of the causes of child abuse cannot proceed very far when governed by the preconception that the perpetrator is an Everyman.

In fact, many leaders of the campaign against child abuse—who make much of their willingness to break past taboos of silence— are keeping strangely quiet about important research into the typical setting and the underlying causes of child abuse. Contrary to the claim that child abuse occurs indiscriminately among all social groups, Besharov reports that "compared to the general population, families reported for maltreatment are four times more likely to be on public assistance and almost twice as likely to be black. . . . [M]altreating parents tend to be the 'poorest of the poor.' . . . About 30 percent of abused children live in single parent households and are on public assistance; the comparable figure for neglected children is about 45 percent."

Further, if those leading the crusade against child abuse have been largely quiet about the link between abuse and poverty, they have been even more skittish about acknowledging that much of today's child abuse can be traced to a cultural revolution under-mining marriage and weakening restraints on sexual behavior. David G. Gil, author of *Violence Against Children*, observes that "the data. . . suggest an association between physical abuse of children and deviance from normative family structure, which seems especially strong for non-white children." In a controlled investigation of 214 parents of battered babies, British researchers Selwyn Smith, Ruth Hanson and Sheila Noble discovered that "battered babies are likely to be reared in broken homes" and that premarital pregnancy, illegitimacy, and absence of the child's father were among the most common "precursors of baby bat-tering."

Child Abuse and Stepparents

In a 1982 study, researchers at Pennsylvania State University found that stepparents and their stepchildren are much more at risk to child abuse than are parents and their offspring. The re-searchers remarked that the statistical strength of the association between child abuse and stepparents was "quite high" and that "given the choice between abusing a stepchild and a biological offspring, these individuals *never abused their own kin.*" In the same vein, political scientist Jean Bethke Elshtain points out that "in two-thirds of all cases of 'father-daughter incest,' the offender is not a biological parent but a stepfather or live-in roommate of the mother." To dispel any lingering doubt, Professors Martin Daly and Margo Wilson of McMaster University established in 1985 that "preschoolers living with one natural and one stepparent were *40 times* more likely to become child abuse cases than were like-aged children living with two natural parents." In contrast, a 1985 study for the National Institute for Mental Health found that violence against children actually appears to be *decreasing* in

America's intact families. Generally supportive of sexual freedom and of the no-fault divorce laws passed in the early 1970s, most government officials and journalists would rather not pursue such findings to their logical conclusion. . . .

Working Mothers

In a 1988 study at the University of New Mexico, Professors Robert Fiala and Gary LaFree discovered "a remarkably clear, positive relation between female labor-force participation and child homicide. The six countries with the highest homicide rates all have relatively high female labor-force participation rates, while four of the six countries with the lowest homicide rates have relatively low female labor-force participation rates." Apparently, "greater female labor-force participation resulted in higher homicide rates for both children less than one and children one to four." In surprising contrast, the researchers reported that "inequality and unemployment, more commonly associated with child abuse in the literature, have no impact on child homicide."

Being Honest About the Problem

No reform is possible without first being honest about the problem, something child welfare professionals have been afraid to do. To make the case for change, they would have to tell the American public that almost 85 percent of the one million maltreated children we hear about have not been brutally battered, sexually abused, or physically endangered by serious neglect—even though it is these heartrending cases that have gained them continued increases in funding. Instead, they would have to argue for more social services for poor families—something for which there has been little public or political support.

Douglas Besharov, *Policy Review*, Winter 1987.

Perhaps to allay any suspicion of reactionary motives, Fiala and LaFree argue that "greater levels of welfare spending" have apparently held down the level of child murder in Scandinavian countries like Denmark and Sweden, even as maternal employment has risen. Fiala and LaFree did not comment on the depressed fertility—far below replacement level—of Sweden and Denmark, but Professor Mikko A. Salo of The University of Turku in Finland has concluded that "there is an association between the simultaneous appearance of child abuse and low fertility in the welfare societies." Both depressed fertility and child abuse, he believes, may spring from "common sources of stress and frustration."

Even if state subsidy of day care does help hold down the number of children killed when mothers go to work, it creates new risks for child abuse. When an employed mother drops her children off at the day-care center, she may be leaving them with a pedophile. The prevalence of this problem accounts for the frequency with which state officials must investigate day-care centers for allegations of child abuse. At any one time, officials of the Department of Social Services in California are investigating between two and three hundred day-care centers, primarily for allegations of sexual abuse. And at a time when child psychologists are discovering that day care weakens maternal bonding to infants, researchers are finding that events which disrupt parent-infant bonds increase the risk of child abuse. Worse, the evidence suggests that the "bonding failure" which causes abuse can create a pattern that persists from generation to generation.

Other scholars likewise argue that child abuse has emerged in modern culture for reasons not generally acknowledged. Social psychologist Edward M. Levine believes that child abuse and other forms of family violence are fostered by "major sociocultural changes that have seriously weakened the moral standards" governing American life.

In particular, he ponts to the pursuit of self-fulfillment and individual interests, to the weakening of parental authority, and to "the impact of the themes of violence and sexuality that are emphasized by the mass media and popular culture." "It is open to question," he concludes, "if the rate of family violence will recede unless those moral standards that constitute the basic social constraints against such horrible forms of aggression are restored." At a conference sponsored by The Royal Society Of Medicine, Dom Benedict Webb went even further: "It is only by the application of the Christian ideals of love, service, marriage, reverence for man and forgiveness that we will find a solution for child abuse."

Cultural Causes

The cultural causes of child abuse have also received attention from Yale historian John Demos, who argues against "the consensus view" that "children have always been abused" in America. Surveying the records of colonial New England, Demos finds almost no evidence of child abuse, nor of abuse "disguised as accidental injury." Noting that other studies have similarly found no child abuse in "traditional non-Western societies," Demos suggests that child abuse (as opposed to harsh discipline) is uniquely a modern phenomenon, caused by urbanization, industrial development, unemployment, on-the-job alienation, and the collapse of "the 'providential' world-view of our forebears—their belief that all things, no matter how surprising and inscrutable, must be attributed to God's overarching will."

Since the media and the modern state have collaborated in the secularization of American life, it is perhaps understandable that they would now ignore the evidence that their past efforts have fostered the child abuse they now loudly deplore. . . .

Social Changes, More Crime

Those who tout the theory that traditional relationships promote crimes against women are left with an uncomfortable question: If gender differentiation stimulates sex crimes, why are we experiencing far more of these offenses today than a generation ago?

The feminist agenda has triumphed. A majority of women now work outside the home. There are severe legal constraints against discrimination in the work place. Women are invading what once were all-male bastions. Normative sex roles are out of fashion, and the dogma that the sexes are psychologically identical is widely accepted. Yet crimes against women are on an upward spiral.

Don Feder, *Conservative Chronicle*, July 12, 1989.

Interpreting child abuse as proof of various ideologies, some utopians, feminists, and socialists welcome the opportunity to turn the state against family autonomy and parental authority (especially if exercised by fathers)—with only incidental concern for reducing child abuse. For feminist Renate Bridenthal, the discovery of "remarkably widespread" abuse and violence in the home has "demystified the home," exposing its "oppressive relations" and so defining it as "a political arena in which individuals compete and form alliances." Nor is it reassuring that feminists still find reasons to praise the 19th-century "child-savers," who often removed children from poor immigrant homes for the flimsiest of reasons. Writing recently in *Feminist Studies*, Linda Gordon conceded that "on one level" the child-saving of the 1870's "did represent oppressive intervention into working-class families." Yet, she sees merits in the kind of "social control" pioneered by the child-savers if "evaluated within a feminist framework." Gordon points out that the child-savers were "part of the original definition and construction of family violence as a social issue" and that "feminist thinking exerted an important influence [on] original formulations of the problem of family violence." "Child protection work," observes Gordon, "was an integral part of the feminist as well as the bourgeois program for modernizing the family." Gordon especially emphasizes that "the very undertaking of child protection was a challenge to patriarchal relations" in the traditional family. For her, the "antipatriarchalism" of the child-savers made their work beneficial to immigrant women, even as the child-savers denigrated and misunderstood the immigrant culture.

113

Inevitably, an ideologically distorted view of the past gives a distorted view of the present. Recently social workers R.L. McNeely and Gloria Robinson-Simpson have complained that the whole issue of "domestic violence" has been "falsely framed" by almost exclusive focus on masculine behavior. Such bias has "contributed to men's increasing legal and social defenselessness." . . .

A Distinctly Modern Problem

Despite the evidence that child abuse counts as a distinctively modern problem, ideologues use the issue to wage war on the traditional authority of parents, so pushing society further into the wasteland of modernity. Historian Christopher Lasch has remarked that modern bureaucracies tolerate—even foster—a "new permissiveness, [which] extends largely to expression of libidinal instincts, not to aggression." His observation helps explain why state officials can preach against the evils of child abuse while simultaneously supporting "value-neutral" sex education and school-based clinics for dispensing contraceptives. The inconsistencies in such policies remain hidden so long as the cultural causes of abuse are not exposed.

No wonder, then, that many contemporary child-savers promote the "myth of classlessness." To render all parental authority suspect, child abuse must somehow be attributed to all sorts of households, rich and poor alike, not under the care of enlightened therapists. "Why," Elshtain wonders, "are we so willing to put our faith in individuals who clearly have an interest in defining the problem [of child abuse] and its solutions in terms that will enhance their own influence and power?" . . .

Intervention Is Harmful

According to a team of researchers at Yale University and the Hampstead Child-Therapy Clinic, "any interference with family privacy alters the relationships between family members and undermines the effectiveness of parental authority. . . . Children. . . react even to temporary infringement of parental autonomy with anxiety, diminishing trust, loosening of emotional ties, or an increasing tendency to be out of control. The younger the child . . . the stronger is his need to experience his parents as his lawgivers—safe, reliable, all-powerful, and independent." But for enemies of the family, reduced parental authority is a desirable goal, even in homes where children have not been abused.

3

"Officers, their supervisors and prosecutors and judges more often than not treat the crime of domestic violence less seriously than they treat any other crime."

Police Sanction Wife Abuse

Sheila James Kuehl

Controversy often erupts when battered women who seek and are denied police protection are later murdered by their abusive partners. In August 1989 in Los Angeles, Maria Navarro was murdered by her husband after she telephoned the emergency number 911 and was refused help. In the following viewpoint, lawyer Sheila James Kuehl criticizes the police for failing to respond effectively to battered wives' pleas for protection. Using the Navarro case as an example, Kuehl argues that police sanction violence against women when they do not believe women who are threatened by their husbands. Kuehl is the managing attorney for the Southern California Women's Law Center, an organization that provides legal services for women.

As you read, consider the following questions:

1. What evidence does Kuehl use to support her argument that domestic violence is relatively common in the U.S.?
2. Why does Kuehl contend that police officers take reports of wife beating less seriously than reports of other crimes?
3. What does the author believe law enforcement officers could do to prevent and reduce domestic violence?

Sheila James Kuehl, "911 Must Bring Protection, Not Just Post-Mortem," *Los Angeles Times*, August 31, 1989. Reprinted by permission of Sheila James Kuehl, Managing Attorney of the Southern California Women's Law Center.

When Maria Navarro died, shot by the estranged husband she was trying to escape, she didn't die alone. Not just her aunts and a friend died with her, but so did untold numbers of women across the country. They, like Maria, have been shot by their husbands or boyfriends, and, like Maria, are basically left unprotected by a law-enforcement system that turns a deaf ear to the real dangers and fears of women who are the victims of violence by a "loved" one.

"How does this happen?" I heard everyone asking themselves. How? It happens because the priorities of the law-enforcement response system are based on a series of fundamental untruths. Law enforcement generally reflects a deeply held societal belief that women are not credible, that they exaggerate the danger of their situation. Such a myth serves very handily to protect the men who commit incest, rape or battering, or who threaten murder.

Nothing in women's experience supports this myth. In fact, the opposite is true. Women who have been battered or threatened, as Maria Navarro was, are the ones best placed to judge the severity of their own situation. No one knows better than the woman who has lived with him when this man will blow up, or when he will really carry out his threat. Law enforcement would do well to listen to the victim's assessment of her danger.

Society's Denial

Law enforcement's response also reflects the larger denial of a society that treats the death of Maria Navarro as news, as if such a death at the hands of an estranged husband is unusual. The horrifying truth is, nothing could be more usual.

Time magazine ran the pictures and names of all those Americans who had been killed by handguns in one week. All but three of the women who had not killed themselves had been shot to death by a husband, boyfriend, ex-husband or ex-boyfriend. Almost half of the women died this way. If you extrapolate from the statistics in that article, it is easy to see that this is an everyday occurrence in women's lives.

Law enforcement's response to domestic violence also reflects a widely held belief that men have a right to control the behavior of women and children, even if they "must" use violence to do so. This is the only possible explanation for the fact that officers, their supervisors and prosecutors and judges more often than not treat the crime of domestic violence less seriously than they treat any other crime.

A corollary to this myth is one that teaches that the women themselves are responsible for causing the violence against them. No crime is taken seriously if the victim may have brought it on. Of course, it is only when the crime has been against a woman, as in rape or domestic violence, that you hear such a statement.

Perhaps the greatest problem typified by Maria Navarro's death is the bankruptcy of law enforcement's commitment to protecting female victims of violence. . . .

Although Maria Navarro touchingly believed, when she naively dialed 911, that the sheriff's deputies were there to "protect and serve" her, the truth is that law enforcement has almost entirely given up on protection and has basically opted only to punish. "More prisons!" cries the Legislature, and "More prisons!" the governor echoes. Wait until somebody kills somebody, then show up and arrest. This is not the answer. Law-enforcement resources could be more effectively used to prevent crime.

The Police Are Unsympathetic

Not surprisingly, stereotypes about women—that they are masochistic, 'asking for' or 'deserving' their battering—also surface during police intervention. Studies in both the US and Britain confirm that even when confronted with severe violence, police still produce these stereotypes. In 1976, the New York City Police Department was sued for its policy in handling domestic disputes by seventy-one battered women who had been 'repeatedly and violently threatened, harassed, assaulted, beaten, and brutalized by their husbands, in clear and absolute violation of the laws of [New York] state.' 'Throughout their marriage,' the legal brief in Bruno v. Codd stated, 'these women have been slapped, punched and kicked by their husbands, in the head and all over their bodies. . . . They have been struck and beaten with fists, chairs, pots, ropes, bats, hammers, wrenches and iron bars.' One woman claimed that when a police officer responded to her call for help, he said to her assailant, 'Well, maybe if I slap my wife around a couple of times she might behave too.' The lawsuit, settled out of court on the agreement that police would intervene in domestic crisis situations, still leaves the decisions on how to handle situations firmly to the discretion of street patrol officers. . . .

Day after day on the job, fed by traditional attitudes about male violence, coupled with constraints of time and resources, police are unlikely to gain any sympathetic understanding of men's violence to female intimates.

Elizabeth A. Stanko, *Intimate Intrusions: Women's Experience of Male Violence*, 1985.

"What can we do?" the 911 dispatcher said to Maria Navarro. Well, for one thing, law enforcement can stop being so fundamentally dishonest about its inability to protect. When Maria called 911, she was told, "We can't have a unit sit there and wait and see if he comes over." No one says that when politicians, candidates and celebrities need protection after threats. Police protect, but they select when they protect.

Law-enforcement officers must make fundamental changes in the way they see their duty to the public. It is simply bad policy to refuse to respond until a crime is actually in progress. By that time, women are unable to protect themselves. But they could be protected if law enforcement took a victim's assessment of the potential danger seriously. They could be protected if society would awaken from its unsupported denial of the prevalence of the violence of husbands and boyfriends against women.

That may lead us to the answer to the question posed by the 911 dispatcher to Maria Navarro: "What can we do?" Some would say that we simply need more officers. But more officers is an answer only if they are committed to protecting and not just showing up too late and punishing.

Establishing a Policy That Protects

More training? Definitely. Officers will tell you that once they understand the reality of violence against women, they can never go back to their own denial or, as so often happens, to their identification with the husband. That seems natural to so many of them. But that training must also include the need for a fundamental change in response policy, one that truly protects. Law enforcement has to face the truth before the next Maria Navarro and countless other women die of its myths.

"Looking to police to prevent and solve domestic violence is both naive and deadly."

Police Cannot Be Expected to Prevent Wife Abuse

Susan Yocum

Susan Yocum is a police officer with the Van Nuys Division Patrol of the Los Angeles Police Department. Yocum argues in the following viewpoint that police officers cannot respond to every threat an abusive husband makes against his wife. Most threats are never carried out, she writes, and there are not enough police officers to respond to the threats anyway. Yocum concludes that police action alone cannot protect a woman from a crazed husband with a gun who is determined to murder her.

As you read, consider the following questions:

1. Why does Yocum object to allegations that police officers are sexist?
2. What policies adopted during the 1980s have changed how police respond to domestic disturbances, in the author's opinion?
3. What steps does Yocum advocate abused women take to protect themselves?

Susan Yocum, "Police Can't Prevent Domestic Killing," *Los Angeles Times*, October 4, 1989. Reprinted with permission.

In the continuing media flurry over domestic violence, prompted by Maria Navarro's grim and tragic murder, attention has focused on police protocol, training, sensitivity and action. The public cannot understand why a police car was not dispatched the moment that Navarro relayed her fears to the 911 operator. Police are paid to protect and serve. Why didn't the Sheriff's deputies respond immediately to the reported threat by her estranged husband? Why don't police take domestic violence seriously?

Maria Navarro told police that her husband had threatened to kill her, and tried to convince them that he would carry out that threat. She knew that she was right. She *was* right. And the police refused to respond to her call.

The fact of the matter is that most of the threats arising from domestic disputes are just that: threats. Intended to frighten and intimidate, but seldom carried out.

Too Much Crime

If police were to sit outside the homes of people who have been threatened, there would be no one to respond when you hear a prowler in your home. There would be no one to respond when you see a robbery in progress and no one to respond when your life is visibly in immediate danger.

It is not a matter of police apathy. It is not a matter of police insensitivity toward domestic violence. It is not a matter of sexist police policy. It's a matter of too much crime and too few police. It's a matter of practicality.

More Awareness

Domestic violence has always existed. The decade of the 1980s can take credit for recognizing, defining, naming and publicizing it. State and national governments have given effort and money to research; statistics have been compiled. We now are aware that every six hours somewhere in this country, a woman is killed by her husband or boyfriend.

As a police officer, I can testify that police training in domestic violence is complete. It has to be; answering calls to scenes of domestic violence involves great risk to our own lives. The Los Angeles Police Department's program is comprehensive and well-taught. We learn how to recognize cycles of domestic violence and how to counsel women who are victims of it. We are required to provide women with information on how to obtain restraining orders and with referral phone numbers for help ranging from psychological counseling to temporary shelter.

Further, court interpretations of California law have left very little to a street cop's discretion. For example, if you punch your neighbor, leaving a bruise on his arm, the officer called to the scene may try to get you and your neighbor to resolve the situation without legal intervention. If your neighbor insists on prosecution, you will be arrested, taken to jail and booked on a misdemeanor charge of battery.

However, if a man hits his wife and a similar bruise appears on her, the police officer called to the scene has no option. Regardless of the wife's desires or the husband's explanations, he will be taken to jail immediately and booked on a felony charge of spousal abuse.

Witnesses Who Will Not Testify

Although the law now requires them to make arrests, police officers say, the courts toss out many domestic cases for the same reason that long hampered police.

"Unfortunately, many women just want the case dropped and fail to recognize they're in a dangerous situation," says Anthony J. Salius, director of the family division of Connecticut Superior Court. "If she really doesn't want to prosecute, it's very difficult to have a trial because we don't have a witness."

Howard Kurtz, *The Washington Post National Weekly Edition*, May 16-22, 1988.

With the accused in jail, police action becomes secondary. He will be released by the court system in a matter of days or hours. It is up to the victim to prosecute, something abused women seldom do. Even when they do prosecute, the case is often resolved with a plea bargain or a token prison term, both of little use to women who justly fear for their lives.

Police officers strive to protect everyone in society, but we cannot always prevent. In Navarro's case, had police been on the scene to stop her husband, they would have taken him into custody for, at most, carrying a concealed weapon. That would have kept him in jail overnight, assuming he couldn't make bail. Anyone who believes that a person determined to kill another can reliably be prevented from doing so by the police—or anyone—is dreaming.

Women Must Protect Themselves

Success in dealing with domestic violence demands action from the abused women themselves and from the courts. Women who have been beaten or threatened too frequently decide to give the abuser another chance. All too often the cycle begins anew. These women must want to extricate themselves from abusive relationships and they must seek the prosecution of their abusers. Those who are abused must also take steps to protect themselves.

The legal system must really punish those men whose wives and girlfriends are brave enough to prosecute. At present, a man convicted of spousal abuse will spend little time in jail. Dist. Atty.

121

Ira Reiner has made a strong statement by directing his office to prosecute gang members in Los Angeles County to the fullest extent of the law. If we are truly serious about protecting women from abusers and potential murderers, we must demand that prosecutors do the same.

Police Cannot Be Held Accountable

It is difficult to say that a woman should have to leave her own home, but in the case of Navarro and many other abused women, that is the action most likely to keep them safe after a serious threat. Why did Navarro and her guests stay in her home, even when she believed her husband's threat, and the police had explained they could not yet take action?

Maria Navarro was a victim. But police cannot be held accountable for the actions of a crazed person who has a gun. Looking to police to prevent and solve domestic violence is both naive and deadly.

"We tolerate sexual abuse of children. . . because we continue to process cases through an adversary system that is overwhelmingly weighted against the child victim at virtually every level."

The Legal System Exacerbates Child Abuse

Billie Wright Dziech and Charles B. Schudson

Billie Wright Dziech is assistant to the dean and professor of language arts at the University of Cincinnati. Author of *The Lecherous Professor* and co-author of *On Trial*, she has lectured frequently on sexual harassment, women's issues, and higher education. Charles B. Schudson is a circuit court judge in Wisconsin. A member of the faculties of the National Council of Judicial and Family Court Judges, Schudson is an expert on laws and techniques affecting children in the courtroom. In the following viewpoint, they argue that most cases of child abuse are never reported, and the few that are rarely result in the punishment of perpetrators. This happens because the legal system intimidates and works against child victims of abuse.

As you read, consider the following questions:

1. How many children are sexually abused in the U.S., according to Dziech and Schudson?
2. What social changes do the authors contend have led to an increase in child abuse?

Statistics indicate that one American female in every three or four is likely to be sexually victimized before she is eighteen years old. Data for males is more sparse and less reliable, but most experts agree that the lowest frequency is between one in ten and one in six; and there is growing suspicion that male children may be as often involved in sexual activity with adults as females because they are the preferred victims of habitual pedophiles. The American Humane Association's figures, which are from 1984, indicate that 200,000 cases of child sexual abuse were reported in that year. The first nationwide study of the extent of child molestation was conducted by the *Los Angeles Times* in 1985. That poll found that at least 22 percent of Americans (27% of women and 16% of men) were sexually victimized during childhood. The *Times* poll and studies by other researchers indicate that at least half of adult perpetrators are unrelated to the children they victimize.

These statistics are conservative when compared to two other studies regarded by experts as more methodologically rigorous. Diana Russell, a sociology professor at Mills College, reported that 38 percent of women in her 1978 survey indicated they were victimized before eighteen. In a 1985 study Gail Wyatt, a professor of medical psychology at the Neuropsychiatric Institute at UCLA, found that in cases involving some form of body contact, one in approximately two females had experienced sexual abuse prior to age eighteen. . . .

The point on which experts agree is that child sexual abuse is one of the most underreported of all crimes. Fewer than half of the respondents to the *Los Angeles Times* poll told a close friend or relative about their victimization within a year, and only 3 percent reported the incident to legal authorities or public agencies. This statistic is similar to Russell's findings that only 2 percent of intrafamilial and 6 percent of extrafamilial incidents were reported to the police.

The Agony of Children Goes Unheard

This means that in a culture frequently described as "child centered," the agony of thousands of children goes unheard each year. The results are devastating—not simply for the victims but for everyone who comes in contact with them. The trauma of victimization is not confined to the child and his or her family. The *Chicago Tribune* interviewed some of the most prominent professionals who work with convicted intrafamilial and extrafamilial sexual abusers and concluded from "a sampling of recent or ongoing clinical studies in different cities. . . that a clear majority of males who sexually abused children were sexually abused as children." The *Tribune* reported that experience with thousands of offenders leads researchers to estimate that between 70 percent and 85 percent of child victims become sexual abusers themselves. In addition, other social ills—rape, prostitution, drug addiction, and crime—have been attributed to former victims of child sexual abuse. Thus the silence of the abused is eventually broken and their despair and rage are acted out in ways that threaten not only other children but all of society. . . .

Ignorance and indifference to the problem, acceptance of the status quo, are comfortable and undemanding. If the public doesn't realize how pervasive the problem is, it won't feel compelled to learn about children, about their capabilities and limitations, their powerlessness in society and especially in the legal system. If the public doesn't know about children in courtrooms, it can abandon the legal system to police, attorneys, judges, and legislators, who have little motivation to question it. If acceptance of the status quo prevails, society won't have to analyze legal misinterpretations that often render the justice system incapable of providing justice for child victims. Comfortable in its ignorance, the public can avoid the challenge of Suzanne Sgroi, whose *Handbook of Clinical Intervention in Child Sexual Abuse* is a classic in its field. Sgroi reminds us that "we tolerate sexual abuse of children in our society because we continue to process cases through an adversary system that is overwhelmingly weighted against the child victim at virtually every level.". . .

Keeping Child Witnesses Out of Court

Every child has the right not to be abused—physically, sexually or emotionally. For a child abuse victim, the trauma of testifying about the abuse in open court may exacerbate the harm already suffered. To protect children from needless, additional harm of this sort, more than forty states have adopted evidentiary rules or procedural statutes affording alternatives to in-court testimony.

Gregory P. Joseph, *Human Rights*, Summer 1989.

VOCAL, Victims of Child Abuse Legislation, [is] a group which claims to be composed of several thousand people falsely accused of child molestation and abuse. VOCAL and its supporters oppose legal reform and, to some extent, public education about child sexual abuse. Many of their arguments are variations on the denial approach; others are more sophisticated.

Perhaps VOCAL's least credible contention is that there is a child sexual abuse industry financially dependent upon discovery, prosecution, and conviction of offenders. The view that innocent people are being destroyed in vast numbers by bureaucrats and politicians seeking to score "points toward a promotion, a pay raise, or a federal grant" is developed in *The Politics of Child Abuse*. This book contains primarily remarks by child sexual abuse defendants, their relatives, and attorneys, and records a series of personal attacks on professionals working with child victims. One attorney quoted in the book contends:

> These people [working with victims] are afraid of losing money. The real explosion [in reporting of child abuse] is related to money. It took a few years for it to crank up, but with all this money going into the system, that's what makes the social workers so anxious to start new cases. It's their job that's on the line. . . . And then you have the ripple effect. [The social workers] send [children] to one of their favorite agencies or doctors, some of whom—without mentioning any names—have a reputation among attorneys doing juvenile law, as being *professional child abuse finders*. . . . And these agencies then make a lot of money from the county. They not only get paid per case or per child, but they get grants!. . . Look for the profit motive if you really want to know what this thing is all about. Most of these schools carry liability insurance of one million dollars per child. And all these militant parents are pushing and pressuring the District Attorney's office to convict these people so they can sue for millions.

The facts belie these claims. Social workers' jobs are hardly "on the line" because they lack work. From the largest cities to the most remote rural areas, social workers are overworked and underpaid. The 58 percent increase in reports of child sexual abuse over a two-year period demonstrates only one facet of the ever-increasing demand on their time and energy. The vast majority of social workers are civil service employees whose salaries are constant and not affected by caseloads or grants; the annual minimum salary recommended by the National Association of Social Workers for a beginning professional with a bachelor of social work degree is $17,000, and many do not receive that much. . . .

Child Abuse Legislation

Opponents of child abuse legislation argue that innocent people are being punished because of false allegations by children. But a major purpose of the new legislation is to provide better means of communicating with child witnesses to help assure more informed judgments about their veracity. Once an accusation is made, it is vital to an innocent suspect that the system use every means possible to communicate with and encourage responses from the accuser. The reforms—using anatomically correct dolls and hand puppets in questioning children, allowing children to be seated on the laps of trusted caretakers, permitting them to be questioned via closed circuit television or by an impartial court representative—do not threaten the innocent. They facilitate discovery of truth. . . .

There is also no validity to the claim by VOCAL and other opponents of legal reform that attention to child victims' rights somehow threatens the constitutional rights of defendants. Child advocates have not argued that American courts should abandon traditional protections for defendants. Responsible professionals have not advocated rejecting the constitutional principle that the accused is innocent until proven guilty. They have not maintained that defendants be denied the right to confront their accusers. They have argued only that sometimes in order to facilitate

"Just keep walking. . . . She's not going to believe us, either!"

discovery of truth, confrontation of a child must occur in ways not usually employed in court rooms. Child advocates have not maintained that admittance of hearsay evidence should be the rule in sexual abuse trials. They have argued only that, in special instances, certain hearsay statements by children should be considered under the long-accepted category of exceptions to the hearsay rule. Respect for the rights of child victims does not limit the rights of defendants; it helps to balance the scales of justice so that the system can foster the quest for truth. . . .

A Father's Experience

"Don't talk to me about the legal system," says a father whose five-year-old daughter was raped by a neighbor. "I know all about the legal system. The legal system lets the guy who used to live next door get up and leave the house every morning after we've been up all night dealing with [Jenny's] nightmares. He saw a psychiatrist once a week for six months, and now life is back to normal for him. [Jenny's] been in therapy for years, we had to move across town because she was so afraid he'd come and get her, and sometimes I think she'll never be able to lead a happy life. That's the way the legal system protected us."

How did we reach a point where America's cherished legal system has become an enemy of a five-year-old rape victim? Stinging critiques of the system are as familiar on television talk shows as they are in lengthy scholarly treatises. Citizens, social critics, and journalists locate injustice in the very place where justice should be pursued. . . .

Social Changes

In the late 1970s, greater awareness of the dangers of child sexual abuse pushed it to the fore of America's consciousness. In part, heightened sensitivity to child victims was the result of dramatic and unprecedented social forces that altered the life styles of Americans and their children. Some of those forces had been building gradually for years; but for most, their impact came with extraordinary power and speed. And it was only a matter of time before they blended to produce new sets of court consumers and a new outcry over the legal rights of children.

One of the most significant forces was the changing character of the family. Until the 1960s, Americans considered divorce an exception to the rule of normal family life. A painful acknowledgment of failure, divorce was relatively rare for many reasons, including the emotional costs it exacted from spouses, extended family, and most of all, children. But the frequency of divorce and attitudes about divorce quickly changed. Prior to 1965, there were approximately 2 divorces per 1,000 people. By 1979, the rate increased to 5.2 per 1,000, the highest in the world. More than two million children are involved in divorce every year. . . .

With divorce came new life styles for children that exposed them to more outsiders and potentially threatening circumstances. Through the 1960s, children with working mothers were often considered victims of family misfortune for whom special day-care or after-school arrangements were required. But in the 1980s, "latch-key" children and day-care centers were common. In 1950, only 11 percent of women with preschool children worked outside the home; by 1980, that figure had risen to 43 percent. Divorce was not, of course, the only force responsible for the increase in working mothers. A changing national economy forced married mothers, often against their wills, out of the home and into the work force; others, influenced by feminism, determined to combine careers and parenting; and still others chose to have children without marrying.

A Rare Occurrence

Children rarely use an allegation of child sexual abuse to get back at adults. More than 99 times out of 100, allegations of child sexual abuse by children are in fact true. Keep in mind that most victims of child sexual abuse are 12 and under; when those children give details about abuse, the descriptions are neither figments of their imagination nor products of watching cable television, but rather a recounting of a very real experience. And, although one can imagine that such an allegation is a potentially powerful weapon in the hands of a malcontent youngster, this simply turns out to be a rare occurrence.

Alan Trager, in *Mental Health and Violence*, 1985

Almost overnight there appeared a new norm—the working parent. Television, the mirror of American values, recorded the transition. Shows like "My Three Sons," "Bachelor Father," "One Day at a Time," and "Kate and Allie" portrayed the single, working parent with fascination and admiration. "Family Ties" and "The Cosby Show" romanticized working parents successfully combining careers and family. Even surrogate parental figures— from a British butler ("Mr. Belvedere") to an alien life form ("Alf") led some of televisions's nontraditional families. In fact, of the sixty-eight regular TV series in 1986, only three depicted the traditional nuclear family. The Nelsons, Cleavers, Andersons, Petries, and Flintstones of earlier years were history.

On television these new familial arrangements always work. Children are never neglected; they are never confused and unhappy for longer than thirty minutes; and in the end love, understanding, and harmony sustain them and their families. Real life is quite different. With the phenomenon of the working parent came new demands and new compromises. In a society unprepared to cope with the enormous influx of mothers of young children into the work force, something had to give—or rather, someone had to give up something. With employers offering little flexibility in job demands and hours, parents had little choice but to leave employment behind, or leave their children behind with others. Their children, however, were not consulted. Children's time with friends, recreation, lessons, and most important, parents was compromised; and American society, in order to accommodate the social and economic demands of a new era, established a haphazard network of facilities and programs—some excellent, some dismal—to care for children. Infants and toddlers filled day-care centers. School-age children found themselves in after-school programs. Responsibility and exposure came early and sometimes at great cost.

Teenagers Having Children

During roughly the same period, unprecedented numbers of poor teenage children were having their own children. Unmarried, uneducated, unemployed, and emotionally immature, these teenagers were now attempting to be parents. Abuse and neglect of infants and toddlers increased so rapidly that, in some states, social workers could not even respond to cases within twenty-four hours, as required by law. They described the problem of teen pregnancy and resulting child abuse as "mammoth" and "overwhelming." One county social worker told of an eleven-year-old mother and thirty-four-year-old grandmother, "You ask them if they tuck little Joey in at night and they look at you like you're crazy. Those words don't mean anything to them." Another social worker explained, "I say, 'Does your mother tell you she loves you?' They've never heard those words before."

By 1983, in many parts of the country for the first time, the birth rate of single women exceeded 50 percent. From 1981 to 1985, reported child abuse in America increased at unprecedented rates almost everywhere—445 percent in Arizona, 137 percent in Mississippi, 142 percent in Ohio, 367 percent in Oregon, 196 percent in Rhode Island. The actual numbers are even more frightening—for example, there were 18,000 substantiated cases of abused and neglected children in Wisconsin from 1985 to 1987, many involving sexual abuse. While increased reporting undoubtedly accounts for some of the increase, child protection social workers relate most of that reporting to actual increases in child abuse and neglect, often in families with poor, young, unmarried parents. . . .

Although the legal system was increasingly compelled to acknowledge the presence of children, the courts remained ill-equipped to deal with child witnesses and victims.

"Under the watchwords 'the best interests of the child,' 150,000 kids are taken from their parents each year by a system geared to act first and ask questions later."

The Legal System Overreacts to Child Abuse

Dan Zegart

While many people criticize the legal system as insensitive to child abuse victims, others argue that it is insensitive to adults and victimizes parents falsely accused of abuse. In the following viewpoint, Dan Zegart examines the case of the Kracht family. Jenny and Paul Kracht had their children taken away from them for a year because their seven-year-old son told his teacher that his father had hit him. According to Zegart, social workers are so anxious to prevent child abuse that they sometimes have children removed from their homes when there is insufficient evidence to indicate abuse. Zegart is a reporter for *The Evening News*, a daily newspaper in Newburgh, New York.

As you read, consider the following questions:

1. What proportion of child abuse accusations are unfounded, according to the author?
2. In Zegart's opinion, how do the legal provisions used in child abuse cases differ from those used in cases involving adult victims?

Dan Zegart, "Soloman's Choice," *Ms.*, June 1989. Copyright Ms. Magazine, June 1989. Reprinted with permission.

Jenny Kracht stood in the living room of her sister-in-law's house in Newburgh, New York, dialing frantically, trying to reach a lawyer. A nervous woman, she had always had trouble keeping her head in emergencies. Now she struggled for control as a tense little group of relatives consoled her five terrified kids. Outside the house a small army of state and local police blocked off any escape.

It was late afternoon on September 26, 1986. Jenny Kracht had just been accused of child abuse.

A few hours earlier, as she drove to Meadow Hill Elementary School to pick up three of her children, she had been anticipating a big Friday night dinner and the season premire of *Dallas*. But some time before she arrived, seven-year-old Michael Kracht had told school authorities that a bruise on his back was the result of a beating. Michael had warned his father, Paul, on several occasions that if he made him go to school, he'd be sorry. But that afternoon, watching his mother on the phone, Michael was scared—this wasn't at all what he expected to happen.

A Few Bruises

Based solely on a few bruises and Michael's explanation of where they came from, all five of the Kracht children—Michael, his brother Matthew, 10, Jessica, five, Ashley, four, and Justin, seven months—were split up that evening and placed in foster homes. It took five weeks and thousands of dollars in lawyers' and therapists' fees to get them back home and a year and a half to regain full legal custody. The child protection unit of the Orange County Department of Social Services, which acted so promptly to rescue the children from their mother, was agonizingly slow to respond when Michael and Matthew told their caseworker they were being physically abused in foster care. The long separation was more puzzling to the family given the fact that Michael recanted his story soon after reaching the foster home.

"Social services tore this family apart," said Jenny Kracht, sitting in the kitchen of her two-story home with Paul, who recently retired as a prison guard. "I used to tell the kids, you've got nothing to ever worry about, nobody can ever hurt you, don't worry about the bogeyman, you're safe here with Mom and Dad. You can't tell them that now."

That fall, the Krachts became one of thousands of American families devastated by a false accusation of child abuse. Tragedies such as the death of Lisa Steinberg in New York City have focused attention on the vulnerability of children, and the National Committee for Prevention of Child Abuse reports a continuing rise in child abuse fatalities. But the Krachts also were victims of a child welfare system where overburdened caseworkers face often impossible choices.

Under the watchwords "the best interests of the child," 150,000 kids are taken from their parents each year by a system geared to act first and ask questions later. However, two thirds of the 2.2 million reports of child maltreatment in 1986 turned out to be unfounded. And of the substantiated reports, only 15 percent involved any serious risk to the child's safety, according to Douglas Besharov, a resident scholar at the American Enterprise Institute and first director of the National Center on Child Abuse and Neglect. It's this 15 percent, he concluded, that need the kind of intervention the Krachts received but Lisa Steinberg didn't—immediate removal from the home. An atmosphere of well-justified concern for maltreated children has bred a monster that can traumatize both parents and kids, trampling their rights to a parent-child relationship.

Family Abuse

Emotional stories about false accusations of child abuse, what might be called family abuse on the part of social welfare agencies, are now appearing with the same prominence as stories of the child abuse "plague" of the eighties. . . .

Incidents of child abuse allegations continue to abound and many, perhaps most, are true. However, in an increasing number of cases the alleged "abuse" is of a nature that strikes many observers as firm parental guidance and direction to children, the exact opposite of child abuse.

Tim Lawrie, *Family, Law & Democracy Report*, August 1989.

It can happen most easily to families that are poor, out of the media's spotlight, and afraid to speak out when faced with the authority of the social service agencies. In Newburgh's East End, which is across town from Jenny and Paul Kracht, I spent time with families who had none of the resources of the middle-class Krachts. Within a two-week period, five of these families lost their children for various periods of time. The federal Adoption Assistance and Child Welfare Act of 1980 requires that "reasonable efforts" be made to keep families together and that only children in real danger of maltreatment be placed in foster care. But there is a considerable gap between theory and practice, according to Mary Lee Allen, director of child welfare and mental health for the Children's Defense Fund (CDF) in Washington, D.C. Citing antifamily bias in the child welfare system, she expressed concern that children are placed inappropriately when preventive services should be offered instead to poor parents having difficulty caring for their kids. . . .
The legal system that underlies the machinery of removal is

quite unlike that which applies to criminal cases.

Child protective investigations often start with an anonymous phone call to a hotline number, and the parents will probably never learn who turned them in. Alice Williams, another Newburgh mother, said she has been investigated by child protective services on and off for three years because of two of these calls, both, she suspects, made by acquaintances with an ax to grind. No evidence of abuse or neglect has ever been found.

Many states have legal definitions of maltreatment that are vague enough to leave a lot to the discretion of the protective worker. Family and juvenile courts, which provide the legal authority for removing children, operate under flexible rules of evidence that would be unacceptable in criminal cases. Some hearsay evidence is admissible. Parents questioned by social workers are not advised beforehand of any rights they might have. Police can seize evidence without a warrant when a child is considered at immediate risk. The system of charging the parents is also strangely flexible, giving the agency the ability to remove the child and determine the precise reasons later. . . .

Odds Stacked Against Parents

The Krachts found the odds heavily stacked against them. Before any evidence had been presented, Jenny and Paul Kracht had been forced to begin counseling, at a cost of $185 per week, as a condition for having Jessica, Ashley, and Justin returned to them and to win weekly visits with Matthew and Michael. Even the children's court-appointed law guardian, Michael Schwartz, agreed that the case against them was extremely flimsy. "It was always my position, as the Court is well aware . . .that I thought perhaps the County acted presumptuously in removing the children from this home," he told Judge Victor Ludmerer.

Nevertheless, the Krachts, like many other parents interviewed, say they were advised that the surest way to get the kids back was to confess to something. At a hearing on October 31, 1986, they put themselves on record as having engaged in excessive corporal punishment by admitting that they had "with an open hand, physically disciplined the child Michael Kracht," unintentionally causing bruises. Neighbors and friends of the Krachts say the couple has never been abusive. "If anything," said Jenny's sister-in-law, "she's too good to those kids."

The family was ordered to continue counseling and was placed under an unlimited order of supervision, giving the department continued access to their home. Michael and Matthew returned home the day of the hearing, but the legal custody that had passed over to DSS [Department of Social Services] was only restored to the Krachts in the spring of 1988.

The two boys came home traumatized by their experience in

foster care, a nightmare they had been telling their helpless parents about during phone calls and weekly home visits. The Krachts had learned another dismal failure of the child welfare system: Besharov and others say significantly more children are maltreated in foster care or in institutional settings than in their natural homes. . . .

Manipulation

Armed with the belief that under no circumstances would a child claim to have been molested unless it were true, child protection agencies are ready to send a child for "therapy" before any kind of thorough investigation has been done. Even worse, those interviewing a child allegedly molested (whether investigators or therapists) frequently manipulate the child. They do so because they do not take very seriously the possibility of a false allegation.

Lee Coleman, *California Lawyer*, July 1986.

Child welfare administrators say they have quite enough work to do without manufacturing cases. But Matthew and Michael described considerable prodding when they were initially questioned by a social service worker and then by state police. And none of the children confirmed Michael's story.

Matthew remembers being asked about Michael's bruise. "They said, 'Did your dad hit him there? Because Michael said that he did.' And I said no, he just spanks him. He doesn't pound him on the back or anything like that." Matthew said he was never asked if he knew how his brother had been hurt. Had anyone asked he could have told them the bruise was inflicted by Matthew himself while the boys were roughhousing in the yard. . . .

Sexual Abuse Cases

In sex abuse cases, especially when the charge is fondling, the only basis for the removal may be the word of the child. It's not hard to imagine how a social worker, who by training and inclination may focus on making a client feel comfortable enough to talk about painful stories, might cross the line between questioning and coaxing a young witness.

Sara says she was interrogated several times a day about fondling after she told her teacher at the Mark Twain Elementary School in Colorado Springs in February 1986 that her stepfather, Clark, had tickled her. On the basis of statements made by Sara to social service workers, Clark Gabriel was charged with what he now jokingly refers to as "felony tickling." The charge was fondling—sexual assault on a child—and had he not been acquitted, Gabriel could have gone to prison for 16 years.

135

Susan Gabriel, Sara's mother and a technical writer with TRW Corp., said she was mystified when she first learned from DSS that Sara had been taken from her school and placed in foster care: "They said she specifically said it [the tickling] wasn't between the legs, wasn't on the breast area or anything. And then they said, this is molesting. At that point I really felt like I had been dropped onto an alien planet."

Unlike many parents in similar situations, the outraged Gabriels refused to admit to any wrongdoing and insisted on a trial. The judge told them to get a second opinion from his former law partner, J. Gregory Walta. In a letter to their attorney, Walta wrote that the case fit a "disturbing pattern in which child protection workers induce the child to make allegations not originally made, then resist the child's efforts to recant, and ignore reports by qualified experts questioning the truth of the child's allegations."

More Reports

As a result of her experience, Susan Gabriel founded southern Colorado VOCAL, Victims of Child Abuse Laws, which has more than 70 chapters nationwide and a membership of roughly 5,000, according to Margaret Gran, who helped establish the group in 1984. Child protectors do most of their work among the poor, but VOCAL's membership, according to Gran, is almost entirely middle class. The American Enterprise Institute's Besharov suggests a major reason for this is a tenfold growth in reports—not necessarily occurrences—of sexual abuse since 1970. And while neglect charges tend to be leveled against poor parents, sexual abuse has proven to be an equal opportunity accusation.

Reports of all types of child maltreatment are more than 14 times what they were in 1963, but neither child abuse nor child removal is a new phenomenon. In *Heroes of Their Own Lives*, a history of family violence from 1880 until 1960, Linda Gordon, a professor of American history at the University of Wisconsin, wrote that concern over maltreated children has risen and fallen many times over the past 100 years, but there is "no evidence the problem is actually increasing." Gordon's book focuses on the Massachusetts Society for Prevention of Cruelty to Children. Before government entered the picture, a relatively recent involvement, it was up to private agencies like the MSPCC to protect children, and their clientele was almost exclusively poor. Most of the legal tools used to remove children today originated with the MSPCC and its sister organizations. And in the nineteenth century, as now, "hostile neighbors and relatives often turned in false accusations," Gordon wrote, adding that from 1890 until 1960, the proportion of false complaints never fell below 65 percent.

Since 1974, as a result of federal mandate, states require almost all professionals who deal with children—from child-care workers and teachers to doctors, psychiatrists, and social workers—to report suspected abuse. These professionals are liable to criminal and civil penalty if they fail to report but are shielded if they do.

Parent advocates complain that because of this, the therapeutic and helping professions are being turned into spies, violating the confidentiality of people who come for help. Robert VanCleave, director of the El Paso County Department of Social Services, said "children rarely fabricate stories," but, he added, "it would be an unusual kid who was not intimidated by a group of authority figures" asking questions. . . .

Whatever the accuser's credibility, the odds are that key decisions about whether a child will be taken from a home will rest with overburdened, underpaid, and inexperienced caseworkers. In New York City, the turnover rate for caseworkers was almost 70 percent in 1987, and each of those workers was carrying an average of 40 cases at one time. No social worker wants to be responsible for the next Lisa Steinberg. Agency workers in general feel if they are going to err, they will err on the side of protecting the child.

Damaging Effects

But the effects of such an error can be damaging and long-lasting for both children and families. More than two years after the fact, it is still extremely painful for the Kracht children to discuss what happened to them. Until recently, Matthew had frequent nightmares about his experiences at the hands of [his foster parents] Madge and Johnny. And the three older children all told me they are afraid it could happen again.

Child psychology experts say the experience of being taken from the family is so devastating, removals should be performed only in the most extreme cases of abuse or gross neglect. "It will be very, very, terrifying," said Lorraine Siegel, a Pleasantville, New York, social worker who deals with children who have been placed in foster care. "They will lose their confidence. They will lose their sense of trust in others."

Distinguishing Bias from Reason

When dealing with controversial issues, many people allow their feelings to dominate their powers of reason. Thus, one of the most important critical thinking skills is the ability to distinguish between statements based upon emotion or bias and conclusions based upon a rational consideration of the facts.

The following statements are taken from the viewpoints in this chapter. Consider each statement carefully. *Mark R for any statement you believe is based on reason or a rational consideration of the facts. Mark B for any statement you believe is based on bias, prejudice, or emotion. Mark I for any statement you think is impossible to judge.*

If you are doing this activity as a member of a class or group, compare your answers with those of other class or group members. Be able to defend your answers. You may discover that others come to different conclusions than you do. Listening to the rationale others present for their answers may give you valuable insights in distinguishing between bias and reason.

> R = *a statement based upon reason*
> B = *a statement based on bias*
> I = *a statement impossible to judge*

138

1. Dark alleys, strange cities, and the night are full of danger, ready to leap upon an innocent, unsuspecting victim.

2. Child witnesses are often intimidated by courtrooms and legal procedures. It makes sense to try and modify court procedures so they will be able to testify.

3. Statistics show that stepparents and their stepchildren are much more at risk for child abuse than are parents and their offspring.

4. Child abuse never occurs in good, Christian homes.

5. In our violent, sexist society, the marriage license is a hitting license.

6. The real danger of personal attack is in the home.

7. Because an injured child with poor parents is more likely to be labeled abused than a middle-class child with the same injuries, the poor suffer at the hands of a biased child welfare system.

8. The whole issue of domestic violence has been falsely framed by focusing on masculine behavior. Such bias has contributed to men's legal and social defenselessness.

9. Parent-to-child violence is so common and so widely approved that one needs few case studies to make the point.

10. There is a child sexual abuse industry financially dependent upon discovery, prosecution, and conviction of offenders.

11. Underfunded, understaffed police forces cannot be held accountable for the actions of every crazed person with a gun.

12. Men have economic and social power in our society. Thus they can hit their wives without fear of punishment.

13. Anyone who believes that a person determined to kill another can reliably be prevented from doing so by the police—or anyone—is dreaming.

14. As divorce rates have increased, so has child abuse. Thus child abuse occurs because of a cultural revolution that undermined marriage and family values.

15. Law enforcement officers are interested only in punishment.

Periodical Bibliography

The following articles have been selected to supplement the diverse views presented in this chapter.

James and Phyllis Alsdurf	"Battered into Submission," *Christianity Today,* June 16, 1989.
Bryce J. Christensen	"By Blab Befuddled," *Chronicles,* July 1989.
Rita-Lou Clarke	"Hand-Me-Downs," *Daughters of Sarah,* January/February 1989.
Karen Diegmueller	"The Battered Husband's Case Shakes Up Social Notions," *Insight,* March 7, 1988.
Kathleen Doheny	"Sexual Abuse: When Men Are Victims," *Los Angeles Times,* January 10, 1989.
Neil Gilbert	"Teaching Children to Prevent Sexual Abuse," *The Public Interest,* Fall 1988.
Ellen Goodman	"Curtains for 'The-Bitch-Deserved-It' Defense," *Los Angeles Times,* May 23, 1989.
George Hackett	"A Tale of Abuse," *Newsweek,* December 12, 1988.
Sonia Johnson	"Feminism: The CenterPeace," *Friends Journal,* October 1, 1985.
Phil Kushin	"Child Abuse: A New Twist on an Old Problem," *Eternity,* March 1988.
Lois Gehr Livezey	"Sexual and Family Violence: A Growing Issue for the Churches," *The Christian Century,* October 28, 1987.
The New Republic	"The Battered Child," March 20, 1989.
Susan Schechter, interviewed by Mary Suh	"Understanding Battered Women," *Ms.,* April 1989.
The Phyllis Schlafly Report	"Family Violence Is Everyone's Concern," June 1987. Available from The Eagle Trust Fund, Box 618, Alton, IL 62002.
Joseph P. Shapiro	"Whose Responsibility Is It, Anyway?" *U.S. News & World Report,* January 9, 1989.
Janice C. Simpson	"Beware of Paper Tigers," *Time,* March 27, 1989.

What Causes Teen Violence?

Chapter Preface

Decades ago, when a juvenile in the U.S. committed a serious crime and was brought before a court, the criminal justice system treated that juvenile as an adult and in many cases, sentenced him or her in the same way it would an adult. Gradually the U.S. justice system changed its view of children and violent crime. Illinois in 1899 became the first state to pass a criminal code that established a juvenile justice system to treat juvenile offenders separately from adults. The system emphasized care, treatment, and rehabilitation of youthful offenders. Other states followed Illinois's lead. The reasoning behind the change was that children, unlike adults, might not fully understand the difference between right and wrong and might not understand the consequences of their actions. Furthermore, supporters believed that children could be reformed if they received specialized attention and treatment, something they would probably not receive if they were in large, institution-like prisons that also held adults.

Increasingly brutal juvenile crime has made the public question this view of children. Several events in 1989 drew media attention and made many people wonder whether children who commit heinous acts should receive the same punishment as adults. One such incident occurred when five teenage boys raped and savagely beat a woman jogging in Central Park, leaving her for dead and showing no remorse when they were apprehended. Also in New York, a group of high school football players sexually assaulted a mentally retarded classmate, while others observed and encouraged the attackers. In Pennsylvania, a nine-year-old boy shot his seven-year-old neighbor who had said she could play the video game Nintendo better than he could. The boy was charged as an adult, and if the case goes to trial, he will be the youngest person tried for criminal homicide in an adult courtroom since the turn of the century.

Contributing to the reevaluation of the treatment of juveniles is the high recidivism rate among youthful offenders. The U.S. Bureau of Justice Statistics found that 11,347 youthful offenders were arrested again for other serious crimes within six years. These youths were charged with 36,726 new crimes.

Should juvenile criminals be treated with leniency and society try to reform and rehabilitate them? Or must juveniles be prosecuted to the full extent of the law? These are some of the questions discussed in the following chapter.

"The present system is based on the idea that [juveniles] can be rehabilitated and yet fails to provide the deterrents, structure, and supervision."

The Juvenile Justice System Encourages Teen Violence

Rita Kramer

In 1988 journalist Rita Kramer wrote *At a Tender Age*, a book which examined the juvenile justice system and teenagers who have committed violent crimes. In the following viewpoint, excerpted from *At a Tender Age*, Kramer describes cases of violent teenagers who received minimal, ineffective sanctions for the crimes they committed. She contends that juvenile courts actually encourage further violence because they fail to punish violent acts. As a result, violent teenagers continue to victimize society, Kramer concludes.

As you read, consider the following questions:

1. What points does the author make by describing Billy's experience with juvenile court?
2. What approach toward violent teenage offenders does Kramer believe might work?
3. Why does Kramer disagree with the sharp distinction between the way the justice system treats adults and the way it treats juveniles?

Rita Kramer, *At a Tender Age: Violent Youth and Juvenile Justice*. New York: Henry Holt and Company, 1988. Reprinted by permission of Henry Holt and Company.

143

When an individual actually enters upon a criminal career, let us try to catch him at a tender age, and subject him to rational social discipline . . .

—Charles H. Cooley, "'Nature v. Nurture' in the Making of Social Careers," *Proceedings of the National Conference of Charities and Corrections*, 1896.

At twelve years of age, Billy L. stands five feet eight and weighs 128 pounds. In the early morning hours of a Friday late in August 1984, Billy and two companions, sixteen-year-old Frankie W. and thirteen-year-old Jimmy P., came on a bag lady asleep on a bench in Central Park. According to Frankie's later account, Billy hit her on the head with a piece of pipe . . . and told the others to hold her legs. They took turns holding her down and repeatedly raping and sodomizing her. Later they reported dispassionately that she kept crying out, "Oh, God, please help me," and that afterward they beat her with their fists and kicked her on the body and face, and that then Billy found a stick in the bushes with which he hit her, stopping only when a light scared them off and the boys ran out of the park. The woman's blood was on Billy's hands and clothing when the three were apprehended by police officers. They were taken in for questioning, and the two youngest were eventually tried in New York's Family Court; there, Billy was found to have committed an act "which if committed by an adult [a person over the age of sixteen] would constitute the crime of attempted rape in the first degree" and was given the maximum penalty provided for any act—even murder—committed by a person twelve years of age or younger: placement for a period of up to eighteen months. There is no legal minimum penalty.

While at the upstate facility, rather like an austere boys' camp, at which he was serving his eighteen months, Billy L. was brought back to Manhattan to be arraigned on an armed robbery charge. The robbery had occurred the previous April. Had that case been heard earlier, rather than having been scheduled on the court calendar some months after the time of his arrest, Billy might not have been in Central Park in August. . . .

Frankie's Story

Frankie, the sixteen-year-old involved in the August rape of the bag lady in Central Park, had four previous arrests, three of them for assault, including one incident in which he had thrown a woman teacher down a flight of stairs. Interviewed at the precinct house after being apprised of his rights in the presence of his father, Frankie offered some further information. He and Billy and another boy, Wayne M., fourteen, had raped another homeless woman in the park a month earlier "and did the same thing as

they did to the lady last night." Not quite the same, actually, since the first woman had been killed after she had been raped. Billy had beaten her to death after he and Frankie and the other undeniably troubled youth, Wayne, had raped and sodomized her and attempted to set her on fire. . . .
On the New York City Police Department's Juvenile Arrest Report filed on the August morning after the boys had been taken to the precinct house, Billy L. was charged with second-degree murder and assault in that he "w/2 others did assault one Evans, Mary, causing to her death . . . weapon poss/used: blunt instrument."

Crime Can Pay

The general message in New York and other states with crowded prisons and soft-hearted, hope-for-the-best family court judges has been that crime can pay.

The kids, being kids, know it, too. Like "terrible 2s" (and 3s and 4s) who are determined to test the limits of their permissive parents by repeating obnoxious behavior, violent children test the limits of society's institutions.

Suzanne Fields, *The Washington Times*, May 4, 1989.

He was not charged with first-degree murder because it is a capital offense and New York State has no death penalty. However, even the second-degree murder charge did not stick. Billy never admitted to the July killing, about which there was only the evidence of his two companions against him. The statements of co-perpetrators are not sufficient to convict without independent corroborating testimony. Although both Frankie and Wayne had told the same story with the same details in separate interviews without having had a chance to talk about their versions of the events beforehand, it was Billy who had the last word. He maintained coolly, "I don't know nothing about no killing," and added, "You ain't got nothing on me." In the matter of the August rape, in which he had beaten the victim bloody, and her blood was found on his shoes, he pleaded guilty to attempted rape in the first degree. The victim, who had lived on the streets and in the park since being released from a mental institution, was unable to testify against him, since it was her belief that the attack was part of a government plot against her. Billy was sent to Camp Tryon, an open facility in upstate New York, for a period of up to eighteen months.
A little over a year after the rape of the bag lady, Billy was moved from the upstate camp to a facility called a youth development center, the first step in DFY's [Division for Youth] community reentry program. The center was further upstate, but there were

145

more frequent home visits. On one of these, Billy disappeared. A member of the Corporation Counsel staff, who remembers Billy, thought she saw him in Central Park one morning while she was jogging, the day after a derelict was found beaten to death and sexually mutilated. "It was his m.o.," she says. . . .

Focus on Chronic Offenders

We know now from the findings of *Delinquency in a Birth Cohort* and *The Violent Few*, the Columbus, Ohio, study . . . that violent juvenile offenders are a very small fraction of youth—even a very small fraction of those youth who break the law—and that these juveniles do not typically progress from less serious to more serious crimes. They start out committing serious crimes. . . .

It is the *chronic* offenders who should be the focus of federal, state, and local efforts, from the funding of various attempts to design preventive projects in the community to programs within the existing justice system. These chronic offenders are the boys who start early, go on interrupted only by time spent locked up, and wind up in the adult criminal system.

These findings also call into question the logic of the sharp break that now exists between the juvenile and the adult systems, where, in New York, for instance, a boy may commit an act with relative impunity a day before his sixteenth birthday for which he can be severely punished the day after it. Instead of a "juvenile" system that treats a delinquent boy with leniency and then suddenly closes its books on him when he reaches the arbitrary age of sixteen, seventeen, or eighteen, turning him over to a new "adult" system, we should consider ways of integrating the two systems. Since we know there is a continuity between the chronic youthful offender and the adult criminal, we ought to change the courts, the correctional facilities, and the non-institutional programs so that there is a continuity in them as well. A unified system would create some sense of accountability in the juvenile programs, the results of which could be clearly tracked as individuals grow up and either continue to appear in the court system or stop their criminal activities. This accountability would create some pressure to do things right—to show some results for public money in terms of public good. That means improving the public safety, but it also means improving the chances of some young men growing up to lead useful lives who now grow up to be criminals—or don't grow up at all.

Violent Offenders' Childhoods

We know what they are like, these violent few, and even something about how they got that way.

We know that these children who are not children, those with an early history of serious criminal and deviant behavior, who attack, rape, rob, sometimes kill, are alienated and hostile, with

146

anti-social values and attitudes, unable or unwilling to control themselves. We know they often come from backgrounds that seem to support their criminal behavior; that they have had inadequate parenting; that the only models they have had for what it is to be a man are those they have found on the street; that they feel no connection with family, school, church, or other socializing institutions of society and have no sense of a stake in the system; that their impulsiveness and poor judgment reflect their failure to grow up. They remain infants in a child's and then a grown-up's body. Missing from their development from the very begin ning have been those identifications that define character, create conscience, and organize the mature personality in stable family relationships. Language and thought development have lagged, too, in their chaotic worlds, and, without insight, empathy, or verbal skills, they are not reachable through psychotherapy. . . .

A Serious Challenge

American juvenile courts continue to face a serious challenge from youthful offenders. From 1975 to 1981, the number of delinquency cases handled by juvenile courts increased by 2.5 percent, while the proportion of the U.S. population between the ages of 10 and 17 decreased by nearly 9 percent. . . .

Especially disturbing is the fact that a small number of juveniles appear to commit most of these offenses. Data from Marvin Wolfgang's second cohort study indicate that 7.5 percent of the juvenile population committed 68 percent of the cohort's offenses. This group was responsible for 61 percent of the homicides, 75 percent of the rapes, 73 percent of the robberies, and 65 percent of the assaults committed by the cohort. Wolfgang found that this second cohort (born in 1958) was more criminally active and violent than the first cohort he studied (born in 1945). The second cohort, he concluded, contains "a very violent criminal population of a small number of brutal offenders."

Christopher P. Manfredi, *Juvenile Justice Reform*, 1987.

There is some evidence that incapacitation—the euphemism in juvenile justice literature for imprisonment—works. Punishment does indeed seem to be the best deterrent we have found so far for the persistently dangerous delinquent. The Chicago Unified Delinquency Intervention Services project of the mid-1970s studied juveniles sentenced to training schools who had an average of over thirteen arrests with more than eight of them for the most serious and violent offenses. Their later arrest records were compared with those of "reasonably comparable" juveniles who received educational and vocational training in the community or were placed in group homes where they received counseling.

The authors of the study found that both kinds of intervention worked. All kinds of placements and sentences, according to the authors of the study, influenced delinquents' perceptions of the consequences of continued delinquency. Prior to placement in one program or another, they had been in and out of juvenile court repeatedly, often for violent offenses, but nothing had ever happened to them. At worst they were expected to show up for a weekly appointment with an overburdened probation officer. They might have had to listen to a lecture from a judge. Not infrequently they may even have been encouraged to "beat the system" by a lawyer committed to their defense and more concerned with their legal rights than with their futures.

Those who were given the less drastic placements were put on notice that the next step for them was the training school. And those sent to the training school were subject to the regimentation and other indignities and pains of incarceration, not the least of which is the inevitable victimization of the weak inmates by the strong. This aspect of institutionalization is not planned, but neither should it be a reason for not using incarceration as a last resort for dealing with those who, as one sociologist puts it, "will have killed, raped, robbed or beat their way into" such places.

The Fear of Punishment

The Chicago study found that both the juveniles sentenced to the training schools and those receiving less drastic alternative treatment showed "reasonably comparable" results as measured by number of arrests before and after intervention. In both cases the researchers found a decline in the number of arrests afterward, the so-called suppression effect being 53 percent in the case of the alternative placements and 68 percent for the training school subjects. Their conclusion, which is supported by studies of other programs in California and Utah, is that many kinds of intervention tend to suppress delinquency. Incarceration seems to have the strongest effect, but less drastic residential placement and community-based training programs have an effect too. No one can say for certain to what extent the deterrent effect is a result of the education or training offered in these programs and to what extent it results from the fear of being locked up once all the pains and humiliations of that situation become clear. The authors of the Chicago study concluded that awareness of the possibility of being sent to a locked institution has a deterrent effect both on those who have experienced it and those who have heard about it from others.

So incarceration and the fear of punishment do appear to reduce crime in that chronic group of repeaters from whom the violent few emerge. And while it obviously does not deter that hard-core few, who go on behaving violently no matter what, there seems to be reason to believe it keeps some youngsters from becoming part of their number. Institutionalization takes the worst criminals out of circulation, and the available evidence indicates that it deters some of them and some others as well by showing them that society means business and their criminal acts are likely to have painful consequences. . . .

To the objection that incarcerating more young criminals would be expensive, there is no answer. To the familiar complaint that it costs as much to keep a kid in a training school as in a prep school, one can only answer that we hope they learn something there, because it costs much more in victims' lives and victims' suffering to leave them out on the streets. . . .

Judge M. Holt Meyer thinks it "foolish and socially dangerous" to discard the present juvenile system in favor of the adult criminal-justice model, "which seems neither to rehabilitate criminals nor to deter crime." Can he possibly think that the present juvenile justice system does so? It would, on the contrary, seem to be thoroughly discredited by rising juvenile crime rates, partly the result of larger social conditions—the disintegration of the family, the proliferation of drugs—but at least partly the result of the system's failure to distinguish the violent few from the rest and its inability to deal with them effectively.

"He blames it on the alienation of youth, the lack of urban renewal and the copycat effect of the media."

As long as the "treatment-rehabilitation approach" remains in place for all juveniles regardless of the nature and number of their crimes, it seems that the violent few will go on committing crimes with impunity while the community suffers. . . .

At the present time, the system seems to teach the violent few that there is almost no chance they will be punished for their first or second offense. Their worst punishment is likely to be having to listen to the exhortations of judges, social workers, and psychotherapists. It is no surprise that they go on doing things for which they pay no penalty and hardly even incur any disapproval. . . .

An Obsolete System

The juvenile justice system doesn't work because it is obsolete and inappropriate. The Family Court Act as written in 1962 is designed to cope with 1950s-style delinquents, youths who stole cars, picked off fruit stands, or carried zip guns. Today, confronted with teenagers who commit random killings, robberies, and rapes, beat up old people, and scoff at all authority, it is powerless. It can only find them to have committed "an act that would constitute a crime if committed by an adult" but for which they are "not criminally responsible . . . by reason of infancy" and can impose only minimal sentences after "hearings" (not trials) that guarantee the most minute procedural rights of the accused while ignoring the more general ones of society.

Defining them as children, it emphasizes their age and not the nature of their acts. As Alfred S. Regnery, former Administrator of the Justice Department's Office of Juvenile Justice and Delinquency Prevention, put it, violent sixteen-year-olds "are criminals who happen to be young, not children who happen to commit crimes." Ignoring the rights of their victims, the present system is based on the idea that they can be rehabilitated and yet fails to provide the deterrents, structure, and supervision that are the only demonstrable ways to influence their behavior and thus provide a realistic chance for eventual rehabilitation. It ignores previous acts and is concerned with not stigmatizing wrongdoers rather than with changing them. And all of this goes on without press and public attendance at the proceedings in order to protect the confidentiality of the young accused—incidentally assuring that the excesses and abuses of the system, the incompetence of officials at many of its levels, and the many ways in which it fails to work or works against the community's interests as well as against the real interests of the youthful criminal remain hidden from public view and immune to public criticism and impulse for change.

"Broad demands to 'get tough' with juvenile offenders often make it more difficult for the juvenile justice system to concentrate its limited resources on violent offenders."

The Juvenile Justice System Does Not Encourage Teen Violence

National Council on Crime and Delinquency

Members of the National Council on Crime and Delinquency work in corrections and advocate community-based programs and the family court system for handling cases involving juvenile offenders. The following viewpoint is excerpted from a pamphlet published by the San Francisco-based Council. The authors argue that the problem of violent juvenile crime has been exaggerated and distorted. They write that juvenile violence has not increased significantly. The authors disagree with proposals to lock up juvenile offenders; they believe such a policy is dehumanizing and encourages bitter teens to be violent when they are released.

As you read, consider the following questions:

1. Who is most likely to be victimized by violent juvenile crime, according to the Council?
2. Why do the authors criticize the belief that locking up violent teenagers would reduce the crime problem?

From *Facts About Violent Juvenile Crime*, a brochure published by the National Council on Crime and Delinquency, May 1988. Reprinted by permission of the National Council on Crime and Delinquency.

V iolent crime is one of America's severest social problems, and it is particularly shocking when such crimes are committed by youths who seem to have no understanding of the serious harm they have caused.

Sometimes, especially in the wake of heinous and highly publicized crimes, the public becomes convinced that large numbers of our young people are predatory criminals who think nothing of killing or maiming innocent victims. At times like these citizens clamor for protection against young lawbreakers, and public officials respond with stiffer penalties for those offenders who are caught and convicted.

But this periodic cycle of public outrage followed by harsher punishment apparently has not reduced violent juvenile crime. Nor has it diminished the public's fear of such crimes. Therefore, it is now appropriate to reexamine our assumptions about youth violence to determine if our responses to the problem are based on the best available information. . . .

The Nature of Violent Juvenile Crime

Assumption: Juvenile offenders are responsible for much if not most of the violent crime in this country.

Fact: The overwhelming majority of violent crimes are not committed by persons under age 18, and the most serious violent offenses are the least likely to be committed by juvenile offenders.

One common method of measuring crime is to look at arrest rates (although this method is imperfect because suspects who are arrested may not be representative of all those who commit crimes).

The *Uniform Crime Reports*—which are compiled by the Federal Bureau of Investigation based on statistics from local police departments—show that persons under 18 accounted for 17 percent of the 1985 arrests for the most serious violent offenses: murder, non-negligent manslaughter, rape, robbery and aggravated assault. Among the more than 1.7 million arrests of juveniles in 1985, some 4 percent were for these serious violent crimes.

The federal government also sponsors annual National Crime Surveys in which interviewers ask a representative sample of citizens about their experiences as victims of crime. In the survey for 1979, victims attributed about 25 percent of the rapes, robberies, assaults and larcenies to offenders under 18 years old.

However, even though they commit fewer violent crimes than adults, because juveniles are a relatively small part of the United States population, as a whole their *rate* of committing such crimes is higher than the rate for adults, though it is lower than the rate for persons aged 18 to 20. . . .

Assumption: Violent juvenile crime is increasing sharply.

Fact: Violent juvenile crime did increase substantially during

152

the 1960s and early 1970s but the best available evidence suggests that it has stabilized and may have even declined in the past few years.

Between 1980 and 1985 the number of juvenile arrests for violent crimes remained almost constant, with violent crimes accounting for 4.1 percent of all juvenile arrests in 1985 (compared to 4.2 in 1980).

Assumption: Violent crimes committed by juveniles usually result in death or serious injury.

Fact: Fortunately, the overwhelming majority of violent crimes

committed by juveniles do *not* cause serious physical injuries to the victims.

Most juvenile crimes that are categorized as violent cause little physical harm to the victims. National Crime Surveys have indicated that 72 percent of the rapes, robberies and assaults committed by juveniles caused no injuries, 22 percent caused injuries that did not require medical attention and 7 percent did require medical attention. A study of 811 Columbus, Ohio youths with at least one violent crime on their records showed that 73 percent had neither threatened nor inflicted significant physical harm during those crimes.

Nevertheless, all violent crime must be taken seriously because even those victims who escape physical injuries often suffer psychological harm from being victimized.

Use of Weapons

Assumption: Juveniles are usually armed with guns or knives when they commit violent crimes.

Fact: Most violent crimes committed by youths do not involve the use of weapons, although the use of guns and knives may be increasing.

Researcher Marvin Wolfgang and his colleagues examined the police records of all boys born in Philadelphia in 1945 who lived in that city between their tenth and eighteenth birthdays. (This type of statistical grouping is known as a "birth cohort.") The records showed that weapons were used in 263 of the 9,934 offenses known to police. Similarly, a Vera Institute of Justice study of juvenile court records in three New York and New Jersey counties showed that weapons were present in fewer than 17 percent of the violent juvenile crimes.

Finally, an analysis of data collected in the federal government's National Crime Surveys indicated that juvenile offenders used weapons in 27 percent—and guns in fewer than 5 percent—of the rapes, robberies, assaults and larcenies described by victims.

Assumption: Juvenile delinquents tend to commit their violent crimes against the more vulnerable members of society, particularly the elderly.

Fact: Most violent juvenile crime is committed by males against other young males. The elderly are the least likely age group to be victimized by juveniles, but crimes involving the elderly seem to be somewhat more serious.

Data from the National Crime Surveys indicate that juveniles are seven times more likely to commit rapes, robberies, personal larcenies and assaults against other juveniles than against any other age group. (Purse snatching is the one crime where the victims are more likely to be elderly and female.) Data from police records also show that young males, as a group, are by far the most likely victims of violent youth crime. . . .

Assumption: Once a youth has committed a violent crime he or she will probably commit more of them, and the crimes are likely to become increasingly serious.

Fact: If a juvenile offender commits one violent crime he or she is not necessarily prone to commit more such crimes, nor to commit increasingly serious violent offenses.

About one-quarter of the youths in a Columbus, Ohio cohort study—all of whom had been arrested for at least one violent crime before the age of 18—had committed a serious violent offense. Of the 218 youths who had committed at least one serious violent offense, 90 percent had not committed more than one such crime. Similarly, a study of 282 Pennsylvania youths referred to juvenile court in 1977 for violent offenses found that two-thirds had no subsequent offenses during the follow-up period.

The Pitfalls of Getting Tough

"Get tough" policies are popular with politicians who are responsive to persistent public fears about crime. But, the most immediate results of "get tough" policies are overcrowded facilities and demands for increased funding for corrections agencies. There is no evidence that tougher penalties actually reduce youth crime.

Barry Krisberg, *The Juvenile Court: Reclaiming the Vision*, 1988.

Studies of juvenile crime records in Philadelphia, Columbus, Minnesota, New York, and New Jersey found no uniform tendency among delinquents to escalate from less serious to more serious offenses. . . .

Assumption: Locking up more juvenile offenders would teach them a lesson and discourage them from committing additional crimes.

Fact: The bulk of the evidence suggests that incarceration does not deter delinquents from committing additional crimes after they are released from confinement.

The Columbus cohort study found that after being released from incarceration delinquents committed additional crimes at a faster rate than they had before. Similarly, Marvin Wolfgang's Philadelphia cohort study concluded:

> Not only do a greater number of those who receive punitive treatment (institutionalization, fine or probation) continue to violate the law, but they also commit more serious crimes with greater rapidity than those who experience a less constraining contact with the judicial and correctional systems. Thus, we must conclude that the juvenile justice system, at its best, has no effect on the subsequent behavior of adolescent boys and, at its worst, has a deleterious effect on future behavior.

One interpretation of these findings is that judges were correctly selecting for incarceration those youths most likely to commit further crimes after release. Another interpretation is that the experience of incarceration itself encourages further delinquency because prisons and jails serve as "schools for crime." Biographical reports and fiction such as Clifford Shaw's *The Jack-Roller*, Claude Brown's *Manchild in the Promised Land*, and John Allen's *Assault with a Deadly Weapon*, do depict youths learning to become hardened criminals in such institutions. . . .

Whatever the effects of incarceration on future criminality, there is abundant evidence that such institutions cause long-lasting psychological damage to many youths.

The Pitfalls of Incarcerating Youths

Assumption: Even if locking up violent kids doesn't deter them from future crimes, at least they can't commit crimes while they are behind bars.

Fact: It would take a vast increase in the number of juveniles incarcerated to produce even a small drop in crime, and the human and financial costs would be extremely high.

Data from the Philadelphia cohort study indicate that putting twice as many juvenile offenders behind bars would result in a 1 to 4 percent reduction in theft, property damage and sexual assaults. Similarly, an Ohio study concluded that large increases in the incarceration of adult and juvenile offenders would have only minimal impact on the crime rate.

In deciding how often to resort to incarceration, the benefits must be balanced against the high human and financial costs. In 1986, it cost from $20,000 to $51,000 per year to incarcerate each youth, which is far greater than the cost of community-based programs such as restitution and community service work. Thus, a study prepared for Congress proposed that secure confinement ought to be treated as a "scarce resource" to be used only when all other possibilities have been exhausted.

Assumption: Courts should stop coddling these kids; it's time to punish them for a change.

Fact: There is no objective standard to determine whether a sentence is too lenient or too harsh, but there is evidence that more juveniles are placed in institutions than is necessary for public safety.

Nationwide, a study estimates, at least half of the 450,000 juveniles held in detention each year could be released to supervised non-secure settings without endangering public safety if recognized national detention standards were enforced. . . .

Assumption: It ought to be possible to identify youths who are likely to become violent and to nip their criminal careers before they do serious damage.

Fact: It is true that a small proportion of youths commit a large part of the violent crime, but it is very difficult, if not impossible, to predict which youths will become repeat offenders.

When scholars examine juvenile arrest records they can identify relatively small groups of juveniles who appear to be responsible for a disproportionately large number of crimes. But, while researchers can find these chronic delinquents after they have developed substantial arrest records, it has not been possible to identify them before they have committed multiple crimes. . . .

The Real Issues

The puzzle of how to approach youngsters committing violent acts has never been more difficult. At one end of the spectrum are those calling for removal of these predators from the streets. One researcher has calculated that doubling sentences would increase the jail population about 6 percent and simultaneously lower the amount of crime in the street by 5 percent. The 5-percent reduction is an appreciable gain, but the impact would not address the full scope of the crime problem.

Another factor to consider is the ability of the subculture to replace lost leaders. Somehow, no sooner is one member of the corner crowd lost than a replacement appears. Regardless of a surge in police arrests, the supply seems inexhaustible. . . . Arrest does not deter. Among chronic offenders, it is only a condition to which one must accommodate. Hard-liners can find little solace in incarceration. It neither stems the tide nor creates a sense of security. A few individuals are put out of commission temporarily, but the real issues are never faced.

Seymour Gelber, *Hard-Core Delinquents*, 1988.

Assumption: If they're old enough to kill and rob like adults, violent juveniles should be punished like adults.

Fact: Treating juvenile offenders like adult criminals has proven to be largely ineffective and unjustified.

Since 1978, more than half the states have enacted legislation to "get tough" with juvenile offenders. The goal of the legislation was to make it easier to waive juvenile cases into adult court. Statutes included: permission for prosecutors to direct file selected cases in the adult court; lowering the age of waiver; and excluding certain offenses from juvenile court jurisdiction.

For the most part, the decision to waive a case to the adult court is highly idiosyncratic and not necessarily limited to the most serious offenders who go to court. For example, [even after] implementing new juvenile sentencing guidelines in Washington state, studies showed little or no change in the sentencing practices of judges. Research indicates that some youths waived to

157

adult court may receive lighter sentences than if they had remained under juvenile jurisdiction, thus dispelling the myth that juveniles placed in the adult court will be more severely punished.

Assumption: It seems that nothing works with these delinquent kids so the best we can do is lock them up.

Fact: Some approaches have worked with some kinds of delinquents, although there is no panacea.

Just as there is no single cause of juvenile delinquency, there is no single effective treatment for all youths who break the law. But the consensus of the recent research is that some programs do steer some youths away from criminality.

An ideal way to deal with violent juveniles has yet to be developed. But, the current trend leans toward a combination of community-based programs and small secure facilities for the few violent juvenile offenders. As a result of research, a number of juvenile systems have successfully decreased their secure bed capacity. Community programs offer opportunities to learn social skills, education and the chance for the offender to stay in the community while attempting rehabilitation. . . .

In order to respond most effectively to violent juvenile crime it is necessary to keep the problem in proper perspective. The facts outlined above show that most delinquency does not involve violence.

Nevertheless, it is clear that a relatively small proportion of juvenile lawbreakers does pose a serious threat to the safety of society. They need special attention from the juvenile justice system—intensive programs run by highly qualified staff. In some cases they need secure custody, but it should not be dehumanizing.

The juvenile justice system has limited resources. As long as it is swamped with hundreds of thousands of cases involving minor and even noncriminal offenses, it will not be able to deal adequately with the frightening but numerically small problem of violent juvenile delinquency.

Making Juvenile Justice Effective

Yet, broad demands to "get tough" with juvenile offenders often make it more difficult for the juvenile justice system to concentrate its limited resources on violent offenders. The "get tough" philosophy is so diffuse that it affects almost all youths who come into contact with the juvenile justice system. Harshness increases for both petty offenders and serious ones. The system soon finds its institutions crowded with young people who should not be in them.

Only when the juvenile justice system deals more efficiently with the large numbers of less serious offenders will it be able to respond more effectively to the serious dangers posed by repeat and violent offenders.

"Researchers . . . found that a diet of television violence was the best predictor of convictions for juvenile delinquency."

Television Promotes Teen Violence

Thomas E. Radecki

Psychiatrist Thomas E. Radecki is the chairman and research director of the National Coalition on Television Violence, an organization that has long worked to reduce violence on television broadcasts. In the following viewpoint, Radecki contends that several studies have shown that children who watch violent TV programs become more accepting of violence and are more likely to act out the behavior they see on the screen. He concludes that violent television programs have significantly contributed to the problem of juvenile delinquency.

As you read, consider the following questions:

1. Why does the author contend that evidence proves TV does promote violence?
2. How much has violence on television increased, and in what types of programs, according to Radecki?
3. What does Radecki recommend be done to reduce TV violence?

Thomas E. Radecki, "Violent Behavior Images Diet of Media Violence." Excerpted with permission from *engage/social action* magazine, May 1987. Copyright 1987 by the General Board of Church and Society of the United Methodist Church.

Violence in the United States generally decreased from the 1820's, from when the earliest records are available, to the 1930's, 40's and early 50's when violent crime reached its lowest point. There appears to have been a sizeable epidemic of domestic violence associated with the Civil War, but it abated 10 years or so after hostilities ceased. However, starting in 1956 and 1957, violence in America shot upward, slowly at first and then very rapidly. The increase stalled in 1974, but has increased again sporadically since that year. Even in the 1980's violence continues to grow, especially if the figures are corrected for the aging of the postwar baby boom, which is now rapidly taking people out of the most violence-prone ages of 18 to 25. The expected 35 percent decrease in violence between 1978 and 1985 due to this factor did not occur.

More Television, More Violence

It is significant to note that television ownership in the United States was growing rapidly during the 1950's and passed the 50 percent mark in 1956. Early television programming was relatively low in violence with only an estimated 8 percent focusing on violence. This changed dramatically in 1956 when the adult western took the television ratings by storm. Since then, the percentage of television programs high in violence has fluctuated between 30 percent and 55 percent of all prime-time hours.

One study has gone back and analyzed FBI [Federal Bureau of Investigation] data from 1951 and 1952 to see what the impact of early television was on crime rates. In 1952, the television signal finally spread from limited areas on the east coast to the entire nation. Using the cities already receiving television in 1951 as controls, the researchers were able to document a significant increase in petty larceny due to the arrival of television even though only 10 percent of Americans had television sets.

Research on the impact of television violence started in 1956. Earlier studies did note correlation between movie, radio, and comic-book violence and juvenile delinquency. However, the number of hours of violence consumed per person per week was quickly dwarfed by television. By 1972, US Surgeon General Jesse Steinfeld concluded that the research evidence of harmful effects from television violence was strong enough to dictate immediate public action.

Since 1972 further research has accumulated with dozens of sophisticated field studies to complement the careful laboratory studies. Now over 1,000 research studies and reports on television violence exist. More than 75 percent of the studies report finding harmful effects and only 1 percent claim to find beneficial effects. When two of the studies claiming beneficial effects from television violence were reported with more careful controls, television violence was found to increase, not decrease, violent behavior.

A statistical review of the research concludes that the studies show conclusively that at least 3 percent of all violence comes from the impact of violent entertainment on the subjects in the studies. However, this is a minimum estimate with the certainty that the actual impact is still larger. A review, done by Scott Andison, of the 67 best studies through 1976 found that three-quarters of the studies documented harmful effects. These studies found on the average a 25 percent increase in whatever harmful behaviors or attitudes were being studied in the violence-viewing group.

Even the best studies we have can only give us a partial estimate of the full impact of violent entertainment. Jerome Singer and Dorothy Singer of Yale University had parents keep a careful record of the programs children watched at home, and the researchers recorded anti-social playground behavior. Up to 25 percent of the variance in playground aggression could be attributed to the viewing of television violence. Interestingly, the children most harmfully affected were the children watching the violent programs with their parents. These parents were also more likely to take their children to violent sporting events. Even the saying

"WELL, I SAY TV VIOLENCE WON'T HAVE A DETRIMENTAL EFFECT ON ANYBODY!"

Wayne Stayskal. Reprinted by permission: Tribune Media Services.

of bedtime prayers was found to be of no protection to the harmful impact of violent entertainment.

A detailed field study by William Belsen with 1600 randomly selected adolescent boys in London, England found strong evidence that serious interpersonal violence is increased by violent television, movie, and sports entertainment. Between 10 percent and 12 percent of violent behavior could be linked directly to violent entertainment with cowboy violence and programming in which the good guy wins through the use of violence being found to be particularly harmful.

Leonard D. Eron and L. Rowell Huesman of the University of Illinois at Chicago have completed three-year field studies in the United States, Israel, Australia, Poland, Finland, and the Netherlands. In each instance they have found increases in violent behavior in school children due to a diet of violent entertainment. They completed a 22-year study, starting in 1960 with over 700 middle class school children, whom they followed as they grew up into adulthood. The quarter of the children with the heaviest diets of violence in 1960 at ages 9 and 10 were found to be convicted of criminal offenses during their adult lives 150 percent more often than the quarter of the children with the smallest diets of violent television entertainment. Even after controlling for various important factors, such as the level of aggressiveness the children already had at the beginning of the study, the researchers still found that a diet of television violence was the best predictor of convictions for juvenile delinquency 10 years later and that there was a cause-effect relationship. . . .

Increase in Violent Entertainment

Research from the National Coalition on TV Violence (NCTV) and others have documented a gradual but steady increase in various forms of violent entertainment since early in this century and especially since 1970. Hollywood films in 1985 reached a new high average of 30 acts of violence per hour with two-thirds being high violence. Prime-time television also reached an all-time high in 1985 with 13 violent acts per hour and 55 percent of programming high in violence. It has since decreased to 40 percent thanks to recently declining ratings for violent programs. Rock music lyrics more than doubled its use of violent lyrics between 1963 and 1983.

Explicit violence in pornography has gone from being almost non-existent in 1970 to comprising 19 percent of all porn in 1982. Hockey violence in both Canadian amateur and professional leagues has increased by over 300 percent in the past 40 years. Violent themes in best seller books have increased dramatically since 1970, going from 15 percent to 45 percent of all best selling titles. Even bubblegum cards have turned violent with 800 million

Garbage Pail Kid cards selling in 1985 and 1986 featuring intensely sadistic themes.

Perhaps the most disturbing trend has been the massive 700 percent increase in the sales of war toys since 1982. This surge is directly linked to the most massive promotion of war to America's children that has ever occurred in reported world history. Toy companies are now financing the production of 29 different series of war cartoons that air nationwide from one to five times weekly. Led by G.I. Joe, Inhumanoids, Centurions and Transformers, these cartoons have gradually become more and more violent, averaging 48 acts of violence per hour. Inhumanoids is a line of satire toys from Hasbro, America's second largest toy company. In a cartoon episode, the US military made a temporary pact with the satanic forces to defeat sadistic Russian communists who were trying to destroy the world. Centurions recently featured nuclear and chemical gas warfare breaking out in Yugoslavia.

The Evidence

The evidence on television violence is in. And it comes in many forms.

It comes in studies—over 3,000 of them—almost all of which show that children who watch television violence are more prone to use physical aggression than those who don't.

It comes in somber warnings from child psychologists who can tell after one visit which preschool age children watch violent television and which do not.

It comes in the configurations of the corpses, mutilated by disturbed teen-agers to resemble victims in slasher movies that find their way onto television.

Finally, it comes in the emotionless testimony of violent youngsters who may not realize they are fingering an accomplice.

"Oh, I don't know. I just seen it on TV."

Carl M. Cannon, *St. Paul Pioneer Press Dispatch,* June 18, 1989.

The average four-to-eight-year-old American child will view 250 episodes of war cartoons and 1,000 commercials for war toys this year or the equivalent of 22 days of classroom instruction in exciting, pro-war entertainment. And that's just the cartoon diet. . . .

Military fantasy role-playing games have been popular for adolescent males in the US since the early 1980's; 75 homicides and suicides have now been linked to game play according to press reports, police investigations, and family studies gathered by NCTV. Dungeons and Dragons (D&D) is the most popular of these. I have personally participated in five D&D murder trials. It has been easy to see the dramatic impact of entertainment violence on these adolescent murders. War films, heavy metal music and martial arts weapons skills all interface with an intense involvement with D&D.

Immediate Action Needed

The question about what can and should be done is crucial. The first television generation has grown up to be the most violent generation in our history. We have been murdering each other 300 percent more often per capita, assaulting each other 500 percent more often and raping women 600 percent more often per capita than our parents' generation. Now, the second television generation is growing up on much stronger stuff.

First we must strongly protest the massive promotion of violence by certain desensitized members of the entertainment industry, as well as protesting our own desensitization. However, protests aren't enough. They are not going to bring about a lasting decrease in the consumption of violence. America is a democracy. We have a right to and need for reasonable legislation, compatible with the First Amendment, to turn back this tide of violence. The most critical legislative goal is to educate children and adult viewers. . . .

We need to help children and adults realize that using violence as a means of entertainment is a bad idea. We need to recommend that they turn the channel or turn off the set. We need to educate viewers to differentiate when violence is being used to educate the viewer, such as in the documentary series *World At War*, from when it is being glorified, distorted and used to entertain.

The main objection to doing anything about entertainment violence is the First Amendment. However, numerous steps can be taken fully compatible with the First Amendment. Actually the First Amendment argument is simply a smoke screen used by the entertainment industry, which blocks any appropriate governmental action through its tremendous political might and large campaign contributions. . . .

In view of the seriousness of the problem, I urge each and every one of us to get involved to correct this situation. We must help turn back this growing culture of violence as quickly as possible. The human toll it is taking on our society is too great to look the other way.

4

"Many social scientists specializing in this area maintain that the evidence relating aggression to television violence is essentially flawed."

Television Does Not Promote Teen Violence

Barry W. Lynn

Members of Congress have often discussed the problem of violence on television and some have introduced bills to reduce violent broadcasts. Such efforts, however, raise several questions. First, is TV violence truly harmful enough to warrant a law? Second, would such a law infringe on the First Amendment right of free speech? Barry W. Lynn, the author of the following viewpoint, argues that the harmfulness of TV violence has never been proven and maintains that a law limiting it would be harmful. This viewpoint is taken from Lynn's testimony before the Senate Judiciary Committee. Lynn serves as legislative counsel for the American Civil Liberties Union, an organization that works to protect freedoms guaranteed by the Bill of Rights. his background

As you read, consider the following questions:

1. According to Lynn, what types of studies have been done on TV violence?
2. What does Jonathan Freedman's research show, according to the author?
3. What does the author believe would be a better approach to handling the problem of violent television programs?

Barry W. Lynn, prepared testimony before the Senate Judiciary Committee, July 25, 1987.

The American Civil Liberties Union (ACLU) appreciates the opportunity to testify regarding exempting from antitrust laws television industry efforts to alleviate the negative impact of violence on television. The ACLU is a national non-partisan organization of 250,000 members dedicated to defending the principles embodied in the Bill of Rights. For over sixty years the ACLU has sought to preserve and strengthen the First Amendment as a bulwark against all forms of government censorship.

In our view, the proposed exemption is both unwise and unconstitutional. A legislative decision to enact such an exemption would invariably be based on judgments which are ultimately inconsistent with the principle of full freedom of expression. . . .

Unpleasant and unpopular speech, as well as speech we favor, is safeguarded by the First Amendment. There is no precedent excluding depictions of violence from full First Amendment protection. Moreover, even speech which is not afforded full constitutional protection—such as obscenity—is still guaranteed certain safeguards as the Supreme Court made clear in *Bantam Books*:

> [U]nder the Fourteenth Amendment, a State is not free to adopt whatever procedures it pleases for dealing with obscenity . . . without regard to the possible consequences for constitutionally protected speech (citations omitted).
>
> Thus, the Fourteenth Amendment requires that regulation by the States of obscenity conform to procedures that will ensure against the curtailment of constitutionally protected expression.

Support for Senate bill S. 844 must be founded upon the assumption that exposure to television violence causes antisocial, aggressive behavior, in children or adults. However, the available research on this topic is inconclusive. Certainly, there has not been sufficiently strong evidence of a causal link between television violence and aggressive behavior to warrant the type of legislative action proposed here.

While some researchers contend that there is evidence of a causal link, many social scientists specializing in this area maintain that the evidence relating aggression to television violence is essentially flawed. Some have even reported findings which point to the conclusion that such a link is nonexistent. . . .

Research Techniques

Three main research techniques have been used to produce the social scientific data in this field: laboratory studies, natural setting studies, and correlational studies. Laboratory research has serious limitations.

It is not clear to what extent findings of experiments in laboratories are generalizable to the "real world." In laboratory experiments, aggression (fake "shocks" or hitting toy dolls) is tested under conditions where the experimental design may foster aggression because the subject knows that this is "only an experiment," and the subject may feel that the experimenter expects or even wants an aggressive response. Even so, laboratory studies suggest that the negative effects measured are more marked in subjects already predisposed to violence. The question of how television violence affects aggressiveness in natural settings is an empirical one that involves many complex interacting variables that cannot be reflected in the results of "controlled" laboratory experiments. Accordingly, the laboratory research, while perhaps demonstrating that viewing television violence may increase aggressiveness under specified, limited conditions, may tell little about the effect that television has in the world outside the laboratory.

Freedman's Research

Jonathan Freedman, in his review article, "Effects of Television Violence on Aggressiveness," (1984) devoted his primary attention to field studies and correlational studies. Field studies are studies which take place in natural settings. Subjects in these studies are exposed to various kinds (violent and nonviolent) of programs, and then changes in actual aggressive behavior are measured over a period of time ranging from a few hours to several years.

No Compelling Evidence

I am the vice president of program practices of the CBS broadcast group. We at CBS do not believe that there is yet any convincing evidence that depictions of violence on television create criminals or increase crime in our society. The causes of crime and violence are complex and are deeply rooted in our society and in the world at large.

Alice M. Henderson, testimony before the Senate Judiciary Committee, June 20, 1986.

Correlational studies are studies in which data on television viewing behavior (such as quantity of viewing, and proportions of violent to nonviolent programs viewed) is related to data on aggressiveness. The goal of such studies is, first, to determine whether *any* relationship exists between viewing and aggressiveness. If a relationship is found to exist, then it is necessary to determine whether or not that relationship is causal. This is so because two measures which are found to be correlated may both be caused by some third factor. For example, a correlation might be found between driving a Mercedes and sending one's children to private school. But that does not mean that driving a Mercedes *causes* one to send one's children to private schools, nor that sending one's children to private schools *causes* one to drive a Mercedes. Rather, both driving a Mercedes and sending one's children to private school may be a function of some third variable—such as wealth. Thus, establishing a causal relationship in correlational studies is a process including at least two separate steps: establishing a correlation, and establishing that the correlation is causal.

Freedman concludes that, 1) there is a consistent, small positive correlation between viewing television violence and aggressiveness; and 2) there is little convincing evidence that in natural settings viewing television violence causes people to be more aggressive. Field studies have demonstrated only a very modest positive statistical correlation between viewing of violent television programming and actual aggression. Freedman acknowledges this slight connection while still maintaining that sufficient support has not been provided to justify the conclusion that viewing television violence has any effect on subsequent aggression.

Television Viewing May Be the Problem

Dennis Howitt, an English social psychologist, has suggested that the viewing of nonviolent television has as much effect on aggressive behavior as exposure to violent television. In other words, it could be argued that it is television viewing and not violent content as such which may increase aggression. One study conducted by Seymour Feshbach and Robert D. Singer (1971) goes a step further by actually demonstrating that subjects who are permitted to watch only *non*violent programs were generally *more* aggressive than those who viewed strictly violent television for six weeks.

The findings of correlational studies have not been more conclusive than those of field research. To address the question of whether television viewing has an effect over time, years or decades of exposure, which it might not have from just a few minutes or hours of exposure, Dr. Rowell Huesmann has proposed a "cumulative effect hypothesis." According to this hypothesis, the correlation between television viewing and aggression would be expected to increase with age of subject. Children who have just begun to watch television should be affected very little, but as they are exposed to more and more violent programs the correlation would be expected to increase. However, the available data do not support this cumulative effect hypothesis. Neither Huesmann's 1982 study on correlations collected on Finnish and Polish schoolchildren nor Milavsky's study completed in the same year indicate a cumulative trend. Likewise, Jerome Singer and Dorothy Singer's 1980 study claimed no tendency for correlations to increase with age.

The available social scientific data is, to say the least, inconclusive. But beyond the inconclusiveness of the social scien-

· 168

tific data regarding any causative link between media violence and violent behavior, the danger inherent in S.844 runs far deeper than a mere absence of empirical evidence of causation. Acceptance of a principle that speech should be restricted based upon what some viewers might do after exposure to the speech entails a dangerous backsliding in First Amendment jurisprudence. The most significant development in obscenity law, set forth in the decision in *Roth v. United States*, a generation ago, was the rejection of the idea that sexually-oriented material should be judged by its effect on the most suggestible person who might be exposed to it. If the measure of permissible suppression becomes what one or two people might do in response to particular speech, we will all be reduced to sitting in darkened rooms in order to prevent violent (or other) images from crossing the eyes or mind of someone who might react in an antisocial manner. The fundamental issue is not violent imagery; it is whether we can afford to curtail speech because of its possible overt effect on a few people. . . .

More speech instead of less speech may be the optimal course to follow in the area of media violence. As Bruno Bettelheim, professor of child psychology, has suggested, "There is hardly a program from which a child could not learn a great deal, provided some responsible adult does the necessary teaching. Even violent programs are no exception. . . . It is very important for children to develop the right attitudes toward violence, and closing one's eyes to its existence can hardly be considered the most constructive attitude. Every child needs to learn what is wrong with violence, why it occurs, and how he ought to deal with it in himself and others." Children of all ages are constantly being bombarded with data from mass media. The constructive way of helping them to absorb this information is through critical viewing—teaching children to analyze and evaluate what is seen on television—not through the encouragement of television censorship. The introduction of media presentations which foster a realistic and mature attitude toward violence, without infringing on the first Amendment, may do far more good than would the elimination of violence from the public view.

"Our economy does not provide enough opportunity . . . for the young. We pay for this neglect in drugs, alcohol and crime."

Poverty Promotes Teen Violence

The Washington Spectator

The following viewpoint is an excerpt from *The Washington Spectator*, a semimonthly publication that covers a variety of economic, political, and social issues. The authors argue that poverty in the U.S. is increasing, particularly among children. As more and more children are born and raised in poor families, they suffer from the instability caused by the parents' lack of money. As these children grow older, the authors write, they despair that they will ever be able to find work for themselves. Thus, *The Washington Spectator* concludes, teenagers' violent behavior is an expression of frustration and an effort to take some of the wealth they are denied.

As you read, consider the following questions:

1. How do the authors describe the typical young person who commits a crime?
2. How does unemployment affect young people, according to *The Washington Spectator*?
3. How can government programs help children, in the authors' opinion?

The Washington Spectator, "Violent Crime: Cause and Cure," May 15, 1989. Reprinted by permission of The Washington Spectator.

Homicides take the lives of more children in the District of Columbia than any other single type of injury, including car accident, house fire or drowning. This is not an exclusive phenomenon of Washington. The overcrowded slums of other big American cities, such as New York, Miami and Los Angeles, are ridden with senseless violent crime. It is a form of incoherent, unplanned rebellion against a society which, the young complain, deprives them of the good life they see on TV. It is also a symptom of what Noam Chomsky says is the mass alienation of Americans.

The violence springs from four factors:

• The sullen rage of mostly boys and young men who live in poverty and squalor and are taunted by visions of affluence and ease which they have no hope of reaching. They are in part victims of the stress on materialism and self-interest of the Reagan era.

The young understand the spur that goads them. They spoke their minds at a meeting in a Washington high school called to discuss the crime crisis. Some comments: "We have to show there's more to life than shooting or stabbing someone, or wearing clothes that cost a fortune. . . . Our biggest problem is that teen-agers in this city have low self-esteem. If you don't respect yourself, how can you respect other people?"

• The easy access to guns, which become the substitute for fists, the usual weapon of the young. Murder is so common in the ghettoes that the social horror has been lost. A mother who has kept her son from Jordan High School in the Watts area of Los Angeles explains, "I don't want my son killed up there. It's as simple as that."

• The desperate craving for drugs to relieve boredom, melancholy, self-doubt and want.

• Gang warfare built around profits from crack, a derivative of cocaine.

Reasons for the Violence Epidemic

The cure is not only to build more prisons, for they have become too often graduate schools of crime. Rather, we must change the social and economic reasons for the epidemic of violence and get rid of guns and drugs.

First, a look at the young fellow who wantonly shoots to kill or wound, and the environment in which he lives.

• He is male, in his teens or 20s. The early years of his life, a time when character is formed, were spent in poverty. The Children's Defense Fund points out, "Our children are growing poorer and poorer while our nation is growing richer." (Average income of the lowest fifth of all persons in the U.S. dropped nearly 11% from 1973 to 1987, while average income for the highest fifth rose 24%, according to a House Ways and Means Committee study.) Within a few years, suggests the National Education Association, 40% of all secondary students will come from families living in poverty. This is due in part to the high birth rate among the poor.

The National League of Cities finds that poverty in inner-city slums has become more persistent and concentrated over the last 20 years, and its victims have less chance of escape. The *Philadelphia Inquirer* reports that families living in inner-city poverty areas nearly doubled between 1980 and 1985, from 884,000 to 1.7 million households.

• He is of a minority, black or Hispanic, and has felt the sting of rebuff. As a child he had little of the tender, loving care that a close-knit family can offer. His father was nowhere to be seen. His mother was so intent on finding the bare necessities that she had little time for him. His schooling was superficial. His moral values came largely from the street and TV.

Rage at Being Excluded

Young people in poor, black urban areas start out with a belief that they can make decisions about what happens to their lives. They believe that they can be President of the United States. Then they walk out into the street, put their hand up for a cab and it passes them by. The guy at the grocery store says he can't hire them. The landlord won't rent them the apartment they want. As these young people begin putting all the pieces together, the feeling that they are part of society begins to erode.

The strong sense of possibility slowly turns into a kind of rage. . . . The fury and violence of the individualist survivor's rage is usually turned back on the poor blacks in the community. The violence is aimed at the black neighbor. As a black male living in Harlem, for example, my chances of dying violently are 1 in 25.

While otherwise unnoticed, the rage of this lost generation is ominously broadcast to the society at large during degradation ceremonies in the "halls of shame," called courts, where, in the flash of camera lights, these kids are led away to jail, heads down, arms shackled. These kids are only visible through that imagery.

Terry Williams, *New Perspectives Quarterly*, Summer 1989.

NEA president Mary H. Putrell says, "We are finding that poverty and lack of parental support, money and language are the norm rather than the exception." From 1974 to 1983, more than 21% of blacks in big cities were poor; among non-blacks, less than 3%.

A teacher tells the *Washington Post* that she has been "moved by children who fill up on water or steal sandwiches out of their friends' lunch boxes because they are hungry, or fall asleep in class because they do not have the proper nutrition."

The Children's Defense Fund states: "It is the lack of loving care that turns children into savage teen-agers and adults. . . . The number of youths held for alcohol and drug offenses increased by 56% between 1985 and 1987. . . . The rage and pain of these homeless, hopeless, abused, alienated children will continue to explode in our faces."

Their health has deteriorated. "When the savings and loan industry has a crisis, political leaders find at least $60 billion to bail them out. When our children are dying and being disabled from preventable causes, our political leaders. . . say we cannot afford the few billions to build a health floor."

The *New York Times* describes a lodging for the poor in Washington: "Scarred and unkempt, the motel is now shelter for 200 adults and 700 children. One family to a room, month after overcrowded month, even for years. . . . Teachers from the elementary school frequently come in search of absent pupils, often finding that the children are embarrassed by their clothing and status in life."

The *Los Angeles Times* describes a lodging there: "Torn blankets, piles of rags, old clothes, dirty pillows, a few scattered utensils or cups—the detritus of a privileged city in which pauperized men and women try to create a normal life." . . .

A Hopeless Situation

What about the kids when they grow into adolescence? The story is told of a black mother in Washington, proud of her son who won excellent grades in high school and was determined to make his way up. Six months after graduation and a diligent search for a job, he was still idle. She was afraid he would "quit" his resolve and sink back into the hopelessness that held so many of his peers.

The *Los Angeles Times* tells of two such men: "Wilson and Butler now walk the tough streets of Skid Row wondering what to do. They pass by thousands who have 'quit,' people not much different from themselves. 'Quitting' offers relief from the constant struggle for housing and employment, but often it means battling with nightmares of crime, crack, cocaine and alienation." . . .

Drugs are a prelude to much of the violent crime. After a bloody night in Washington when four were killed and five wounded by gunfire, the *Washington Post* reported: "Police said most of the slayings have been drug-related killings that involved territorial disputes, buyers and sellers who are fighting, persons acting under the influence of drugs or thieves seeking money to buy drugs."

The use of crack is concentrated among the urban poor, while drug use in more well-to-do communities has decreased, according to recent studies. Crack is cheap, as little as $5 a "rock," and it offers a momentary escape from the degrading life of the ghetto. Yet, as Barbara Ehrenreich writes in *Ms.*: "Drug frenzy is not. . . a quick and harmless high. It is an obsession, overshadowing all other concerns, and capable of leaving a society drained, impotent and brain-damaged."

A New York drug enforcement agent says, "I can tell you that crack is clearly the most pernicious drug we've ever seen." A Miami homicide detective calls it "the worst drug ever," with users "terribly addicted. Young people are willing to kill for it."

So overwhelming is the use of crack that treatment centers cannot care for the torrent of addicts, who tend to be young and poor.

Anyone Can Buy a Gun

An obvious trigger to violence is easy access to guns. A comparison with British crime and gun control is revealing. "Britain, whose population is nearly 100 times Washington's, has fewer than twice the number of murders, despite a slowly but steadily worsening drug problem." (*Washington Post*) England and Wales, with 50 million people, had 635 homicides in 1987, "with one in eight victims shot." The District of Columbia, with a population of 622,000, had 372 murders in 1988.

Why? Firearm laws in Britain are strict. An applicant for a gun of any kind must get a certificate from the local police chief and explain why he needs the gun. He must supply four photographs of himself and provide a character witness. Gun licenses are valid for only three years, but may be renewed.

Minorities and the American Dream

The humane solution to the problem of excluding young minorities from a stake in the American dream is simply to include them, which, of course, might not be so simple. The nation's young crack dealers are merely pursuing the American dream along what they see is the only channel open to them—drug-dealing entrepreneurial ventures. True, it's a high-risk endeavor, but so is life in America for minority youth. As they see it, what alternatives do they have?

Claude Brown, *St. Paul Pioneer Press Dispatch*, May 22, 1988.

Almost anyone in the U.S. can buy a gun. The result: "Almost by the hour, some awful event in an American city or town hammers home the terrible consequences of this country's gross national arsenal of firearms sold on the spot, not just to legitimate buyers but to any deranged or empty-headed client.

"The excuses for permitting unchecked on-the-spot sales of almost anything with a trigger are still wrapped in righteous rhetoric by the world's greatest promoters of munitions, the leaders of the National Rifle Association." (*Washington Post* editorial) . . .

The children of the slums, even at a very young age, need a program that offers the affection, attention and training that most of them lack in their homes. One such program is Head Start. The Committee for Economic Development estimates that every $1 spent on early training results in a saving of $5 otherwise spent on crime control, welfare, school dropouts and remedial education.

In a House debate, Rep. Thomas J. Tauke (R-Iowa) pointed out: "Head Start serves primarily 4-year-olds from disadvantaged families, providing them with comprehensive health, education and social services prior to entering school. It is an excellent example of how Government can enhance the opportunities of low-income children and families. It gives these children the opportunity to enter school on an equal footing with other children. . . . Also, parents are helped as well as the children in the program."

The effect of such pre-school programs was noted by Senator Ted Kennedy (D-Mass.): "When compared with students from similar backgrounds who had not taken part in early education programs, the preschoolers were twice as likely to go to college, twice as likely to be literate, twice as likely to have a job. They were a third less likely to be school dropouts, half as likely to have a teen-age pregnancy, half as likely to be on welfare, and much less likely to have a run-in with the law.

"These results translate into a sound financial investment as well. An expenditure of $4,800 per child saved $29,000 in later welfare, social services, crime and other costs—or $6 saved for every dollar spent."

By the time inner-city kids are teen-agers, they need job training and employment. As of January 1988, 23.8% of black and 13.6% of Hispanics 16 to 24 years old were idle. A study suggests that 3.5 million jobs could be filled each year by young service workers improving the worn infrastructure.

Federal Youth Corps

Today, there are 50 full-time youth service and conservation programs, sponsored by states and local governments. Sixty-four members of Congress have sponsored a Federal Conservation and Youth Service Corps. Rep. Leon Panetta (D-Ca.) pointed out, "Our economy does not provide enough opportunity to find a productive and respectable place in society for the young. We pay for this neglect in drugs, alcohol and crime."

"The broken home produces many of the nation's most violent young criminals."

Family Breakdown Promotes Teen Violence

Bryce J. Christensen

Several commentators have argued that there is a link between the rising number of single-parent and nontraditional families, and the number of violent crimes committed by teenagers. In the following viewpoint, Bryce J. Christensen contends that children raised without both parents do not learn to respect authority. Without firm rules from parents, many of these teenagers use violence to get what they want. Christensen is the director of the Rockford Institute Center on the Family in America, a conservative organization which supports research on families. He also edits the Center's monthly *Family in America* bulletin.

As you read, consider the following questions:

1. What factors does Christensen believe lead teenage boys to join gangs?
2. How does Christensen refute arguments that drug use and poverty encourage teen violence?
3. Why does the author oppose government programs directed at families?

Bryce J. Christensen, "From Home Life to Prison Life: The Roots of American Crime," *The Family in America*, April 1989. Reprinted by permission of the THE FAMILY IN AMERICA, a publication of the Rockford Institute, Rockford, Illinois.

Crime appears as a large and troubling stain on the fabric of American society. Almost twenty-one thousand people were murdered in the United States in 1986, up from 19,000 in 1985 and 18,700 in 1984. Similarly, 543,000 robberies were committed in 1986, compared to only 498,000 in 1985 and 485,000 in 1984. A similar pattern may be discerned for aggravated assault, burglary, car theft, and larceny. Crime now touches a quarter of all American homes each year.

As crime has intruded into their lives with growing frequency, Americans have responded by developing sophisticated security systems and by demanding tougher laws and judges, bigger prisons and police forces. The budget for the nation's criminal justice system stood at over $45 billion in 1985 and continues to grow. . . . The need to reduce crime also inspires those trying to reduce poverty and improve education. But a close look at crime reveals that neither American legislators nor the general public have yet faced up to one of its primary causes: our national retreat from family life. Most contemporary commentators regard divorce, illegitimacy, and singleness as lifestyle choices that should be left to individual preference. But researchers are accumulating evidence linking family dissolution to the intolerable crimes occurring in American streets and homes. . . .

Family Life and Juvenile Delinquents

In a study released in 1988 by the Department of Justice, researchers found that of the juveniles in state-operated institutions in 1987, only about 30 percent had lived with both parents while growing up. More than half (54 percent) had lived in single-parent households, while another 16 percent lived with grandparents or in some other arrangement without both parents. In contrast, over 70 percent of the nation's children were living with two parents in 1986. . . .

A number of analysts likewise perceive a linkage between family life and juvenile delinquency. Since many criminals begin their antisocial activities as teens, the domestic causes of delinquency deserve particular attention. One of those causes is maternal employment, which has risen sharply since the late 1960's. In a study completed in 1950, Sheldon and Eleanor Glueck cited "unsuitable supervision of boy by mother" as one of the prime causes of delinquency, finding that employed mothers were especially likely to provide such unsatisfactory supervision. In their comparison sample, almost half (47 percent) of the delinquent youth had mothers with "gainful employment," compared to only one third (33 percent) of the mothers of the non-delinquents. "Entirely apart from the problem of delinquency, there is a strong hint that working mothers, at least of low-income groups, are not as conscientious about arranging for the supervision of their children as are those who remain at home."

New studies confirm the importance of maternal supervision for preventing delinquency. In a 1987 study at the University of Toronto, sociologists noted particularly high rates of delinquency among female teens in two kinds of households: 1) single-parent households; 2) households in which the mother is employed in a career or management position. Maternal employment can affect the criminality of sons, too. "It's tougher for mothers who are busy earning a living to control their teenage boys," according to Professor Alfred Blumstein of Carnegie-Mellon University. Criminologist Roger Thompson believes that one of the primary reasons that young boys join gangs is that "their parents work, and if they didn't have the gang, they'd just have an empty home."

The Single-Parent Family

Such family measures as the percentage of the population divorced, the percentage of households headed by women, and the percentage of unattached individuals in the community are among the most powerful predictors of crime rates. Consistent with these findings, in most (but not all) studies that directly compare children living with both biological parents with children living in "broken" or reconstituted homes, the children from intact homes have lower rates of crime. These differences amply justify concern about current trends in divorce and illegitimacy rates. The likelihood that the biological parents of a particular child will marry and stay together throughout the period of child rearing is lower today than at any time in the past.

Travis Hirschi, in *Juvenile Delinquency: A Justice Perspective*, 1985.

But family disruption overshadows maternal employment as a cause of juvenile delinquency. In their landmark study of the problem, the Gluecks found a strong correlation between delinquency and parental divorce and separation. Nor have their findings lost their relevance. In a 1982 study at the Behavioral Research Institute, Rachelle Canter examined the effects of family life on delinquency for a nationwide sample of youth. She discovered that delinquency shows up relatively infrequently among teens deeply involved in family life, particularly when parents have established strong norms for conduct. On the other hand, delinquency occurs frequently in homes broken through divorce or illegitimacy. "Youths from broken homes engage in significantly more delinquent acts than youths from intact homes," Canter reports. Canter established a statistical tie between family structure and every form of delinquent behavior except minor theft. . . .

A keen observer of youth for more than a decade, Francis Ianni attributes the appearance of youth gangs in America's inner cities to the deterioration of families. After in-depth examination of a number of urban street gangs, Ianni reports that "almost all of the street-gang members came from broken or severely disturbed and deprived homes." In numerous interviews, Ianni and his colleagues repeatedly heard gang members express a desire "to distance themselves from inept or uncaring home environments which lacked even the most rudimentary family structure to support some form of a competent parent-child relationship. Many were from single-parent families where the mother had been unable or unwilling to establish adequate behavioral controls over her male children. In many other cases, there was a stepfather present against whom the teenage gang member rebelled." At a time when intact families have become an endangered minority in many inner cities, it should come as no surprise that according to the estimates of the National Institute of Juvenile Justice and Delinquency, there are approximately 120,000 youth gangs with about 1.5 million members in the 2,100 American communities with populations of at least 10,000. This means that for every five male teens in such communities, one is a gang member!

  Seedbed for gang activity, the broken home produces many of the nation's most violent young criminals. In a study of 72 adolescent murderers, researchers at Michigan State University found that 75 percent of them had parents who were either divorced or had never married. Among nonwhite teen murderers in this sample, only 12 percent had married parents. Violent rapists come from similar family backgrounds. In a 1987 study of 108 violent rapists, researchers established that 60 percent came from single-parent homes. . . .

Criminologist Travis Hirschi complained in 1983 that many of his colleagues were too obsessed with poverty and unemployment, while they "ignore family considerations." In his view, specialists were choosing to neglect the family partly because of "'modern' theories of crime, which assume that people are good by nature and that individuals would be law-abiding were it not for the flaws in society around them. This kind of stance toward the family is one I think we should avoid," he declares. "If nothing else, research on crime and the family may help prevent us from making a bad situation worse—for example, by adopting policies that, perhaps unwittingly, make the parents' job harder."

Drug Abusers' Families

Reasons for heeding Hirschi's argument are not hard to find. Many of the documented antecedents of crime are influenced by family disruption. Consider drug use, for example. Unfortunately, despite widespread concern over drug-related crime, the family backgrounds of drug users have received little attention. In a 1964 study of heroin addiction, researchers discovered that young men

"It's ten o'clock. Do you know where your parents are tonight?"

were particularly vulnerable to drug addiction if they had suffered from "the absence of a warm relationship with a father figure." Mother dominance showed up frequently in the families of addicts. In a 1972 assessment of drug use, researchers found that those least likely to use drugs were those who came from religious, father-led families in which "the strength, love, and sometimes glory of father is presented as a reflection of the father before him.". . .

Often cited as a cause of crime, poverty is frequently the result of family breakdown. More than one third of all children living in female-headed households live below the government's official poverty line, with many more living perilously close. In contrast, only about one in twenty two-parent households live in poverty. In a 1988 study conducted at the University of Wisconsin, Professor Sara McLanahan found that daughters raised in single-parent households were far more likely to become welfare dependent than daughters of two-parent households. On the other hand, researchers at the State University of New York at Stony Brook have found that among young people born in poverty, marital status defines the best predictor of economic mobility. Their study showed that among people born into poor households, 63 percent of those who remained in the lowest income bracket (bottom 20 percent) were single, while almost 95 percent of those who made it into the upper income bracket (top 40 percent) were married.

Even fundamental qualities of character reflect family structure and upbringing. Sociologist Steven Nock has recently argued that children in two-parent homes are much more likely than children in one-parent homes to learn how to recognize and accept authority. Lawbreaking will come easier and social success will come harder for those who have never learned this lesson. Nor can the dishonesty evident in "insider" stock trading and other white-collar crimes be fully understood unless viewed against the backdrop of family deterioration. In the opinion of Father Theodore Hesburgh, former president of Notre Dame University, "To the extent family life is disintegrating, kids are not being taught values about lying, cheating and stealing." In line with Father Hesburgh's view, a new study at the University of Cincinnati and Xavier University finds that among young male delinquents, those whose fathers were present "attained higher moral maturity" (and thus presumably were more amenable to reform) than those whose fathers were absent. . . .

Only those with a strong desire to be deceived can persist in the belief that Americans can retreat from family life without fostering lawlessness. A decisive reversal of that retreat from the home will require profound shifts in American culture, including a renewal of religious faith and a rediscovery of the limits of individualism. Such things are not effected through government action.

Unwise Policies

On the other hand, the nation's family woes have been exacerbated by a number of unwise government policies that deserve to be challenged by all who seriously desire to reduce crime in America. Some sociologists still resist the notion, but it has become almost conventional wisdom that the growth of the welfare state has fostered illegitimacy. Nathan Glazer notes that "ordinary people (including the poor)" have long suspected that welfare benefits serve as "an incentive for fathers to leave their families, or, in a more sophisticated version, for mothers to push fathers out of the home, and for young girls and older women to have illegitimate children because of the assurance that support would rise with need, measured by the number of children."

Schooled by his own experience in New York City's welfare system, Charles Morris believes that current policies have the effect of "subsidizing . . . teenage pregnancies." Morris observes that "for a generation of lower-class black and Hispanic girls, having a baby is an opportunity for an illusory independence. They can go on welfare in their own apartments with an annuity for the rest of their adult lives, and their boyfriends are able to escape completely the consequences of casual sexuality." Morris stresses that broken homes and illegitimacy were less common among blacks during the 1940's and 1950's, even though most blacks were considerably poorer than they are today. If 1988's welfare reform may be taken as any indication, the nation may lack the political will necessary to do anything more than move illegitimate children from broken homes into day-care centers (hardly an improvement), while directing their mothers not toward marriage but toward employment. Such dubious reform will neither strengthen the nation's families nor reduce our crime rate.

Sweden's Example

Admittedly, there are those who still believe that crime would be reduced by further enriching the welfare system to eradicate poverty. The refutation of this argument is a country called Sweden. An affluent country with few hard-to-assimilate minorities, Sweden has developed one of the most generous welfare systems in the world. But according to Professor David Popenoe of Rutgers University, the growth of the Swedish welfare state has seriously weakened family life. He goes so far as to suggest that "the very existence of the welfare state compromises the institution of the family" and that the "acceleration of welfare-state power weaken[s] the family further." Naturally, this erosion of Swedish family life has fostered lawlessness. Not only does Sweden suffer from a "relatively high rate of juvenile delinquency (including school vandalism)," the country suffers from a widespread "youth malaise," manifest in 1987 in several days of youth riots in a number of its cities.

Rather than imitate the Swedes by expanding our welfare system, Americans would do better to try to return some integrity to our marriage laws. There can no longer be any question that when lawmakers adopted a "no fault" standard for divorce, they helped push divorce rates up dramatically. Since millions of these divorces created single-parent households, many of them newly impoverished, these liberal divorce laws helped foster crime as well. . . .

Most crimes are acts of despair. Marriage and family life provide a focus for hope. Laws which strengthen marriage and the home can make it easier to retain that focus. But more than good laws are required. Building families requires personal commitment, discipline, and sacrifice. Until Americans relearn these lessons, they can expect the boom in prison construction to continue.

"What distinguishes these boys [involved in the Central Park rape] is not their anger . . . but their lack of any moral faculty."

A Lack of Morality Creates Teenage Rapists

Charles Krauthammer

In April 1989 a group of teenage boys raced through New York City's Central Park, accosting people they met. When they spotted a young investment banker out jogging, they chased her down, beat and raped her and left her for dead. The brutality of the crime and the nonchalance of the boys who were apprehended stunned the nation. In the following viewpoint, Charles Krauthammer argues that this rape, and others committed by teenagers, occurred because many teenage boys lack a conscience that tells them such behavior is immoral. Krauthammer is a well-known columnist and a contributing editor to the weekly magazine *The New Republic.*

As you read, consider the following questions:

1. What similarities does Krauthammer see between the Bonnie Garland case and the Central Park incident?
2. How does the author define "wilding"?
3. Why does Krauthammer object to arguments that society must share some of the blame for brutal acts like the Central Park rape?

"I'm depraved on account I'm deprived."

—West Side Story

In 1977, Bonnie Garland, a pretty, upper-class Yale student, was murdered. Her estranged boyfriend went up to her bedroom one night and with a hammer cracked her head open "like a watermelon," as he put it. Murders are a dime a dozen in America. But the real story here, the real horror, chronicled in painful detail by Willard Gaylin (in *The Killing of Bonnie Garland*), was the aftermath: sympathy turned immediately from victim to murderer, a Mexican American recruited to Yale from the Los Angeles barrio. Within five weeks he was free on bail, living with the Christian Brothers and attending a local college under an assumed name. Friends raised $30,000 for his defense. "From my investigation," wrote Gaylin, "it is clear that more tears have since been shed for the killer than for the victim."

In New York City another awful crime. A 28-year-old jogger was attacked in Central Park by a gang of teens from nearby Harlem. Police say the boys hunted her down, beat and raped her savagely and left her for dead. . . .

In New York the instinct to "Garland" the monstrous—to extenuate brutality and make a victim of the victimizer—is more attenuated than in the Ivy League. The New York tabloids, the moral voice of the community, are full-throated in their vilification of the monstrous "wolf pack." It is their social betters, those from the helping professions, who have lost their moral compass. It is they who would Garland this attack if they could.

These children are "damaged," explains forensic psychologist Shawn Johnston. "They are in pain inside . . . acting out their pain on innocent victims. In the case of the Central Park beating, they picked a victim that was mostly likely to shock and outrage. That speaks to how deep their anger and despair is."

"We have to be honest," explains psychologist Richard Majors. "Society has not been nice to these kids."

"They're letting out anger," explains Alvin Poussaint, the Harvard educator and psychiatrist. "There's a lot of free-floating anger and rage among a lot of our youth."

Rage? Upon arrest, police said, the boys joked and rapped and sang. Asked why he beat her head with a lead pipe, Yusef Salaam was quoted by investigators as saying "It was fun." The boys have not yet been taught to say they did it because of rage, pain and despair, because of the sins whites have visited upon them and their ancestors. But they will be taught. By trial time, they will be well versed in the language of liberal guilt and exoneration.

How could boys have done something so savage? We have two schools. The "rage" school, which would like to treat and heal

Land of the free, home of the brave.

Doug Marlette. Reprinted by permission.

these boys. And the "monster" school, which would like to string them up.

I'm for stringing first and treating later. After all, the monster theory, unlike the rage theory, has the benefit of evidence. What distinguishes these boys is not their anger—Who is without it?—but their lack of any moral faculty. Acts of rage are usually followed by reflection and shame. In this case, these characteristics appear to be entirely missing.

The boys were not angry. They were "wilding." Wilding is not rage, it is anarchy. Anarchy is an excess of freedom. Anarchy is the absence of rules, of ethical limits, of any moral sense. These boys are psychic amputees. They have lost, perhaps never developed, that psychic appendage we call conscience.

Conscience may be inbred, but to grow it needs cultivation. The societal messages that make it through the din of inner-city rap 'n' roll conspire to stunt that growth. They all but drown out those voices trying to nurture a sense of responsibility, the foundation of moral character.

For example, the ever fatuous Cardinal O'Connor could not resist blaming the park assault on, well, society. We must all "assume our responsibility," he intoned, "for being indifferent to the circumstances that breed crimes of this sort." What circumstances? "Communities which know nothing but frustration."

When the Rev. Calvin Butts III of Harlem's Abyssinian Baptist Church was asked by CBS about the attack, he spoke of "the examples that our children are faced with." Such as? "We've had Presidents resign, foreign Prime Ministers resign in disgrace. We've had Oliver North lie publicly on television. . . . And many of our youngsters, across racial lines, see that and then act it out."

Richard Nixon, Noboru Takeshita and Ollie North may have much to answer for in the next world, but the savaging of a young woman in Central Park is not on the list. The effect of such preposterous links is to dilute the notion of individual responsibility. Entire communities are taught to find blame everywhere but in themselves. The message takes. New York *Newsday* interviewed some of the neighbors of the accused and found among these kids "little sympathy for the victim." Said a twelve-year-old: "She had nothing to guard herself; she didn't have no man with her; she didn't have no Mace." Added another sixth-grader: "It is like she committed suicide."

There is a rather large difference between suicide and homicide. For some, the distinction is not obvious. They must be taught. If not taught, they grow up in a moral vacuum. Moral vacuums produce moral monsters.

Young monsters. The attackers are all 14 to 17. Their youth is yet another source of mitigation. In addition to class and racial disadvantage, we must now brace ourselves for disquisitions on peer pressure, adolescent anomie and rage.

Spare us the Garlanding. The rage in this case properly belongs to the victim, to her family and to us.

"We've got to trace the crime [of rape] to its roots: patriarchy, misogyny, and childhood sex-role socialization."

Restrictive Gender Roles Create Teen Rapists

Letty Cottin Pogrebin

Letty Cottin Pogrebin is one of the founders of the feminist magazine, *Ms.* She is also a psychologist who often writes on child-raising. Her books include *Growing Up Free, Family Politics,* and *Among Friends.* In the following viewpoint, she argues that many people are puzzled when teenage boys commit brutal acts such as the April 1989 gang rape of a banker in New York's Central Park. Pogrebin maintains that rape occurs because of the way boys are raised. Boys are taught that being masculine means they should be dominant and powerful. Rape, an act of dominance and violent aggression, is one manifestation of that message, she concludes.

As you read, consider the following questions:

1. Why does the author doubt that any serious action will be taken in response to the Central Park rape?
2. What explanations do people offer to avoid examining the real cause of rape, in Pogrebin's opinion?
3. What pressures does the author believe lead boys to rape?

I'm writing this column in mid-June 1989. Two months after the rape of the Central Park jogger, her medical progress is still making headlines. The young men accused of the "wilding" attack remain the subject of talk shows and feature stories analyzing their behavior, their families, the brutality of the crime. All over the country people are comparing other acts of violence to this one, pawing at the facts like a dog with a bone, seeking some marrow of meaning that might explain the unexplainable.

Unlike the attention paid to other nationally publicized victims—such as Bonnie Garland (beaten to death with a hammer by her rejected boyfriend), Karen Straw (raped by her husband at knife point in front of her children), Jennifer Levin (choked by Robert Chambers), or Hedda Nussbaum (maimed and dehumanized by Joel Steinberg)—the outcry in the jogger's case seems to be saying, "Things have gone too far; *something* must be done."

The Rape's Impact

That reaction reminds me of the 1964 murder of Kitty Genovese, when 38 people witnessed a protracted, bloody attack and not one tried to help or even to call the police from behind the safety of their window blinds. As that crime symbolized issues of collective passivity and disengagement, the Central Park rape seems to have crystallized society's fears of violence, moving us beyond horrified fascination to palpable anger and a demand for action.

By the time you read this . . . months will have passed since the rape. Will we still be obsessed and angry? Will the rhetoric of outrage have been translated into anything concrete? Will people in power be ready to change the way violence is understood and treated in our society? I doubt it. Because despite the brouhaha, I don't see any willingness to address the real root of the problem.

Most people deal with unthinkable behavior by seeking causes and finding fault. They submit savagery to the yoke of reason. If they can blame something or someone, they can think about the "contributing factors" rather than the knife at the throat, the kicking and punching, the penis as tool of suffocation or rubbed-raw penetration, the screams and the terror. They don't have to relate this ugliness to their world if they can deplore the "animals" among us and blame the madness on drugs, racial tensions, poverty, family background, TV violence, or educational deprivation. Better still, if they can imagine that a woman "deserved" the assault—said the wrong thing, wore the wrong clothes, went to the wrong neighborhood—then the attack can be made to "make sense."

But in the Central Park case, these formulas don't work. It was rape but the jogger wasn't "provocative." It was a white woman but other "wilding" victims were black and Hispanic and nothing suggests that race was pertinent. It was ghetto kids versus a Wall Street achiever but the woman wasn't parading her status, and the kids didn't seem to be stereotypical "hard cases": addicts, homeless, or on welfare. So how do you figure it? The neighbors shrug. The psychologists speculate. The pundits are stumped.

Facing the Truth

Fury certainly is the order of the day. After the Central Park attack, John Gutfreund, the CEO [Chief Executive Officer] of Salomon Brothers, called for what sounds like martial law to counter the "reign of terror in the streets." Donald Trump's expensive ads cry out for blood. Wealthy, healthy, educated, English-speaking white America just lost one of our own, and we have the means to shake this country up with our rage.

I say Keep the rage! This crime was outrageous. Feel it completely, let it force the truth out. But when we call out our big guns, are we aiming at the real target?

It is true that disenfranchisement predisposes a section of the population to commit violent crimes. But women—of all races and all classes and all ages—are subject to this kind of attack from men—of all races and all classes and all ages. Military crackdowns in Harlem will not change that. The liberal (as in *generous,* also as in *white liberal guilt*) application of money and social programs to a particular group of people is not automatically going to make women's lives safer. Understanding how profound and omnipresent violence toward women is, facing that truth—that is a start.

Andrea Kannapell, *The Village Voice*, May 9, 1989.

That the answer might have more to do with gender than race or class has occurred to a few commentators who recognize that what happened, first and foremost, was an act of violence by males against a female—an occurrence as commonplace and all-American as apple pie. But until we go deeper in our search for causation the jogger will symbolize nothing but another horror story and our calls for action will fade into the wind. Before we can *do* anything, we've got to trace the crime to its roots: patriarchy, misogyny, and childhood sex-role socialization.

Sex Roles Create Violent Boys

Isn't it time to examine why so many sweet, affectionate little boys grow up to be men who feel the need to hurt women? Can't we figure out once and for all what happens to make males so much more violent than females and find a way to neutralize this behavior for the good of both sexes? Isn't it clear by now that the bifurcations of masculinity and femininity lead boys to compensate for being raised primarily by women in a culture where femininity is despised as weak? How can we expect young men to come of age in a society where masculinity is equated with dominance and male supremacy when it is clear that for most young men, dominance is out of reach, concentrated in the hands of older white males? Shouldn't we be exploring the connection between this culturally programmed craving for dominance and the fact that hundreds of thousands of men turn to violence against women to prove their masculine power?

Escalating male aggression has become a form of terrorism in women's lives. For that reason, if no other, these questions, long on feminists' minds, belong up front in public discourse. To guarantee women the basic rights of life, liberty, and the pursuit of happiness, all of us need to rethink the way we raise boys into men, and the meaning of masculinity in America.

a critical thinking activity

Recognizing Deceptive Arguments

People who feel strongly about an issue use many techniques to persuade others to agree with them. Some of those techniques appeal to the intellect, some to the emotions. Many of them distract the reader or listener from the real issues.

A few common examples of argumentation tactics are listed below. Most of them can be used either to advance an argument in an honest, reasonable way or to deceive or distract from the real issues. It is important for a critical reader to recognize these tactics in order to rationally evaluate an author's ideas.

a. *scare tactics*—the threat that if you don't do or don't believe this, something terrible will happen

b. *personal attack*—criticizing an opponent *personally* instead of rationally debating his or her ideas

c. *categorical statements*—stating something in a way that implies there can be no argument

d. *strawperson*—distorting or exaggerating an opponent's ideas to make one's own seem stronger

e. *slanters*—to persuade through inflammatory and exaggerated language instead of reason

f. *testimonial*—quoting or paraphrasing an authority or celebrity to support one's own viewpoint

The following activity can help you sharpen your skills in recognizing deceptive reasoning. The statements below are derived from the viewpoints in this chapter. *Beside each one, mark the letter of the type of deceptive appeal being used. More than one type of tactic may be applicable. If you believe the statement is not any of the listed appeals, write N.*

1. As long as the "treatment-rehabilitation approach" remains in place for all juveniles, we will see their violent and terrible crimes increase while the community suffers as innocent people are hurt and killed.

2. Incarceration itself encourages further delinquency. Fiction such as Clifford Shaw's *The Jack-Roller* depicts youths learning to become hardened criminals in prison.

3. The broad, simple demands of conservatives to "get tough" with juvenile offenders do nothing to help the situation and often make it more difficult for the juvenile justice system to concentrate its limited resources on violent offenders.

4. The Utah reform experience is regarded as an unqualified success.

5. Violence springs from the sullen rage of mostly boys and young men who live in poverty and squalor and are taunted by visions of affluence and ease.

6. An obvious trigger to violence is easy access to guns.

7. A keen observer of youth for more than a decade, Francis Ianni attributes the appearance of youth gangs in America's inner cities to the deterioration of families.

8. Only those with a strong desire to be deceived can persist in the belief that Americans can retreat from family life without fostering lawlessness.

9. We must strongly protest the massive promotion of violence by members of the entertainment industry who recklessly and selfishly continue to show movie violence to reap a profit.

10. Seedbed for gang activity, the broken home produces many of the nation's most violent criminals.

11. The ever-fatuous Cardinal O'Connor could not resist blaming the Central Park assault on society.

12. Those who say that TV violence should be restricted based merely upon what some viewers might do after exposure to it would cause more harm than good, since we would have to curtail everyone's First Amendment rights to free speech.

13. American women should be aware of the danger that they face everywhere: An act of violence by males against females is an occurrence as commonplace and all-American as apple pie.

Periodical Bibliography

The following articles have been selected to supplement the diverse views presented in this chapter.

Garry Abrams — "Defender of the Indefensible," *Los Angeles Times*, June 7, 1989.

Susan Baker and Tipper Gore — "Some Reasons for 'Wilding,'" *Newsweek*, May 29, 1989.

Legrand H. Clegg II — "Why Silence When Mobs Are White?" *Los Angeles Times*, August 30, 1989.

Harry W. Davis Jr. — "South Carolina Study Offers Hope," *Corrections Today*, August 1989.

Nancy Gibbs — "Wilding in the Night," *Time*, March 8, 1989.

Human Rights — "Children at Risk," Summer 1989.

William F. Jasper — "'Students' Who Murder and Rape," *The New American*, December 19, 1988.

Rita Kramer — "New York's Juvenile-Thug Mill," *The New York Times*, July 10, 1989.

John Leo — "The Politics of Hate," *U.S. News & World Report*, October 9, 1989.

Alex Poinsett — "Why Our Children Are Killing One Another," *Ebony*, December 1987.

Katha Pollitt — "Violence in a Man's World," *The New York Times Magazine*, June 18, 1989.

Selwyn Raab — "Central Park Case Puts Focus on Tough Juvenile Law," *The New York Times*, May 15, 1989.

Alfred S. Regnery — "Getting Away with Murder," *Policy Review*, Fall 1988.

Stanton E. Samenow — "Understanding and Helping Antisocial Adolescents," *Education Digest*, November 1988.

Eva Sears — "Skinheads: A New Generation of Hate-Mongers," *USA Today*, May 1989.

Anastasia Toufexis — "Our Violent Kids," *Time*, June 12, 1989.

George F. Will — "Call 'Wilding' Exactly What It Is: Evil," *Los Angeles Times*, May 1, 1989.

5 CHAPTER

What Motivates Serial Killers?

Chapter Preface

Many Americans are gruesomely fascinated by serial killers who often receive a great deal of media attention. *Helter Skelter*, Vincent Bugliosi's book on Charles Manson's murders, remained on the best-seller list for weeks. Letters written by David Berkowitz, the Son of Sam murderer, were published in the national news, making him a notorious celebrity. And Ted Bundy, confessed murderer of twenty-three women, received a great deal of media attention in part because he seemed an unlikely psychopath. Bundy's wholesome and all-American appearance fascinated the American public.

Perhaps the public's attention is drawn to these gruesome cases because serial killings not only raise questions about who will be the killer's next victim, but more profound ones about the nature of violence and the nature of society as well. Are serial killers sick aberrations, people far outside this country's norm of acceptable behavior? Or is a more frightening possibility true: that these people are outgrowths of a perverse society whose media dwell on serial killers because most people surreptitiously admire violence? The following viewpoints address these questions in considering what factors motivate serial killers.

"Charles Manson was neglected and used as a child, setting the stage for the conscienceless adult he was to become."

Painful Childhood Experiences Incite Serial Killers

Ken Magid and Carole A. McKelvey

According to the authors of the following viewpoint, Ken Magid and Carole A. McKelvey, serial killers suffer from Antisocial Personality Disorder. This syndrome can develop in the first few years of a neglected or severely abused child's life. As a result of family disruption or brutality, the infant never learns to bond or trust his or her caregivers. Some of these unbonded children grow up to be serial murderers who kill without remorse. Magid is chief of psychological services at Golden Medical Clinic in Golden, Colorado and codirector of the Behavioral Science Department for Family Practice Physicians at the St. Joseph Hospital in Denver. McKelvey is a journalist whose work has appeared in *Hour Magazine*.

As you read, consider the following questions:

1. What are the personality traits of a psychopath, according to Magid and McKelvey?
2. Why do the authors believe it is difficult to spot a psychopath?

It is 10:30 a.m. in central Florida. Beads of sweat drip from the foreheads of tourists waiting in long, winding lines at Disneyworld for an exciting ride on the Submarine Nautilus.

Less than 10 miles away, 9-year-old Jeffery Bailey Jr. is also waiting. He is waiting for his young companion to die. After making sure that no one else is around, Jeffery has pushed 3-year-old Ricardo "Nicki" Brown into the deep end of a motel pool. He knows the younger child cannot swim and is afraid of the water.

It is taking Nicki a long time to die. Jeffery gets tired of standing, so he pulls up a lawn chair to the edge of the pool. He wants a better view of how someone drowns. Jeffery stays by the pool until Nicki sinks to the bottom, lifeless. Then he puts on his shoes and shirt and saunters toward home.

A short time later he asks another neighborhood child what the "icky white stuff" is that comes out of someone's nose when they're drowning. He doesn't mention that Nicki is at this moment lying at the bottom of a pool.

Nicki's body is recovered from the pool at 6:40 p.m. by the police. Later, after neighborhood children have told Jeffery's mother about the drowning, the youngster tells his mother about the "accident."

Police officer Beth Peturka who investigated the case says she found Jeffery "kind of nonchalant, like he was enjoying all the attention."

On June 3, 1986, the State of Florida charges 9-year-old Jeffery with murder.

Breeding Ground for Psychopaths

America. Land of the free, or a breeding ground for psychopaths? Hundreds of thousands of individuals filled with hatred populate this country. They are people without a conscience, and they hurt—sometimes kill—others without remorse.

They are psychopaths, and they possess a poisonous mix of traits. They are arrogant, shameless, immoral, impulsive, antisocial, superficial, charming, callous, irresponsible, irreverent, cunning, self-assured. They are found in jails and mental institutions . . . but they can also be found in boardrooms or in politics or in any number of respected professions. This disorder evades established definitions of sanity or insanity and there is no cure for adult psychopaths.

Haven't you wondered—as you read the morning newspaper or watched the TV news—why there seem to be ever-increasing accounts of psychopathic killers? Almost daily, it seems, we hear of another conscienceless murderer: Gary Gilmore, who was executed by a Utah firing squad; Charles Manson, who directed the Helter-Skelter murders; Henry Lee Lucas, who claimed he was the worst mass murderer in history; Edmund Kemper III, the Santa

Cruz Coed Murderer; Kenneth Bianchi, the Hillside Strangler; David Berkowitz, the Son of Sam; Richard Ramirez, the Night Stalker; Donald Harvey, the Cyanide Killer; Juan Corona, who murdered migrant workers . . . The Tylenol Killer . . . Theodore Bundy.

Ted Bundy, one of the most infamous mass murderers of modern times, is a classic example of a criminal psychopath.

For years, Bundy outwitted law officers who hunted him across the face of America. He finally was sentenced to death in Florida's maximum security prison for brutally murdering two coeds and a young school girl. . . .

Bundy is the ultimate manifestation of the character-disturbed child. He shares a common trait with the 9-year-old from Florida. Sometime, early in their development, something went terribly wrong. They never developed a conscience.

Bundy and Bailey are typical of certain types of criminals who started life as unattached children, perhaps aided by a genetic predisposition.

What happens, right or wrong, in the critical first two years of a baby's life will imprint that child as an adult. A complex set of events must occur in infancy to assure a future of trust and love. If the proper bonding and subsequent attachment does not occur—usually between the child and the mother—the child will develop mistrust and a deep-seated rage. He becomes a child without a conscience.

Sad Legacy of Abuse

Numerous studies have found those who were victims of child abuse to be more troubled as adults than those who were not. There are disproportionate numbers of victims of abuse among prostitutes, violent criminals, alcoholics and drug abusers, and patients in psychiatric hospitals. . . .

A 1985 study of all 15 adolescents in the United States who were condemned murderers found that 13 had been victims of extreme physical or sexual abuse. In nine cases the abuse was so severe—characterized as "murderous" by the researchers—that it led to neurological damage.

Daniel Goleman, *The New York Times*, January 24, 1989.

Somehow, the normal process that causes attachment to occur—the very process that develops a social conscience—was short-circuited in Bundy and Bailey.

Not all unattached children grow up to be criminals, but most suffer some form of psychological damage. It may be that such children simply are never able to develop a true loving relationship, or they end up "conning" others for their own benefit. These, too, can be considered tragedies, for no child should have to grow up without this trust bond and loving beginning.

In most infants, the affectional bond—the essence of attachment to a parent—develops during the first nine months of life. The most important event occurring during the first year is the formation of these social attachments.

Michael Rutter in *Maternal Deprivation Reassessed* (1981) says the absence of attachment may lead to what Rutter calls "affectionless psychopathy." He describes this as beginning with "an initial phase of clinging, dependent behavior, followed by attention-seeking, uninhibited, indiscriminate friendliness, and finally, a personality characterized by the lack of guilt, an inability to keep rules and an inability to form lasting relationships."

Mary Ainsworth (1973) argues that the most important long-term result of the failure to form an affectional bond is the "inability to establish and maintain deep and significant interpersonal relations."

✳ The consequence of this failure can be individuals suffering from Antisocial Personality Disorder (APD). These people, more commonly known as psychopaths, express no remorse if caught in wrongdoings. They are aggressive, reckless and cruel to others. They leave in their wake a huge amount of human suffering. The pain psychopaths wreak on other human beings can be physical, or it can be the mental anguish often felt by those who try to form relationships with psychopaths.

Frighteningly, a growing number of individuals now being diagnosed as mentally ill fits this particular mental health category. These psychopaths comprise an increasingly large increment of the aberrant segment of our population. And they account for a disproportionate amount of deviancy.

We call them the "Trust Bandits" of modern society. They steal our trust. . . .

The Disease of Psychopathy

It is important, as we explore this illness, to remember that psychopaths run the gamut from mildly impaired to criminal. On a scale showing humanity from its best to its worst the homicidal psychopath, such as Manson or Bundy, would be at one end of the continuum and an exemplary individual such as Mother Teresa of Calcutta would be at the other.

Those on the middle of the scale suffer some problems, but are still able to function in society. Those on the extreme end—those with acute APD—are the most dangerous and inevitably end up doing incredible harm to other human beings. . . .

Particularly among male APD sufferers one will see an arrest record. The marriages of these people often involve verbal or

The Conscience of Humanity

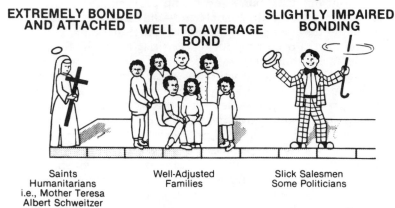

EXTREMELY BONDED AND ATTACHED

WELL TO AVERAGE BOND

SLIGHTLY IMPAIRED BONDING

Saints
Humanitarians
i.e., Mother Teresa
Albert Schweitzer

Well-Adjusted
Families

Slick Salesmen
Some Politicians

---

physical fighting, separation and divorce. Desertion and nonsupport are common. Antisocials also have a higher incidence of alcohol and drug abuse.

Typically school problems are in their backgrounds; Trust Bandits have school records replete with truancy, fighting, suspensions and expulsions. Sexual promiscuity is common, particularly among women where it is true in about 90% of the cases. The antisocial personality is always socially isolated without any true friends, although they may have numerous casual aquaintances. . . .

It often isn't easy, even for a trained therapist, to recognize children or adults who are psychopaths. Even in early years, young psychopaths contain at least two sides to their personalities. The outside, superficial mask is often a likeable character. Usually this charming "public side" is verbally fluent and capable of making short-term friends easily. . . .

Mass-murderer Kenneth Bianchi, for example, was a master at fooling everyone—even the experts. As the Hillside Strangler, Bianchi had terrorized the Los Angeles area for more than a year in 1977. Bianchi, with his cousin Angelo Buono, raped, tortured and then murdered 10 Los Angeles women and girls ages 12 to 28. Bianchi killed two more after moving to Washington State. . . .

An in-depth program on the Bianchi murders was broadcast in 1985 on a special *Frontline* television presentation. The program clearly showed why it is so hard for most people to spot a clever psychopath. . . .

He fooled his common-law wife, Kelli Boyd, who told *Frontline* reporters and police, "The Ken I knew couldn't have hurt anyone. He was helpful with the baby, thoughtful, even helped around

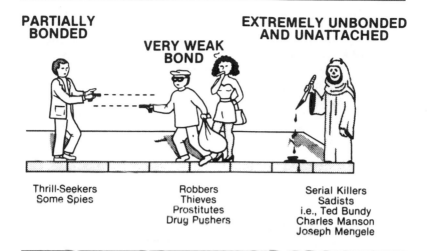

PARTIALLY BONDED	VERY WEAK BOND	EXTREMELY UNBONDED AND UNATTACHED
Thrill-Seekers Some Spies	Robbers Thieves Prostitutes Drug Pushers	Serial Killers Sadists i.e., Ted Bundy Charles Manson Joseph Mengele

the house. He just wasn't the kind of person who could have killed anyone."

In fact, Kenneth Bianchi had suffered from APD since young childhood. Records obtained by the police showed that his descriptions of his mother as a "saintly woman" were far from the truth. (It is typical for adults who were neglected as children—and become unattached children—to deny that their mothers were cruel to them.) Bianchi claimed to have no memory of various events from his childhood, including long periods when he was under psychiatric care.

Fooling the Doctors

"Ken Bianchi had a long history, showing a tremendous amount of pathology and difficulties in the family. He was considered a disturbed child," said Dr. Ralph Allison, who at first believed Bianchi to be a multiple personality. The psychiatrist subsequently changed his mind after doing additional work with prisoners at a penitentiary. "Some of these guys change their story every day," he said. "I guess I was wrong; he fooled me."

Bianchi as a child was trotted from one medical doctor to another when he suffered a series of symptoms, including rolling eyes, tics, falling down after petit mal-type seizures. The doctors referred his mother to a psychiatrist. She took him to Los Angeles' De Paul Clinic where records show doctors found Kenneth to be "a deeply hostile boy who has very dependent needs, which his mother fulfills. He depends upon his mother for his very survival and expends a great deal of energy keeping his hostility under control and under cover.

"There seems to be some basic confusion about his own identity.

201

He seems to try hard to placate his mother, but she always seems dissatisfied. He is a severely depressed boy who seems very anxious and lonely."

Like so many young psychopaths—character-disturbed children—Kenneth Bianchi drew pictures of devils and demons. His lawyer uncovered an old sculpture he had done. One side was the image of a man; the other, a horrible demon. He was a child who bore the brunt of his mother's wrath at her gambling husband. She often hit and badgered Bianchi, who at a young age would hide from her. He said his favorite place—"the best place"—was under his bed. . . .

Without Conscience

Charles Manson has been called the most dangerous, feared man alive. There is perhaps no better example in modern times of a petty thief/con artist whose dark side eventually erupted, shocking a nation. Manson always had a black side simmering just beneath the surface. When it emerged the horrible result was the Tate/LaBianca massacre. The two-day killing spree left 7 people mutilated and dead, including movie actress Sharon Tate.

On the evening of the Tate murders, August 8, 1969, Manson says, "I was aware of being totally without conscience. Though I have pointed to numerous circumstances in my life that may have turned my head in the wrong direction, I can't put a finger on when I became devoid of caring emotion."

In his damning book *Manson in His Own Words* (as told to Nuel Emmons, 1986) Manson lays open the life and thoughts of a man whose acts left us trembling.

There is no better living proof of what can go wrong if the attachment bond isn't formed than Charles Manson. He was born in 1934 in Cincinnati, Ohio, to an unmarried 15-year-old girl. His early life was spent in a succession of different homes and with a number of substitute parents. Finally, his mother asked Indiana state authorities to take over his care when he was 12 years old. Since the age of 12 Manson has lived most of his life behind bars. He was first placed in a reform school and, after escaping from there, was sent to the National Training School for Boys in Washington, D.C. He was set free when he was 19 years old.

"Jails, courtrooms and prisons have been my life since I was 12 years old," Manson says in his book. "By the time I was 16, I had lost all fear of anything the administration of the prison system could dish out." He sees himself as a person who was dealt a hand that couldn't be played by the rules and values of our society.

"Most of the stories and articles written painted me as having fangs and horns from birth. They say my mother was a whore . . . would it change things to say I had no choice in selecting my mother? Or that, being a bastard child, I was an outlaw from birth?

That during those so-called formative years, I was not in control of my life?

"Hey, listen, by the time I was old enough to think or remember, I had been shoved around and left with people who were strangers even to those I knew. Rejection, more than love and acceptance, has been a part of my life since birth."

In explaining why he decided to let Nuel Emmons write the book, Manson says he wanted to answer those who have asked where his philosophy, bitterness and antisocial behavior came from.

There is little doubt that it came from the horrible childhood suffered by the boy who would one day strike terror in the hearts of all mankind. Charles Manson was neglected and used as a child, setting the stage for the conscienceless adult he was to become. "My feeling is, I've been raped and ravaged by society . . . by attorney and friends. Sucked dry by the courts. Beaten by the guards and exhibited by the prisons. . . . My body remains trapped and imprisoned by a society that creates people like me." . . .

At the core of the unattached is a deep-seated rage, far beyond normal anger. This rage is suppressed in their psyche. Now we all have some degree of rage, but the rage of psychopaths is that born of unfulfilled needs as infants. Incomprehensible pain is forever locked in their souls, because of the abandonment they felt as infants.

It is as if a voice inside their heads is saying, "I trusted you to be there and to take care of me and you weren't. It hurts so much that I will not trust anyone, ever. I must control everything—and everybody—to ward off being abandoned again."

"The serial killer . . . and the mass killer . . . can only be accurately and objectively perceived as prime embodiment of their civilization, not twisted derangement."

American Culture Incites Serial Killers

Elliott Leyton

Elliott Leyton is an anthropologist at Memorial University of Newfoundland located in St. Johns, Newfoundland in Canada. In the following viewpoint, he maintains that there are more serial killers today than there were in the middle decades of the 1900s. He believes that today's serial killers tend to be people who are unsuccessful in most areas of their lives. Yet in a culture which glorifies both success and violence, the serial killer can gain fame and notoriety by committing a series of brutal murders, Leyton writes.

As you read, consider the following questions:

1. Why does Leyton object to claims that serial killers are aberrant, freaks of society?
2. How have economic changes contributed to the increase in serial killers, in the author's view?
3. What does Leyton mean by the term "social levelling"?

*"For murder, though it have no tongue, will speak
With most miraculous organ."*

Hamlet

Are multiple murderers merely "insane"? Can such bizarre behaviour be dismissed as simple psychiatric or genetic freakishness? There is an ancient chord in our civilization which insists that such terrible acts be interpreted in terms of possession by evil spirits, or witchcraft (an explanation which reverberates today in the press's frequent, and inaccurate, speculation that occultism is a motive for these crimes); and a more modern variation of this theme similarly dismisses the acts with notions of possession by "mental disease." It would be most comforting if we could continue to accept such explanations, for they satisfyingly banish guilt beyond our responsibility; yet to do so would beg the question—why does modern America produce proportionately so many more of these "freaks" than any other industrial nation? Moreover, if the killers are merely insane, why do they in fact so rarely display the cluster of readily identifiable clinical symptoms (including disorders of thought and affect) which psychiatrists agree mark mental illness? In one important sense, of course, any person who murders another human being has abandoned all reason and sanity; yet such a position is essentially *moral*, and does not help us in an objective attempt to understand the cause and meaning of such a phenomenon.

An Embodiment of American Culture

I first embarked upon this journey into the souls of modern multiple murderers because I was unable to understand the profound personal fulfillment they seemed to derive from their killings. Now, after four years of total immersion in the killers' diaries, confessions, psychiatric interviews, statements to the press, videotapes, and photographs, I see their motives as so obvious and their gratifications as so intense that I can only marvel at how *few* of them walk the streets of America. Nevertheless, their numbers do continue to grow at a disturbing rate: until the 1960s, they were anomalies who appeared perhaps once a decade; but by the 1980s, one was spawned virtually each month. Today, according to unofficial U.S. Justice Department estimates, there may be as many as one hundred multiple murderers killing in America, stealing the lives of thousands. The uncomfortable conclusion is that there will undoubtedly be many more before this epoch in our social history draws to a close. They may still be statistically rare, but I shall try to show that they are no freaks: rather, they can only be fully understood as representing the logical extension of many of the central themes in their culture—of wordly ambition, of success and failure, and of manly avenging violence. Although they take several forms—the serial killer whose murders provide both revenge and a lifelong *celebrity career*; and the mass killer, who no longer wishes to live, and whose murders constitute his *suicide note*—they can only be accurately and objectively perceived as prime embodiment of their civilization, not twisted derangement.

The Most Notorious Convict

There are days when I get caught up in being the most notorious convict of all time. In that frame of mind I get off on all the publicity, and I'm pleased when some fool writes and offers to "off some pigs" for me. I've had girls come to visit me with their babies in their arms and say, "Charlie, I'd do anything in the world for you. I'm raising my baby in your image." Those letters and visits used to delight me, but that's my individual sickness. What sickness is it that keeps sending me kids and followers? It's your world out there that does it. I don't solicit any mail or ask anyone to come and visit me. Yet the mail continues to arrive and your pretty little flowers of innocence keep showing up at the gate. Hell, they don't know me. They only know what your world has projected and won't let go of.

Charlie Manson, *Manson In His Own Words*, 1986.

The mid-1980s were years of unprecedented growth, experimentation, and innovation among multiple murderers, years in which all previous "records" were broken and sacrosanct social barriers were pierced. In 1984 alone, a fortyish drifter named *Henry Lee Lucas* delivered his confessions in which he claimed to have tortured and murdered hundreds of women, a number far in excess of any previous claimant's. Lucas lived with his fifteen-year-old common-law wife in a trailer parked in The House of Prayer for All People campground, a former chicken farm operated as a Pentecostal retreat in a small town in Texas. His eight-year killing spree was terminated only when he murdered an elderly local woman who had befriended him, which provoked his close scrutiny by the local police. Jailed on little more than suspicion, he passed a note to a deputy, claiming that "I have done something terrible, and I want to talk to sheriff." It was only then that inquisitive police began the lengthy interrogations and checking of his claims. Lucas outlined his story to a largely disbelieving audience, spinning an unrivalled tale of rape, torture, dismemberment, and murder, while conceding only that "I know it ain't normal for a person to go out and kill a girl just to have sex with her."

The thirteenth child of a prostitute mother, Lucas began his career in 1960 when, at the age of twenty-three, he stabbed his mother to death in her bed. He spent the following fifteen years in prisons and mental hospitals in Michigan, without obtaining any relief from his homicidal "needs." "I have been to the Ionia State Hospital for the Criminally Insane in Michigan," he told a Texas judge. "I have been to a mental hospital in Princeton, West Virginia. And I tell them my problems, and they don't want to do nothing about it, but there is a hundred, oh, about a hundred women out there that says different." Despite his protestations, he claims, he was released: "I told them before I ever left prison that I was going to commit crimes, told them the type of crimes I was going to commit, and they wouldn't believe it. They said I was going regardless of whether I liked it or not. And the day I got out of jail is the day I started killing." He says he killed two women that day.

Death on Women

"I was death on women," he told a television reporter in his disconcertingly genial manner. "I didn't feel they need to exist. I hated them, and I wanted to destroy every one I could find. I was doing a good job of it. I've got [killed] 360 people, I've got 36 states, in three different countries. My victims never knew what was going to happen to them. I've had shootings, knifings, strangulations, beatings, and I've participated in actual crucifixions of humans. All across the country, there's people just like me, who set out to destroy human life." For eight years he criss-crossed the continent, looking for women alone and defenceless— hitchhikers, runaways, women whose cars had broken down on lonely roads. He explained his behaviour in intellectual constructs borrowed from his culture, which is to say in terms of his childhood. "That's the way I grew up when I was a child— watching my mom have sexual acts. She wouldn't go into different rooms, she'd make sure I was in the room before she started anything, and she would do it deliberately to make me watch her, you know. I got so I hated it. I'd even leave the house and go out and hide in the woods and wouldn't even go home. And when I'd go home, I'd get beat for not coming home. I don't blame mom for what she done, I don't blame her for that. It's the idea of the way she done it. I don't think any child out there should be brought up in that type of environment. In the past, I've hated it. It's just inside hate, and I can't get away from it." What Lucas says *seems* to explain it all: yet he killed his mother first, when he was only twenty-three, and that should have finished her. Why did he have to spend decades in exorcising her ghost by killing "her" over and over again? His explanation seems most imperfect. . . .

After the Second World War, the industrial economies—both east and west—moved into an era of unprecedented expansion and prosperity. With the growth of the industrial sector came a parallel development of social service agencies—running the gamut from education to medicine to welfare. This remarkable growth in both the corporate and social sectors created two post-war decades in which individuals with even the most marginal of qualifications and abilities could enter occupations which offered a measure of dignity and recompense. As might be expected, these were quiet years for multiple murder as the population scrambled to better itself. The explosion in the rate of production of these most modern of killers began in the late 1960s, and it continued in an almost exponential path for the following twenty years. This directly paralleled, and may well have owed its initial impetus to, the *closure* that was taking place in the American economy. From the late 1960s onward, the myriad of middle-class positions that had been created since the Second World War began to be filled, or reduced in number. Inexorably, more and more socially ambitious, but untalented (or unconnected) young men must have found it difficult to achieve their goals of "successful" careers. A proportion of these men—we can never know how large—began to fantasize about revenge; and a tiny, but ever-increasing, percentage of them began to react to the frustration of their blocked social mobility by transforming their fantasies into a vengeful reality.

A Celebrity

Despite [David Berkowitz's] claims of insanity, he was no different from any . . . other multiple murderer: he killed for the same reasons. . . . Looked at in terms of the central propositions of his culture, it made a certain sense to achieve fame and dignity through violent display. Now he would be a celebrity for all time, propelled by his acts from the suffocating anonymity of an illegitimate and friendless postal clerk living in a small apartment in a working-class neighbourhood. "I had a job to do, and I was doing it," he had said manfully. For the price of incarceration—a trifling sum for one who has no social bonds—he had exacted his manhood and achieved a kind of immortality. Such an accomplishment surely buoys his spirits as he lives out his days in prison, holding court with his several biographers.

Elliott Leyton, *Compulsive Killers*, 1986.

All this took place in a cultural *milieu* which for more than a century and a half had glorified violence as an appropriate and manly response to frustration. *The History of Violence In America* documented the public response to a robbery in which a young girl had been shot in the leg: the Kansas City *Times* called the robbery "so diabolically daring and so utterly in contempt of fear that we are bound to admire it and revere its perpetrators." A few days later, the same newspaper commentated that,

> It was as though three bandits had come to us from storied Odenwald, with the halo of medieval chivalry upon their garments and shown us how the things were done that poets sing of. Nowhere else in the United States or in the civilized world, probably, could this thing have been done.

No single quality of American culture is so distinctive as its continued assertion of the nobility and beauty of violence—a notion and a mythology propagated with excitement and craft in all popular cultural forms, including films, television, and print. This cultural predilection must have been immeasurably enhanced by the television coverage of the Vietnam War, which brought real bloodletting and killing into every American living-room, and rendered death sacred no more. Encouraged thus to act out their fantasies, our killers would come to find that their murderous acts would serve both to validate and to relieve their grievances. . . .

More Killers and More Victims

There was essentially no change in the rate of production of multiple murderers until the 1960s, for the decades between the 1920s and the 1950s produced only one or two apiece. In the 1960s, this jumped to six cases during the decade, for an average of one new killer every twenty months. By the 1970s, this had jumped to seventeen new cases, for an average of one new killer appearing every seven months. During the first four years of the 1980s, the total had leapt to twenty-five, for an average rate of production of one new killer every 1.8 months.

The number of victims also experienced a parallel increase. During the 1920s, when thirty-nine people were killed, the average number of murders was 0.325 per month. In the 1930s, with only eight killings, the figure dropped to 0.06 per month. During the 1940s, with a minimum of twenty murdered, this average figure rose slightly to 0.16 per month; and in the 1950s, with eleven killings, the average was 0.09 victims per month. The number of victims began to accelerate during the 1960s: the total of seventy represented a rate of 0.58 per month. During the 1970s, 219 were murdered, a trebling of the rate to 1.83 per month; and during the first four years of the 1980s, the 444 victims represent another quadrupling of the rate, to 9.25 per month, a frequency of victimization *one hundred times* that of the 1950s. . . .

For the production of multiple murderers to reach the unprecedented levels that it has in the America of the 1970s and 1980s, we require the existence of cultural forms that can mediate between killer and victim in a special sense—ridding the potential victims of any humanity, and the potential killer of any responsibility. Both sociologists Christopher Lasch and Barbara Ehrenreich have argued most persuasively that we have developed these forms with no little refinement. Lasch devoted a volume to delineating the nature of this "culture of competitive individualism" which carries "the logic of individualism to the extreme of a war of all against all, the pursuit of happiness to the dead end of a narcissistic preoccupation with the self." Ehrenreich dwelt upon the sources of this ideology which so encouraged the severing of responsibility between people. She saw its roots in the developing post-war male culture of "escape—literal escape from the bondage of breadwinning." Here, men were urged to take part in the superficial excitement of "the nightmare anomie of the pop psychologists' vision: a world where other people are objects of consumption, or the chance encounters of a 'self' propelled by impulse alone."

The Origins of Violence

On the one hand, legislators, practitioners, and the public are willing to characterize some forms of violent crime—the bizarre, the sadistic, the inexplicable—as immanently crazy, as utterly beyond reason and rationality. In such instances it appears that the very fabric of the violence is insanity, that one incorporates the other in an inextricable pattern of unity. On the other hand, we dwell in a society that typically normalizes violence, that celebrates deadly aggression in the sports arenas, cinemas, and battlefields. Violence can be witnessed variously among the chronic psychotics and the unremittingly "normal" of the world, among those confined to maximum-security institutions for the criminally insane and those given ticker-tape parades, among our John Hinckleys and our John Rambos. The line that divides heroic and criminal violence, that separates the rational from the insane, is drawn with a broad and crooked brush. We might be well advised to abandon these efforts at locating danger in the pathological recesses of disturbed minds and to concentrate instead on the global madness and violence that keep us all on the brink of extinction.

Robert J. Menzies and Christopher D. Webster, in *Pathways to Criminal Violence*, 1989.

Thus the freedom for which mankind had struggled over the centuries proved to be a two-edged sword. The freedom from the suffocation of family and community, the freedom from systems of religious thought, the freedom to explore one's self, all entailed heavy penalties to society—not the least of which was the rate of multiple murder. Whether the industrial system was socialist or capitalist, its members were forced to look upon themselves and others as marketable commodities. It can hardly be surprising then that some fevered souls, feeling like automatons, might choose to coalesce their fuzzy identity in a series of fearful acts. Their ambitions crushed, some would lash out in protest at objects (most often sexual) which they had been taught to see as essentially insignificant. Now the question asked by the killer Bundy seems less inappropriate: "What's one less person on the face of the earth, anyway?"

Unable to Live the American Dream

At a certain point in his life, the future killer experiences a kind of internal *social* crisis, when he realizes that he cannot be what he wishes to be—cannot live his version of the American dream. When these killers reach that existential divide, the seed is planted for a vengeance spree. Sometimes their motives are entirely conscious . . . while with others . . . they are only dimly understood. In either case, it is unrealizable ambition that motivates them, as they launch a kind of sub-political and personal assault on society, aiming always at the class group they feel oppresses or excludes them. Some require minimal justification for their acts, obtaining temporary relief from their rage through the killings and then "forgetting" or compartmentalizing their memories, as when Boston strangler Albert DeSalvo remarked: "I was there, it was done, and yet if you talked to me an hour later, or half hour later, it didn't mean nothing." Still others construct elaborate intellectual (Carl Panzram) or spiritual (Son of Sam murderer David Berkowitz's demons) rationalizations to explain and justify their killings. Only a few, (such as Joseph Kallinger, and California's Herbert Mullins, who murdered to "stop earthquakes") detach themselves so much from conventional reality that they construct their own universes, thereby entering that state the psychiatrists call madness.

Yet what they are *all* orchestrating is a kind of social levelling, in which they rewrite the universe to incorporate themselves: no one expressed this more clearly than Charles Starkweather when he said that "dead people are all on the same level." They are all engaged in the same process, punishing the innocent, and in doing so they recreate the dehumanized industrial system in a form that gives themselves a central position. One hundred eyes for an eye: it is by no means the first time in human history that retaliating men have grossly exceeded the degree of the original insult. Neither do they form their missions in a private vacuum, bereft of all advice, for the larger culture encodes in them a respect for violent display—a central theme in the media messages beamed at the working class—and the ready availability of stimulating materials in books and magazines, films and videotapes, teaches them to link their lust with violence. If we were charged with the responsibility for designing a society in which all structural and cultural mechanisms leaned toward the creation of the killers of strangers, we could do no better than to present the purchaser with the shape of modern America.

"Serial murderers have all reported feelings they could not control, voices whose urgings forced them into criminal acts, or sensations from deep within their minds."

Brain Disorders Influence Serial Killers

Joel Norris

Psychologist Joel Norris is a founding member of the International Committee of Neuroscientists to Study Episodic Aggression. He has been a consultant in serial murder cases in Georgia and Florida. In the following viewpoint, excerpted from his book, *Serial Killers*, Norris explains that many murderers report hearing voices that urge them to kill. He argues that these voices come from the murderers' damaged brains. Killers' perception of reality is skewed, he writes; they often confuse the victim with someone from their past. To silence the voice, the murderer kills the victim.

As you read, consider the following questions:

1. Why does the author maintain that serial killers are addicted?
2. According to Norris, why are serial killers unable to determine if they are awake or dreaming when they are caught up in the series of events that leads to a murder?
3. How can the brain's defense mechanism actually encourage a serial killer, in the author's opinion?

In Texas and the neighboring panhandle states, more than three hundred people died, allegedly at the hands of Henry Lee Lucas. Even though questions still remain about the truth and accuracy of Lucas' early confessions, which he later recanted, some of them are so graphic and lurid that even the police refused to believe them. It was reported by the Texas Rangers and law enforcement officials nationwide that he killed hundreds of men, women, and children whom he did not know except for the few brief hours when he had stalked, tortured, put them to death, mutilated their bodies, dismembered them, and buried their remains. In Atlanta an entire community was frozen with terror as each week more and more bodies of its children were found sexually assaulted and buried in the area around the Chattahoochee River. The police in Seattle were baffled for years while they searched for the killer of a score of young, attractive women who had seemed to offer no resistance to the person who took their lives. It wasn't until Ted Bundy was finally arrested in another community that the Seattle killings stopped. It took another series of murders in Utah and then later in Florida, to which Bundy had escaped, to finally bring him to sentencing. Even after their convictions and sentencing, questions still remain about the full extent of their crimes, and families wonder whether their children who have been missing for years will ever be listed among the killers' victims. . . .

Addicted to the Act

Addicted to the act of murder as if it were a drug, serial killers compulsively and silently troll for their victims amid shopping malls at twilight, darkened city streets, or country roads in isolated rural communities. They are motivated by a force that even they don't understand. Once they have sighted a potential victim, they begin to stalk with a dogged relentlessness that does not cease until the victim is cornered and the trap is sprung. Like tormented beasts of prey, serial murderers do not commit simple homicides. They often torture their victims, taking delight in the victims' agonies, expressions of terror, cries of despair, and reactions to pain. Then, in a period of marked depression that follows the high of the murder, the killers plead for help from the police or newspapers as did Richard Herrins, a serial killer in Chicago in the early 1960s, who wrote in lipstick on a dressing-room mirror above his victim's head: "Catch me before I kill again." Always hidden in plain sight, some killers ask to be caught, promise to turn themselves in so that they can receive therapy, but vanish again only to emerge after the next murder. . . .

The serial murderer, unlike the traditional criminal, is addicted to his passion. He is suffering from a disease that is terminal, not only for his numerous victims but also for himself. He is his ultimate victim. On his own initiative, the serial killer can no more

213

stop his killing than a heroin addict can kick his habit. Suffering from waves of a primal pain and fear of the deepest nature after his most recent killing, an unusual set of defense mechanisms emerges. He simply forgets his crime as well as the victim. Soon thereafter, the urge to murder comes upon him again. He may loathe what he does and despise his own weakness, but he can do nothing on his own to control it. . . .

Common Patterns

Serial murderers share a significant number of common medical/psychological patterns that include evidence of possible genetic defect, soft and hard signs of brain damage resulting from injuries or other physical trauma, severe chemical imbalances brought about by chronic malnutrition and substance abuse, an absence of a sense of self which is the result of consistently negative parenting or nonparenting, and an almost hair-trigger violent response to external stimuli with no regard for the physical or social consequences.

Joel Norris, *Serial Killers*, 1988.

"Around fifteen years of age, God came to me with both a voice and visual presence and ordered me to undertake orthopedic experiments to heal myself and save mankind. This was the time when I was having the strange movements, and my parents had put a lock on their bedroom door and a bat behind their door, so I felt hopeless," Joseph Kallinger explained in an interview a few years ago. . . .

"There is something the matter with me," Ted Bundy told his former girl friend, Liz Kendall, after his arrest in Florida. He admitted to a force within him that had begun sucking in his living personality just as the supergravitational pull of a black hole sucks in all light and then the matter from the neighboring stars. He tried to suppress this force that was building in him, but it was too strong. The more energy he applied against it to keep normal, the more the force grew in him. It destroyed his ability to function in school, it continued to warp his relationship with Liz Kendall, and finally it consumed him.

He was unable to lead a normal life, although he presented the appearance of someone who could exert complete control over any situation. Bundy knew when the dark feelings were upon him. He tried to stay off the streets when he felt the urgings start, so that he wouldn't encounter any women who might cross his path. However, as it became increasingly difficult, Bundy felt himself slipping under its control again and again. And the feelings escalated to the point where, if he were on the street and a pretty young woman crossed his path, he would follow her. He tried to fight to remain in control many times by just following down the street until she disappeared into a dormitory or sorority house, but many times he couldn't. Weeks later the girl would be discovered in a shallow grave. . . .

Feelings They Could Not Control

Whether a form of multiple personality or not, Lucas, Bundy, Kallinger, Hillside strangler Kenneth Bianchi, and many of the other serial murderers have all reported feelings they could not control, voices whose urgings forced them into criminal acts, or sensations from deep within their minds that seemed to take over their bodies and hold them hostage. Some killers report that what began in childhood as strange voices or sexual urgings that were different from what other children talked about escalated into rituals within which these individuals would assault other people, rape women, achieve orgasm only when the victim lay helpless before them, and even commit murder and mutilation to hide the evidence and prevent their being caught. The more violent the crime, the more the feelings of violence escalated until the crimes themselves were no longer enough to blot out the disgust and revulsion the killers felt about themselves. Never able to show remorse, never able to experience the feelings of empathy and love other people seemed to experience, these killers lived in their own dark universes until a part of them gave up, attempted suicide, or left a telltale set of clues that led the police to make the arrest. . . .

To understand how someone can be neurologically impaired and still function or how someone like Bundy can lead an apparently normal life, live with a woman and her young daughter, and still have episodes during which he will rape and kill other young women, one has to understand the complex of symptoms that serial killers seem to have. And to understand how that damage controls their behavior, we have to look at how what we call consciousness or sentience is the product of a biological mechanism.

There is nothing magic or mystical about how the brain operates, although it is at the center of the miracle of life. What we call consciousness or awareness is actually the high-speed overlap of millions of electrochemically communicated messages between the senses, areas of recognition, memory banks, and nerves that control muscular movement. The brain is both a parallel processor, accomplishing many things at the same time along the same pathways, and a subordinating processor that prioritizes tasks and loads them into different job queues for completion as necessary. Based on the physical state of the body at any given moment, on the nature of the external world that the brain perceives, the urgency of messages that are stored in different memory stacks, and the emotional level of the organism, the brain allocates an importance factor to each job that it must process and organizes them accordingly. . . .

But this machine model of the human brain oversimplifies the complexity of the organ and the neurological system it manages. Because the system is driven electrochemically instead of only electrically, different types of communication can take place at the same time and actually alter the mind's interpretation of the messages. If a person is tired and hungry, his body is overworked, and his mind is overstressed with concerns about the day's problems and fears not only about tomorrow but about his family and financial situations as well, he will react to the same types of stimuli differently than someone who is unstressed, not hungry or tired, and more confident. . . . Among serial killers whose body chemistry is drastically impaired, the brain can scarcely function normally at all. . . .

The Brain and Loss of Control

If primal displays of violence and a family background of violence are the most identifiable behavioral characteristics of the serial killer syndrome, history of head trauma, degrees of brain or neurological dysfunction, or forms of psychomotor epilepsy are important medical characteristics. . . . These physiological impairments directly affect outward behavior and the social controls the individual is able to exert over behavior. Even minor brain dysfunctions or minor damage resulting from injuries can result in a significant loss of control of violent tendencies.

Joel Norris, *Serial Killers*, 1988.

In the normal brain sensory information from the outside world is relayed electrically to specific centers along pathways of nerve cells. What the nerves transmit to the brain is compared with similar information the brain has stored and the information is recognized and identified. Part of this information process is used to keep the individual oriented spatially and temporally. In other words, to establish what we sense as a continuum from one moment to the next, the brain constantly "flashes" pictures of the outside world. These hundreds of billions of flash cards comprise a conscious reality. Change a major aspect of the outside world in between the flash cards so that it no longer conforms to what the brain expects and the individual can lose the ability to orient himself. . . . We call that reaction momentary panic, and we most commonly experience it when someone unexpectedly jumps out at us into our plane of vision. Children frighten one another like this all the time.

What really happens neurologically when we are frightened in this way is that the suddenness of the appearance is transmitted along a different neural pathway to the autonomic nervous system. This is controlled in the primal area of the brain: the temporal lobe, the limbic region, and the hypothalamus. These areas control the body's prime emotions and hormonal systems. They can and do override any cognitive functions because they maintain the body's metabolic balance. It is in these regions that the biological algorithm is translated from a cellular level to the level of the organism. These areas control fear and rage, the sexual drive, the sense of pleasure or well-being, and the basic sense of self that differentiates one individual from the rest of reality. The autonomic message that someone has appeared unexpectedly triggers a reaction in the hypothalamus of fear and the need for flight.

Under routine circumstances, the brain quickly identifies abnormal sensory experiences and signals a type of alert status until the abnormality is resolved. The logical control exercised by the usually dominant left hemisphere provides a matrix of order and consistency and imposes a structure upon the raw sensory data the brain receives. It serves as a filter, establishing a continuum from one reality flash card to the next, and it judges the validity and content of the information it receives through the sensory receptors. Our ability to discriminate between real and nonreal or true and false is governed to a large extent by the judgmental, logical controls resident in the left hemisphere. This is what keeps even the most emotional person functioning within the social order and behaving according to a consistent set of rules. In dreams, however, the dominance of the governing cerebral hemisphere recedes and along with it the judgmental functions that we rely upon in a waking state. When that happens the logical structure of everyday existence is no longer present and the results are illogical, fanciful dreams that we accept at face value without dismissing them. . . .

Serial Killers' Loss of Logic

Parents, relatives, and friends may be interchangeable in one's dreams, and this can be a source of revelation to the dreamer or to a therapist about the person's assumptions and deeper emotions. However, these moments of insight about dreams are made not by the dreaming mind but by the waking mind or with the help of the therapist. The subordinate hemisphere has no such judgmental capability in the typical adult brain and must be analyzed by some logical entity. During the killing sprees, in the mind of the serial murderer, no such logical entity exists for any extended period of time.

The half-dream/half-waking state that mixes memories and terrors with reality is a true episodic state for the serial killer with a limbic dysfunction or with other symptoms. The aspects of dreams intrude themselves upon waking reality without warning, and the killer finds himself in a world of his own terror-filled fantasies with no basis for determining whether he is dreaming or waking. It is all the same to him. And as in dreams in which people replace people and identities become confused, the delusional or hallucinatory state of the serial killer confuses individuals from the killer's past, such as parents or siblings, with the victim who has just crossed his path or entered his car. As the killer's frenzy silently builds before he springs the trap, he has locked himself firmly into a dream world and the victim before him has no identity whatsoever, except for the identity his mind has already imposed.

The physiological reaction that trips the dream/delusion mechanism can be triggered by an event in the real world. . . .

Bundy's Brain

For Ted Bundy, it was the sight of a pretty coed who aroused a frenzy of sexual feelings. However, Bundy had been rejected by just such a woman. Her confidence in her good looks, and her demeanor, which exuded a belief in her own self-worth, terrified Bundy at the very moment it aroused him. He hated her and lusted after her at the same time, and the two feelings intertwined and became one. He needed to dominate such a woman and destroy the power that had rejected him. To do so excited him sexually and stimulated his entire body. That became the trip wire for the part of Ted Bundy's brain that was out of control. Already trolling for victims, his arm in a cast in a feigned demonstration of weakness, he played upon the very aspects of the woman's self-confidence to entrap her. And as a dialogue between Bundy and his victim was established and he felt the woman being lured into his web, he became more and more aroused. The emotional force that was surging in his brain became more powerful and spiraled him to the next phase of the crime. And at the moment of triumph, when she was beside him in the car, he had her. A quick succession of blows to render her helpless, and Bundy was at the penultimate stage of the crime. Now that she was unconscious and near death, he would rape her—sex and his hatred of this woman had become one and the same—and then he killed her. Now, at the post-mortem of the crime, he was filled with self-loathing. His acts of violence had proved nothing, and he had a body to dispose of. He buried her and placed a late phone call to Liz Kendall in a desperate effort to lurch back to reality and to establish himself as a living being. And this pattern continued through the lives of more than thirty victims in Seattle, more in Colorado, another set of victims in Utah, and a final set of murders in Florida.

For John Gacy the impetus was that he had to destroy something he felt was active and cancerous inside himself. The ritual of slaughtering the young men he encountered was a reenactment of a terrible dream in which his father was slaughtering the boy John Gacy that he had grown to despise for his own weakness and perceived lack of masculinity. Gacy assumed both his father's role and his own role at one and the same time. And, as in a waking dream, his damaged brain allowed the physical playing out of the self-torture and hatred that had been stored in memory since Gacy was a young child. The feelings of helplessness and rage and the childhood need to destroy what was most painful came to the surface when Gacy brought his victims back to his house. But in his own despondence after the failure to achieve a true release from the pain, he buried his victims in the soft mud under his house.

More Than One Cause

Although Gacy, Bundy, Charles Manson, Lucas, Kallinger, Bianchi, Bobby Joe Long, and the others all evidence at least one trip mechanism in each of their particular behaviors, the truth is that there is usually more than one set of causes at work in the individual. If that were not the case, anyone with damage to his limbic brain or to his hypothalamus would automatically become a serial murderer. We know that the brain is a far more resilient organ than that and has a compensating mechanism that tries to correct for deficiencies. If a person has gone for many hours without eating and begins to react with inappropriate violence toward those around him, his normal sense of social order, though diminished, will respond to a direct query such as "Don't you know what you're doing?" or "Why did you do that?" The fear of disturbing the equilibrium of one's family or of losing one's job also serves to counterbalance temper tantrums or violent outbursts. Even alcoholics who are pushed to the brink, if their upbringing has been supportive, can still rebound and benefit from treatment or therapy. . . .

Paradoxically, it is the brain's gyroscopic capacity to right itself and compensate for damage and error that constructs the matrix out of which serial killers are produced. It is a form of defense mechanism which is so complex that when fully operational has turned the individual into a violent predator of other living creatures. To appreciate how a defense mechanism can evolve into a destructively aggressive behavior, one has to appreciate that the prime directive of any living organism is to survive. This is a type of biological algorithm, a biochemical reaction that is basic to the distinction between living and nonliving matter. Reproduction is a manifestation of the biological need to survive: the reproduction of genetic material mirror-like fashion to guarantee the development of another living host for it. Thus, sexual arousal is a primal chemical reaction.

Self-defense in all of its forms is also a manifestation of the need to survive. Therefore fear, violence, rage, flight, terror, and panic are all chemically induced reactions that exist in almost all living creatures in one form or another. They are a part of the compensation process that keeps living entities from simply blundering into death. In human beings, the primal self-defense reactions were socialized very early in the evolution of the species—at about the same time verbal language was developed—so that humans could function in groups and survive the elements and their natural predators in nature. . . .

The behaviors that serial killers display, although they are ultimately self-destructive, are the behaviors that their brains have developed to compensaste for the levels of physiological and emotional damage they have incurred. If the child has not received the sensory stimulation he requires and therefore has not established a boundary between himself and the outside world, the brain will compensate, but a vital component will be missing. A portion of the infant's brain never develops to the point where it can exercise regulatory control over primal emotions. The individual may become all-encompassing and see only himself and nothing else. He recognizes no physical limitations to himself and seems literally to "walk over everyone around him." He has no sense of hurting anyone else, feels no remorse, and shows no sympathy. When the behavior is at its most extreme, the individual exists in his own universe, isolated from the rest of humanity. He may perform violent acts upon small animals at first and ultimately upon people. His own rage is an extension of himself, not capable of being held in check by the part of his brain that never developed properly. . . .

A Defense Mechanism

A close examination of the histories of each of the serial killers researched shows that what society called criminal behavior was in reality a type of defense mechanism against what was confronting him. . . . We perceive him to be a monster, and of course he perceives himself to be almost nonhuman when measured against the normal people he sees around him. Yet, tragically, what he has developed into was not entirely of his own choosing. In order to survive, as Charles Manson has described himself, he had to make a virtue of a necessity and embrace the creature he had become. Thus, in Manson's violent world of chaos, where bad was good and good was bad, his psyche's response was "helter-skelter," the absolute devastation of the external world in a mirror image of the devastation of his own internal universe.

"Killer cults were born and nurtured in the comfort zone of America and are now victimizing it at will."

Satanic Cults Influence Serial Killers

Maury Terry

Maury Terry is an award-winning investigative reporter. The following viewpoint is taken from his 1987 book, *The Ultimate Evil*. In his book, Terry contends that satanic beliefs inspired both the 1970s Son of Sam killings in New York City and the 1960s Charles Manson killings in Los Angeles. According to Terry, many serial murders can be linked to the philosophy of a satanic group called the Process. Although the Process has splintered and parts of it have gone underground, Terry believes its members are behind many brutal killings occurring in the United States today.

As you read, consider the following questions:

1. How do satanic groups recruit members, according to the author?
2. What are the beliefs of the Process, in the author's view?
3. What leads Terry to believe that satanic cults are still operating in the U.S.?

There has been no census of the number of witchcraft and satanic cults active today in the United States. But the number is certainly in the thousands. Fortunately, the majority of these groups are benign, or "white," witchcraft covens, as they are often termed. But not all of them.

The witchcraft phenomenon began in Europe in the Middle Ages. In time, it surfaced in America, and anti-occult hysteria triggered the infamous Salem trials in Massachusetts in 1692.

Legends and beliefs concerning the powers of witches abound in folklore, and to many in the United States, the stories are just that—fables fueled by superstition. But there are believers, and those who practice the "old religion," as it is sometimes called. Some devotees operate alone, others join a coven. In total, there are many thousands of witchcraft advocates casting their spells in modern America.

As indicated, the preponderance of these are relatively harmless. Purists point out that a murderous devil cult should not be confused with the numerous benign covens which dot the landscape of the United States.

To an extent, that admonition is accurate. Not everyone who smokes marijuana advances to heroin addiction; nor does every social drinker become an alcoholic. But just as addicts are initiated on pot and alcoholics emerge from the cocktail party set, hardcore satanists frequently earn their stripes in the lower ranks of occult curiosity or "white" witchcraft.

Homage to Satan

Witchcraft, per se, is not illegal, and most covens ostensibly operate within the law. There has been an ambitious public relations effort undertaken in recent years to present witchcraft in an acceptable light. But the fact remains that while some groups claim to celebrate "nature," many others pay homage to Satan. That is their tradition; and they honor it.

A typical coven consists of thirteen members, but that number varies often. The group will meet regularly, usually at the full moon. These gatherings are known as "sabbats." Several times each year, according to witchcraft calendars, Grand Sabbats—major festivals—are celebrated. Grand Sabbats occur, for example, on All Hallows Eve—October 31—and on April 30—Walpurgis Night.

For the purpose of blasphemy, some major holidays coincide with important Roman Catholic holy days. Others mark the dates of old pagan festivals.

As mentioned, covens pay homage to Satan, just as traditional religions honor God. Accordingly, in defiance of the Catholic Church, the concept of the Black Mass evolved during the Middle Ages. In the Black Mass, satanic prayers were substituted for

222

those contained in the Catholic service; the Lord's Prayer was recited backwards; crosses were inverted; black vestments were worn; chalices and hosts stolen from churches were used in the rituals. . . .

Animals, such as dogs and cats, were sacrificed to Satan and their blood drunk in fertility rites or for other purposes. Some covens, questing for the ultimate sacrifice, offered humans to the devil.

Some contemporary witches, trying to distance themselves from their own traditions, discount the volumes written concerning the Black Mass and human sacrifice. Others readily acknowledge that such rites existed at one time. Some will even concede that militant, drug-ridden, hard-core Satanist covens active today have carried those practices into the 1980s.

It is that element that is of concern in this narrative. . . .

Initially, I was surprised to learn that most of the occult writings I perused were bereft of any substantial information about the cult. Most references were vague. Later, through extensive field research and personal contacts with reliable sources in California, and elsewhere, I was able to complete the biographical picture that is painted here.

Among my advisers was Ed Sanders, author of *The Family*—a superb study of the Manson clan—who graciously sat with me in a wild blueberry patch in an upstate New York meadow one summer afternoon and significantly added to my knowledge of the shadowy cult.

Sacrificed to Satan

Some authorities estimate that 50,000 humans are sacrificed to Satan annually, including babies bred purely for such a purpose. Others dispute the claims, calling it impossible to gather accurate statistics on ritualistic crimes.

But satanism is increasing so rapidly some have labeled it the fastest rising criminal element in the country.

Bernard K. DeRemer, *The Spotlight*, October 2, 1989.

We convened in the open air at Sanders' request. "It's too distasteful a topic to go into anywhere else but out here—where the setting and surroundings are as far removed from what those people stand for as we can get," he explained.

Sanders is not given to hyperbole. He is a thoughtful, sincere man; and an accomplished writer, poet and musician. His band, the Fugs, became well known in the late 1960s, and the group still plays reunion tours on occasion. Sanders spent eighteen months probing the grotesque world of Charlie Manson while researching *The Family*, and he hasn't forgotten what it was like. Neither, for that matter, have other sources—who are still fearful of the group—erased the memories of those days when they came to know of the Process.

The Origins of the Process

The following is an overview of the organization which I, and others, consider to have been one of the most dangerous satanic cults in America.

The Process, as far as is known, has now officially splintered, and its offspring—while still active—have gone underground. But before the Process divided, it spread seeds of destruction throughout the United States. Those spores were carried on winds of evil across the 1970s and into the present. The terror still reigns, with far-flung subsidiary groups united by the sins of the father.

But in the beginning, there was a man and a woman; and they came together in London, England. The year was 1963. . . .

Satanic cults lurk in various guises, and their recruitment techniques also differ. Some harvest via pseudo-legitimate counseling or "self-awareness" groups—actually fronts—which frequently flourish around campuses or military bases or in major cities.

An unsuspecting youth, already possessed of a mind-set ripe for manipulation, will enroll for a series of courses, seminars or therapy sessions allegedly intended to put his or her life into focus. What follows is a period of careful screening and weeding out. In time, the chosen few find themselves drawn deeper and deeper into a web of deceit, rejection of traditional values, and conversion to the twisted beliefs of the group's leaders.

At its outset, the Process was one of these groups.

The Process Church of the Final Judgment was born in London, England, in 1963-64, the Damien-child of two ranking members of the Church of Scientology who split with the parent organization following some philosophical differences with the teachings of L. Ron Hubbard, the developer of Scientology.

The founding couple of the Process, Robert Moore and Mary Anne MacLean, had met while receiving advanced training at the Hubbard Institute of Scientology on London's Fitzroy Street. Divorcing Hubbard, they married one another and adopted the cult name of DeGrimston for themselves. . . .

In late 1967, Robert DeGrimston published a book, *As It Is*, which spelled out the Process's philosophy:

> Christ said: Love thine enemy. Christ's enemy was Satan and Satan's enemy was Christ. Through love, enmity is destroyed. Through love, saint and sinner destroy the enmity between them. Through love, Christ and Satan have destroyed their enmity and come together for the End. Christ to judge, Satan to execute the judgment.

The key to this treatise is contained in the sentence which says that Christ and Satan have joined forces to bring about the end of the world. Christ, according to the Process, was employing Satan as a hit man. So worshipping Satan was akin to worshipping Christ. And killing in the name of Satan was actually killing for Christ: a divine mission.

Naturally, DeGrimston was thought by Process members to be Christ, and they, in adoring Satan, were the agents of God working under divine orders to save the world from itself by hastening the day of the Second Coming. In the end, the cult would survive to build a new world of satanic glory.

A Real and Growing Menace

On September 8, 1985, Sean Sellers, a high school student in Oklahoma City, calmly entered a local Circle K convenience store and shot the clerk to death with a .357 Magnum revolver. No money was taken. Almost six months later, he murdered his mother and stepfather as they lay sleeping.

When Sellers was arrested, on a tip, police discovered occult books in his room, including *The Satanic Bible*. . . . The specter of diabolists on midnight prowl is no longer merely the staple of horror fiction, but a real and growing menace that needs to be taken seriously by all Americans.

John Kenneth Weiskittel, *The New American*, June 5, 1989.

From the Bible, the signs of the Second Coming were evident: the fires of Armageddon, death, chaos and confusion. The Process firmly believed its divine duty was to hasten the arrival of the Final Days—and bastardizing the Bible told them how to do it. This was a blueprint for murder, butchery and other crime cloaked in religious justification.

She disappeared from a nighttime street in Oceanside, Long Island, on March 26, 1985. She was just nineteen. It was a Tuesday evening and she'd come from a girlfriend's home and was walking along a side road to her job at a nearby Burger King. Across the street from Burger King, at Nathan's, it was "bike night," a Tuesday ritual. Although it was just 7:40 p.m., the weekly leathered hordes were revving their Harleys in the parking lot.

But Jacqueline Martarella wouldn't see the bikers; would never reach her job. Jacqueline Martarella vanished in the early spring darkness.

As soon as I read of the disappearance, I suspected foul play. I knew Jacqueline wasn't a runaway. Nothing fit. But I knew more than that. I was already involved in a probe of possible cult complicity in another disappearance and a murder, both involving young girls, in the village of Lynbrook, a few miles from Ocean-side. When the Martarella disappearance was announced, I, and some in law enforcement, thought the cases were probably linked.

In early March, Harry Daley, a writer and stunt coordinator for films, called me at my new residence in Jersey. Aware of what was going on around his community, he asked if I'd come to Long Island to look into the cases. Daley was a friend of Denis Dillon, the Nassau County district attorney. Dillon, Harry said, was concerned about the matter and would be willing to discuss the situation with me. And so I went.

The Fusco Murder

Two teenagers, Kelly Morrissey and Theresa Fusco, had recently vanished from the streets of Lynbrook in the early evening hours. Morrissey, fifteen, was still missing, but Fusco's body was later found buried beneath pallets in a wooded area near the Long Island Rail Road tracks in Lynbrook. She'd been raped, strangled and dumped nude in the cold November air. She lay there a month before her body was discovered. Theresa Fusco was sixteen. . . .

I told Dillon I'd like to visit the Fusco scene, and he gave Harry and me directions to find it. At the site, we examined the pallets which had covered Theresa's body. On one, there was faded writing in Magic Marker. The word "Rush" appeared—the name of a heavy-metal rock group. Beside it was a symbol the group used: the satanic pentagram. On another part of the same panel, a message was written. Some words were obliterated, but what we could decipher said: "Sex . . . No . . . virgin devil . . . allow."

We didn't have to be hit over the head. For years I'd known that the rape of a young "virgin" was an important satanic ritual—and so was murder.

Pulling the planks from the pallet, we turned them over to Dillon.

"Somewhere out here, there's probably a cult working," I said. "I find it hard to believe she just happened to be covered with a pallet that had that crap written on it by accident. But maybe, on a long shot, it is a coincidence. I think we have to learn more."

Dillon readily agreed. He wasn't prepared to call it a cult killing either. But Harry Daley, who'd carefully scouted the village of Lynbrook, pointed out that an unusual abundance of satanic and Nazi graffiti peppered certain hangouts in the town. He thought there was significance in that fact, and there was. Much of the graffiti was sophisticated, and the Nazi connection was important. I was beginning to envision a link to the biker crowd in Oceanside. Many bike gangs are satanically oriented, a fact not lost on the Process and Charles Manson, both of whom actively sought to recruit bikers as the advance troops of Armageddon. . . .

And then Jacqueline Martarella was found. Like Theresa Fusco, she was nude, ligature-strangled and apparently raped. Her body was found in late April 1985 hidden in tall reeds adjacent to the seventeenth hole of the Woodmere Country Club in exclusive Lawrence, Long Island, about five miles west of the spot from which she disappeared. . . .

Harry Daley, "interfering" in police business, was asking questions in the neighborhood surrounding the golf course. He learned from a mailman that behind the course, in a secluded wooden section about six hundred yards from where the body was found, a small cave sat in a clearing. The postman had never looked inside, but he thought we might be interested in knowing it existed. We were.

Inside the cave, which was actually an abandoned root cellar from an estate that had stood on the property years before, we found shocking evidence. The walls were emblazoned with satanic symbols: pentagrams, upturned crosses and other satanic slogans. Outside the cellar, which resembled a bunker, were a white half glove and leotard undergarment that Jacqueline's father, Marty Martarella, soon identified to us as "very similar" to articles Jacqueline owned. When he looked in his daughter's room, her "similar" clothing was nowhere to be found.

"Now we can make a pretty good call on why she was taken about five miles from where they nabbed her," I later said to Harry.

"You mean they took her to that place, killed her there—if she wasn't already dead—and then just drove her out onto the golf course and hid the body in the reeds."

"It looks that way," I agreed. "And they left their calling card near the body."

"These cops have got to be blind," Harry said. "They missed all of this."

Satan Will Return

But the satanic cellar contained another secret, one we ourselves missed at first. It was buried in a pile of leaves on the musty dirt floor. It was a hand-printed note—one composed by a serious Satanist. It was a bastardization of the book of Revelation. . . . Gingerly picking up the damp, aging paper, we read the note:

> Woe to you O earth and sea, for the devil sends his beast with wrath. Let he who has understanding reckon the number of the beast. For it is a human number. Its number is six-hundred-sixty-six.

"Good God," Harry whispered. . . .

"This is big-league stuff," I replied. "And one of their favorite symbols, too. Take a look over your head. That's not General MacArthur up there."

Harry peered upward through the gloom, and the message really began to sink in. Next to a black pentagram and a painted upturned cross were the chilling words: I WILL RETURN.

"That's Satan's return to earth," I said quietly. "Like the note, it's a warning. . . .

Their numbers are growing [and] there is no insulating Middle America. . . . The killer cults were born and nurtured in the comfort zone of America and are now victimizing it at will.

God Help the World

Manson's haunting testimony and a later warning from [Son of Sam killer] David Berkowitz echo loudly across the years. Two statements, made on opposite coasts nearly a decade apart. Yet the dire message is the same.

"What about your children?" Manson challenged a Los Angeles courtroom as the 1970s began. "You say there are just a few? There are many, many more, coming in the same direction. They are running in the streets—*and they are coming right at you!*"

In New York, Berkowitz would write: *"There are other 'Sons' out there—God help the world."*

Sometimes, late at night, one can know the truth of their words. Through the darkness, a foreboding wail can be heard. Faintly at first, then more insistent and nearer, the reverberations ring through urban canyons, roll across the shadowed byways of Scarsdale and Bel Air, and are carried on the night wind to the remote reaches of rural countrysides.

It is a mournful, curdling cry.

It is the sound of America screaming.

a critical thinking activity

Understanding Words in Context

Readers occasionally come across words which they do not recognize. And frequently, because they do not know a word or words, they will not fully understand the passage being read. Obviously, the reader can look up an unfamiliar word in a dictionary. However, by carefully examining the word in the context in which it is used, the word's meaning can often be determined. A careful reader may find clues to the meaning of the word in surrounding words, ideas, and attitudes.

Below are excerpts from the viewpoints in this chapter. In each excerpt, one or two words are printed in italics. Try to determine the meaning of each word by reading the excerpt. Under each excerpt you will find four definitions for the italicized word. Choose the one that is closest to your understanding of the word.

Finally, use a dictionary to see how well you have understood the words in context. It will be helpful to discuss with others the clues which helped you decide on each word's meaning.

1. While some witchcraft groups claim to celebrate "nature," many others pay *HOMAGE* to Satan.

    HOMAGE means:

    a) money   c) themselves
    b) tribute   d) nothing

2. Hundreds of thousands of individuals filled with hatred populate this country. They are people without a conscience, and they hurt—sometimes kill—others without *REMORSE*.

    REMORSE means:

    a) guilt   c) violence
    b) happiness   d) fun

3. Bundy first followed a woman and then captured her. Next, a quick succession of blows to render his victim helpless, and Bundy was at the *PENULTIMATE* stage of the crime. Now he would rape and kill her.

   PENULTIMATE means:

   a) unsuccessful   c) next to the last
   b) first   d) useless

4. Questions still remain about the truth and accuracy of Lucas' early confessions, which he later *RECANTED*. Some of them are so graphic that even the police refused to believe that what he told them, before he changed his mind, was true.

   RECANTED means:

   a) revealed   c) withdrew
   b) checked   d) laughed at

5. I was surprised to learn that most of the occult writings I read, which were supposed to have described all cults, were *BEREFT* of any information about the Process cult.

   BEREFT means:

   a) lacking   c) critical
   b) complete   d) full

6. Mentally-ill criminals constitute an increasingly large part of the *ABERRANT* segment of our population.

   ABERRANT means:

   a) calm   c) contented
   b) deviant   d) normal

7. The creation of serial killers takes place in a cultural *MILIEU* which has glorified violence as an appropriate and manly response to frustration.

   MILIEU means:

   a) vacuum   c) movie
   b) emotion   d) environment

8. Our cultural *PREDILECTION* for violence must have been enhanced by the television coverage of the Vietnam War, which brought real bloodletting and killing into every American living room.

   PREDILECTION means:

   a) uses   c) strategies
   b) taste   d) mission

Periodical Bibliography

The following articles have been selected to supplement the diverse views presented in this chapter.

Garry Abrams — "Portrait of a Mass Killer," *Los Angeles Times*, January 12, 1988.

American Atheist — "Bimbos for Satan," May 1989. Available from American Atheists Inc., PO Box 140195, Austin, TX 78714-0195.

James N. Baker — "Death on the Playground," *Newsweek*, January 30, 1989.

Vern L. Bullough — "On Ted Bundy, Pornography, and Capital Punishment," *Free Inquiry*, Spring 1989. Available from the Council for Democratic and Secular Humanism, 3159 Bailey Ave., Buffalo, NY 14215.

Christianity Today — "Ritual Killings Have Satanic Overtones," September 2, 1988.

Cristina Garcia — "Casting a Net at Green River," *Time*, July 27, 1987.

Jon D. Hull — "Brutal Treatment, Vicious Deeds," *Time*, October 19, 1987.

Nick Jordan — "Spare the Rod, Spare the Child," *Psychology Today*, June 1989.

Kirk Kidwell — "The Crime of the Nineties," *The New American*, June 5, 1989.

Wayne King — "Police Departments Try to Pick Up on Satanism," *The New York Times*, July 16, 1989.

Jerry Kirk — "Ted Bundy Shows Us the Crystallizing Effect of Pornography," *Los Angeles Times*, February 8, 1989.

Richard Lacayo — "Master of Cant and Recant," *Time*, January 12, 1987.

Jeff Meer — "Murder in Mind," *Psychology Today*, March 1987.

Stephen G. Michaud — "The FBI's New Psyche Squad," *The New York Times Magazine*, October 26, 1986.

Tom Morganthau — "Manson," *Newsweek*, July 3, 1989.

231

What Policies Would Reduce Violence?

Chapter Preface

Since experts have widely varying opinions on what factors contribute to the problem of violence, it is not surprising that the solutions they propose to reduce violence differ widely also. One view is that the U.S. suffers from violence because its justice system fails to punish criminals and to send the message that violent crime will not be tolerated. According to writer Robert James Bidinotto, the U.S. justice system no longer punishes violent crime effectively. Bidinotto points to numerous cases in which violent criminals have received light sentences because of plea-bargaining arrangements, or have been released early and then committed new crimes. For example, a Massachusetts man convicted of rape in 1981 spent only three days in jail before being transferred to a halfway house. Bidinotto writes, "That surely taught him an encouraging lesson about the justice system. In 1984 he was arrested for burglary and another rape—and became the prime suspect in seven other attacks on women." Failing to punish criminals, Bidinotto contends, amounts "to playing Russian Roulette with innocent human lives." He advocates establishing fixed sentences for crimes, ranging from imprisonment to the death penalty, as a way of reducing violence.

An opposing view is that focusing on punishment is inadequate because such a focus does not address the social conditions that lead to violence. Tony Bouza, the Minneapolis chief of police from 1980 to 1988 argues, "The insistent calls for more cops, tougher judges, bigger jails, and more macho prosecutors grows shriller. Our Praetorian Guards have never been bigger, stronger, or more efficient, but they're losing." The reason, according to Bouza, is that such policies fail to consider the existence of an underclass—impoverished minorities excluded from the mainstream of American life. He maintains, "Solving the problems of crime, drugs, violence, guns, and urban terror will mean clearing the swamp of poverty and redirecting the funds to programs that ensure education, jobs, housing, income, social service programs, inclusion, and the prospect of making it for America's poor and desperate." To reduce violence, he believes the U.S. must make a commitment to provide better lives for all its people and must increase social spending on programs to fight poverty.

The authors in the following chapter consider several policies they believe could reduce violence in America.

"A ban on handguns is the most effective means of controlling . . . violence."

Gun Control Would Reduce Violence

George Napper

George Napper is the commissioner of the Department of Public Safety in Atlanta, Georgia. He is a former president of the National Organization of Black Law Enforcement Executives. In the following viewpoint, he argues that police officers' jobs have become more difficult because drug traffickers and mentally unstable people have easy access to guns. By instituting a waiting period before people could buy guns, the police could check a person's background, he argues. Napper believes that such a policy would reduce violence.

As you read, consider the following questions:

1. What types of guns are police encountering on the streets, according to the author?
2. Why does the author believe current gun laws are insufficient?
3. What types of violence does Napper believe a waiting period would eliminate?

George Napper, "Firearms Trafficking and Drug Trafficking," prepared testimony before the Subcommittee on the Constitution of the Senate Committee on the Judiciary, August 2, 1988.

I am a law enforcement administrator in Atlanta, a pre-dominantly black city. I am not an objective observer; rather I am one who is very much involved and concerned. I am concerned when I see the disproportionate number of social ills and violent crimes which occur in the black community. I am concerned with the aura of violence which typifies some of our neighborhoods, and which is largely rooted in the accessibility of guns. I am concerned that the leading cause of death among young black males 15-24 is homicide and that most of these are committed with firearms. . . .

Something must be done to keep guns out of the wrong hands. The wrong hands I speak of are those of the depressed employee, distressed family member, petty criminal, truant student, youth gang member, 12-year-old crack house lookout, vicious drug ring member, and the individual drug entrepreneur.

Guns and Drugs

Very alarming and of immediate concern to me, is the ever increasing evidence being generated nationally that the link between firearms trafficking and drug trafficking is becoming more solidly fused. On the one hand, weapons are being acquired daily by drug traffickers to protect their supplies and territories. On the other hand, weapons are directly traded out for drugs or sold at tremendous profits that in turn are used to purchase drugs locally, nationally, and internationally.

In Atlanta, my Narcotics Squad rarely conducts a raid now during which weapons are not found. Like other cities in the country we are repeatedly encountering drug traffickers who have increased both the quality and quantity of weapons they use. No longer are we confronted with Saturday night specials. Instead the trafficker is well armed with expensive handguns, rifles, and UZIs that most often are obtained through legal outlets. We frequently find them in the hands of young, impoverished and poorly educated adolescents with whom they merely become thoughtlessly used tools of death and injury. This is a particular problem in Atlanta's black community which includes some 43 project housing complexes.

Inconsistent State Laws

Nationally variable gun control laws found from state to state perpetuate both interstate and international gun and drug trafficking. A recent Atlanta raid yielded close to 40 guns destined for New York. Guns purchased legally in Florida and Ohio have been traced to Washington DC, New York City, and the Dominican Republic. Guns purchased in Texas have surfaced in Washington DC, Los Angeles, Jamaica, and the Philippines. Guns purchased in my own state of Georgia have surfaced both in Washington DC and New York City. Not surprising is that in the majority of cases the weapons were traced to drug traffickers. It logically follows then that as the drug investment increases so does the perceived need of increased protection.

Less dramatic but also important is the impact of inconsistent laws in our homes and work places. An incident occurred across the street from my office. At 8:30 a.m. on the morning of April 24, 1988 an employee of a public utility opened fire with a .38 caliber pistol. After shooting her supervisor and manager, she turned the gun on herself and committed suicide. Passed over for a promotion, the woman had submitted her notice of resignation earlier in the week. The afternoon before the shooting, the employee bought the .38 caliber snubnose revolver for $135.00 in a neighboring jurisdiction which does not require a waiting or cooling off period. Neighbors later described the woman as a "nice respectable lady." She had been employed by the utility for 8 years.

Though the incident occurred in the Atlanta jurisdiction, it was made possible by the lack of a waiting period in a neighboring location. And that points out the need for national legislation. The patchwork quilt approach has never worked, and it never will.

The guns/drugs connection is one way that we can attack the problem. I believe that a ban on handguns is the most effective means of controlling the violence associated with them. I do not

Wiley. Reprinted with permission of *The San Francisco Examiner.* © 1989 The San Francisco Examiner

believe, however, that I will see such a ban in my lifetime. A less effective but next best step is the establishment of a national waiting period before handgun purchase. In 1981 the Attorney General's Task Force on Violent Crime urged the adoption of such a waiting period, as a part of a larger program of strong federal handgun laws. In March 1987, major law enforcement executives were polled regarding the waiting period for handgun purchases. There was unanimous agreement among those responding that such legislation should be supported.

The waiting period serves two purposes. It provides time for law enforcement officials to conduct background investigations and allows for a cooling off period for potential handgun buyers. The City of Atlanta has had a 15-day waiting period since 1980. This ordinance allows us to deny applications on grounds of criminal record or mental instability. Often the paper work is completed and the handgun can be purchased before the waiting period is over. The 15 days, however, allows us to complete investigations even during peak periods. In the case of history of prior mental illness, it also permits us to get a statement from the treating physician or psychologist regarding the competence of the applicant to own a handgun.

Expanding RICO

I strongly support the adoption of a national waiting period as one means to keep guns from falling into the wrong hands. I realize however, that this is not a panacea. Therefore, I also strongly support the expansion of RICO [Racketeer Influence and Corrupt Organizations Act] to include firearms offenses. RICO has been an effective means of combatting other types of crime because it invokes the power of the purse. It does so by reducing the racketeer's profit while bolstering the resources of the law enforcement agencies involved.

We in law enforcement are in a dilemma. We want to make every street safe for walking or driving day or night. We want to return the sounds of children playing ball and tag to every park. We want to return every parking place in apartment and housing complexes to the law abiding resident.

We're making every effort to do just that. However, as long as the potpourri of gun laws in this country allows our agencies to be outnumbered and outgunned; and as long as we continue to allow our officers to be at maximum risk each day they're on the beat, we can not realistically expect to win and provide you and all of our citizens the total protection [they] deserve.

"Of all the gun laws enacted in the past 10 to 20 years . . . not one city, not one state, not one nation, has experienced a reduction in crime rates."

Gun Control Would Not Reduce Violence

National Rifle Association

The National Rifle Association (NRA) is an organization of gun collectors, hunters, police officers, and others interested in firearms. It has long been a highly influential lobbying group in Congress. In the following viewpoint, the NRA argues that past gun control laws have failed to reduce violent crime. The NRA believes that gun control only takes guns away from law-abiding citizens, while it does nothing to stop criminals, who are unlikely to obey the law and register their guns.

As you read, consider the following questions:

1. What two examples do gun control advocates cite as proof that gun control is beneficial, according to the NRA? What is wrong with these two examples?
2. Why does the NRA contend that many people would disobey a gun control law?
3. What policy does the author advocate to reduce violent crime?

From *Ten Myths About Gun Control,* a pamphlet published by the National Rifle Association of America, 1988. Reprinted by permission.

"The only way to discourage the gun culture is to remove the guns from the hands and shoulders of people who are not in the law enforcement business."

—*The New York Times,*
September 24, 1975

That editorial conclusion by the nation's most influential news journal, one noted for its advocacy of individual liberties, represents the absolute extreme in the firearms controversy—that no citizen can be trusted to own any kind of firearm. This expressed attitude is particularly ironic since the overwhelming majority of the 60 million American firearms owners have done nothing to deserve such a sweeping condemnation. It is the product of a series of myths which—through incessant repetition—has been mistaken for truth. These myths are being exploited to generate fear and mistrust of the decent and responsible Americans who own firearms.

Gun Laws Do Not Reduce Crime

The greatest myth perpetrated by the advocates of repressive gun laws is that such laws reduce crime. They do not.

No empirical study of the effectiveness of gun laws has shown any positive effect—although, to the dismay of the prohibitionists, such studies have shown a negative effect. That is, in areas having lower levels of private firearms ownership, the robbery rates are almost invariably higher, presumably because criminals are aware that their intended victims are less likely to have the means with which to defend themselves.

Further, of all the gun laws enacted in the past 10 to 20 years—each promised by its advocates to result in a reduction of crime—not one city, not one state, not one nation, has experienced a reduction in crime rates, nor even a reduced rate of crime growth in comparison to its neighboring cities and states and nations without such laws.

If gun laws worked, the proponents of such laws would gleefully cite examples of lessened crime. Instead, they uniformly blame the absence of tougher or wider spread measures for the failures of the laws they advocated. Or they cite denials of license applications as evidence the law is doing something beyond preventing honest citizens from being able legally to acquire a firearm. And they cite two jurisdictions' gun laws as "working"—Massachusetts and the District of Columbia. Yet crime in Washington rose dramatically between 1976, the year before its handgun ban took effect, and 1982, the year the city's voters adopted an NRA-endorsed mandatory penalty for misuse of guns in violent crimes. The violent crime rate rose 43% during those years, and the

239

murder rate rose 14%, while the national rates were rising 20% and 3%, respectively. After adopting a law to punish violent criminals, Washington's crime trends have been similar to the nation's.

With a crime rate rising twice as fast as big cities overall, Washington could not even claim a relative change in gun use in criminal violence. No wonder D.C. Police Chief Maurice Turner said, "What has the gun control law done to keep criminals from getting guns? Absolutely nothing. . . . [City residents] ought to have the opportunity to have a handgun."

Massachusetts is an odd example for anti-gunners to choose, since the much-vaunted Bartley-Fox law did not make it more difficult to obtain or carry any firearm legally; it made mandatory a one-year penalty for carrying a firearm without proper authority. For a time, gun-related street robberies rose, and non-gun crimes skyrocketed. Generally, however, the murder-rate fluctuations in the Bay State have mirrored national trends with other violent crimes increasing somewhat faster than in the nation as a whole.

Bureaucratic Red Tape

The major visible effect of gun laws is an obvious burden upon the law-abiding, who pay for the follies of their lawmakers by spending time, money and effort to overcome bureaucratic red tape in order to continue owning and enjoying their guns. Needless to say, the criminal does not bother with the niceties of obeying the law—for a criminal is by definition, someone who disobeys laws.

There is another visible effect of gun laws, one that burdens

Albert Wetzel. Reprinted by permission.

the tax-paying public. Gun laws must be administered by bureaucrats who provide nothing productive while draining the public treasury. Further, such laws are implemented and enforced by law enforcement officers who could far better spend their time and talents in the pursuit of criminals rather than in investigations of the law-abiding and prosecutions for victimless crimes such as simple possession or carrying of a firearm.

Furthermore, restrictive gun laws create a Catch-22 for victims of violent crime. Under court decisions, the police have no legal obligation to protect any particular individual, and under restrictive gun laws, it may be illegal for the person to protect himself. A citizen is thus in the position of having to give up effective self-protection or risk arrest if he or she successfully wards off a violent criminal. In Washington, D.C., according to the author and key supporter of their gun law, self-defense use of handguns has fallen 62% since the virtual handgun ban was put into effect.

Massive Noncompliance

But there is an invisible effect of gun laws that may prove far more important than the visible, direct costs—that is, the social costs of increasing numbers of normally law-abiding citizens disobeying unpopular, irritating or expensive gun laws. Such high social cost was paid during the era of the prohibition of alcohol when a significant portion, if not the majority of drinkers, simply ignored Federal law. That era produced a generation of scofflaws, and provided fertile ground for the growth of organized crime syndicates that plague the nation a half-century later.

The evidence that gun laws are creating scofflaws is evident to anyone willing to look. In New York City, there are fewer than 70,000 legally owned handguns, yet survey research suggests there are at least 750,000 handguns in the city, mostly in the hands of otherwise law-abiding citizens. In Chicago, a recent mandatory registration law has resulted in compliance by only a fraction of those who had previously registered their guns. The same massive noncompliance—not by criminals, whom no one expects will comply, but by the particular minority groups fearful of repression—is evident wherever stringent gun laws are enacted.

In exchange for such high costs, what have the nation's lawmakers achieved? Not an instance of a reduction in crimes of violence. There is evidence of increases in robberies and other offenses where potential victims are disarmed by governmental fiat.

Stiffer Penalties for Criminals

And laws addressed directly to the question of misuse do work. When stiff, certain punishment is levied upon those who misuse firearms—even when it is merely threatened—crime rates go down, particularly for predatory crimes like murder and robbery.

After adopting a mandatory penalty for using a firearm in the commission of a violent crime in 1975, Virginia's murder rate dropped 36% and robbery 24% in 12 years. South Carolina recorded a 37% murder rate decline between 1975 and 1987, and a 9% robbery rate drop, with a similar law. Other impressive declines in homicide rates were recorded in other states using mandatory penalties, such as Arkansas (down 32% in 13 years), Delaware (down 26% in 15 years), Montana (down 18% in 11 years), and Maryland (down 23% in 15 years). And Florida, despite the "Cocaine Cowboys" and rapid urban growth, and with eased handgun purchase and carry laws, saw its homicide rate drop 22% in 13 years (1974-1987).

Yet in none of these areas has the mandatory sentencing been fully implemented, due to the reluctance of prosecutors and judges to give up their discretionary authority. Thus far, such astounding reductions in crime are due mainly to the threat of punishment— once the criminals become convinced that they need to have no more fear of committing crimes with a gun than any other weapon, crime will again climb.

There is ample evidence that there is a solution to the crime problem, and a solution to the problem of criminal misuse of guns. That solution lies in the *promise*, not the mere threat, of swift, certain punishment. So long as the lawmakers refuse to apply that solution, and instead attempt to control crime by controlling law-abiding gun owners, the nation's problems with crime and criminals will only increase.

The Real Task

Our challenge: To reform and strengthen our federal and state criminal justice systems. We must bring about a sharp reversal in the trend toward undue leniency and "revolving door justice." We must insist upon speedier trials and upon punishments which are commensurate with the crimes. Rehabilitation should be tempered with a realization that not all can be rehabilitated.

The job ahead will not be an easy one. The longer gun control advocates distract the nation from this task by embracing that single siren song, the longer it will take and the more difficult our job will be.

"To punish the guilty . . . we must restore the equilibrium to our criminal justice system by building more prisons."

Imprisoning More Criminals Would Reduce Violence

Richard B. Abell

Richard B. Abell is assistant attorney general for the Office of Justice Programs, a division of the Department of Justice. In the following viewpoint, Abell argues that the cost of not imprisoning violent criminals is too high. Abell points out that many felons have been released early because of overcrowded prisons. The majority of these people then commit more crimes. He concludes that only by building more prisons and keeping more people in prisons will the U.S. be able to reduce violent crime.

As you read, consider the following questions:

1. Why have efforts to impose longer, tougher sentences on criminals failed, according to the author?
2. What does the author believe is misleading about sentencing statistics?
3. How does Abell arrive at the conclusion that the U.S. would save far more money by imprisoning people than it would spend on building more prisons?

Richard B. Abell, "The Compelling Economics of Prison Construction," *Human Events*, March 4, 1989. Reprinted with permission.

On Oct. 20, 1973, 28-year-old James Allen of Detroit fatally shot 17-year-old Steven Ellis Taylor in the chest. Allen was arrested three years later, convicted of second-degree murder, and after spending nine and a half months in jail, was sentenced to 15 to 30 years in a Michigan prison in March 1977.

James Allen had quite an impressive prior juvenile record at the time—breaking and entering, armed robbery, assault, and carrying a concealed weapon—all of which had resulted in probation or confinement in a state training school. Allen was paroled in December 1983 after serving only seven and a half years of his original 15 to 30-year sentence.

During a series of robberies in 1984, Allen and two other parolees killed at least four people and seriously wounded two others. After shooting one victim in the face, Allen is alleged to have told an accomplice: "That's the way you play the murder game—leave no witnesses." Allen was convicted of first- and second-degree murder for two of the killings and returned to prison once again, this time for life—we hope.

Criminals Unleashed on Society

Every day, other James Allens are being unleashed on an unsuspecting society, despite the public's demand to crack down on crime.

While 35 million felonies were reported to the FBI [Federal Bureau of Investigation] in 1986, some 1.8 million persons were arrested for those crimes, and only 35,000 were ultimately imprisoned. This translates roughly to a thousand reported offenses for every incarceration and only about two in 100 persons arrested ending up going to prison. In reality, even those "unlucky" few who do get imprisoned will, on average, serve less than one-half of their court-ordered sentence.

Why do the odds so favor the criminal? Obviously, the ascendance of the criminal rights lobby during the 1960s and '70s and the resultant institutionalization of procedural constraints to thwart arrest and conviction have had a major impact in keeping criminals out of prison.

This is confirmed by the fact that prison commitments for the most serious crimes, i.e. murder, non-negligent manslaughter, rape, robbery, aggravated assault, and burglary, dropped from 62 in 1960 to 23 by 1970 and had risen to only 25 by 1980. But, while Reagan-appointed judges have been imposing longer and tougher sentences, "one-man crime waves" are being released back into our communities every day simply because we do not have sufficient places to put them.

The public's demand for harsher punishment is being frustrated by simple arithmetic. Between 1981 and 1988, the number of felons sentenced to federal prisons increased by 92 per cent, reaching an all-time high of 48,300, but the federal prison system's design capacity stood at 29,000. Over the same period, state prison populations increased by 75 per cent, to 533,300, but these facilities had an estimated capacity to hold between 436,000-501,000 prisoners.

Local jails are feeling the crunch as well—operating at 98 per cent of capacity in 1987, up from 85 per cent in 1983. Over 11,250 inmates were being held in local facilities because of lack of federal and state prison space. Even though the opening of 138 new state prisons and the renovation and expansion of existing facilities between 1979 and 1984 increased total housing space by 29 per cent, the number of inmates grew by 45 per cent. . . .

Once legitimate alternatives to incarceration for offenders who posed little threat to the community and who showed likelihood of rehabilitation, such as probation, parole, and the granting of credits for good behavior while incarcerated, are now being routinely granted to dangerous felons as prison escape valves. While we appreciate the fact that our judicial system does a good job of protecting against innocent persons being unjustly imprisoned, we must question seriously why so few found guilty are actually incarcerated and why so many of them are let out early.

Truth in Punishment

If Americans seek to restore safety to our streets and security to our homes and schools, we must restore punishment for crime. We need "truth-in-sentencing," just as we have truth in labeling for foods. A sentence of 10 years should mean 10 years, and a sentence of life in prison should mean life in prison. Those guilty of violent crime should be removed from society and our criminal justice sytem should have as its primary goal the protection of innocent law-abiding citizens.

Allan Brownfeld, *Human Events*, April 22, 1989.

While the public is certainly the victim of these prison release policies, it is frequently an accomplice as well.

For example, when Michigan voters abolished "good time" credits for 80 serious types of crime in 1978, state prison populations began to swell. As a result, the state Department of Corrections was placed under court order to keep its prison population within a 95 per cent capacity ceiling. But, at the same time, the state's voters were forcing tougher and longer criminal sentencing; in 1980, they rejected a $300-million bond issue for prison construction.

The state legislature responded to the court order by enacting

245

the Prison Overcrowding Emergency Powers Act which provided most inmates with 90-day sentence reductions whenever the capacity ceiling was reached.

The act was triggered nine times between mid-1981 and the end of 1984, enabling 10,000 prisoners to get out up to 27 months earlier than they would have otherwise. But in defense of the policy, State Corrections Director Robert Brown was quoted to have said, "Don't complain about who I'm putting out there. Tell me who I should have put out . . . in their place."

The Danger of Releasing Prisoners

A study of over 5,700 Michigan parolees in 1983 revealed that the prisoners released early were worse risks to the community than those who served their minimum sentence. By Jan. 10, 1985, 794 had been convicted of new crimes. The early releasees were convicted of 70 per cent of the crimes against people, 80 per cent of the crimes against property, and 78 per cent of drug and other offenses. Of those convicted, 267 committed their crimes during a time they would have been in prison had it not been for the Prison Overcrowding Emergency Powers Act. James Allen was a typical example.

Tough mandatory sentencing is theoretically supposed to avert such instances, but with too few prison cells, we have created a dangerous game of musical chairs that all too often puts the criminal on the wrong side of the wall. . . .

Today, over one-third of the nation's adult probation population consists of persons convicted of felonies, as opposed to misdemeanors—the types of crimes for which probation was originally designed.

In fact, between 1974 and 1983, while the prison population increased by 48 per cent, the probation population rose by 63 per cent. Incredibly, during 1983, 21 states reported releasing into the community 578 inmates serving "life sentences," of which nearly 25 per cent had served time for a prior felony conviction. The median "life sentence" for those released from prison for the first time was a scant 10 years and nine months.

Repeat Offenders

What happens when felons are released? A study of felony probations in California's Los Angeles and Alameda counties in 1983 revealed that over a 40-month period, only 35 percent managed to stay clean (as far as official records could show). Fifty-three per cent of the group had official charges filed against them, and 75 per cent of their offenses involved burglary, robbery, or other violent crimes. Fifty-one per cent of the sample were ultimately re-convicted—18 per cent for homicide, rape, weapons offenses, assault, or robbery; and 34 per cent eventually were re-incarcerated.

News Item: Average time served in prison at record low

© 1985 THE BLADE KIRK

LIFE SENTENCE?!
BUT JUDGE, THAT
MEANS I WON'T BE
ELIGIBLE FOR
PAROLE UNTIL
5 O'CLOCK!!

ROTHCO

© Kirk/Rothco

In 1986, four out of five state prison inmates were repeat offenders, and over half of them had at least one prior conviction
for a violent offense. An astonishing 20 percent had been either
imprisoned or placed on probation six or more times.

While criminologists, sociologists, and a host of assorted experts
debate the causes of crime, the merits of alternative methods of
punishment, and incarceration costs, one thing is certain—society
will pay the price one way or another—either by accepting the
need to spend more on prison construction, or by continuing to
incur the financial and physical costs of thuggery.

Simply put, our prisons are so crowded that a decision to increase imprisonments will mean either that current prisoners will
have to be released to make room for the new or that new prisons
will have to be built.

The Cost of Prisons

At today's prices, adjusted for geographical variables and level
of security, a single prison bed space will cost between $50,000
and $100,000, including the cost of the land. By the time
maintenance costs are added, the cost to incarcerate one person
for a year runs about $25,000. . . .

The value of an imprisonment decision depends primarily on
the accuracy of how much public safety is purchased for $25,000.
But assessments of this nature can only be made if something is
known about the criminality of the offender population. Unfor-

tunately, the debate over prison construction has typically focused on the first and most visible portion of the equation, the costs of building and operating prisons, while the other side of the equation—confinement benefits—has been largely ignored.

A Misleading Profile

The most readily obtainable statistics on inmate criminality, sentencing statistics, provide a very misleading profile because the sentencing offense is usually the last entry on a long ledger of criminal activity. Remember, the infamous Al Capone was officially sentenced for tax evasion—his "first" offense.

Sentencing statistics do not reveal what offenses were committed by those who turned state's evidence and plea bargained a lesser offense, and because they do not accurately assess past offender behavior they provide little predictive data about their future behavior.

The latest sentencing statistics, which indicate that about 50 per cent of state prisoners and about 70 per cent of federal prisoners are incarcerated for nonviolent crimes, are frequently cited by opponents of prison construction as evidence that we have a wealth of candidates for less restrictive "alternative sentencing," such as community service, restitution, intensive supervision, and house arrest with electronic monitoring.

Although it makes intuitive sense that a drug addict who is convicted of a single property offense probably has committed additional crimes, an important study by the Rand Corp. for the Department of Justice tested this premise.

Based on interviews of a broad sample of prisoners in three states, the study found that those who were primarily burglars averaged between 76 and 118 burglaries per year, and that lesser larceners, such as shoplifters and pickpockets, averaged between 135 and 202 thefts per year. By aggregating the crimes committed outside the offender's conviction status, the study concluded that inmates averaged between 187 and 287 crimes per year, exclusive of drug deals.

The Rand research confirmed that the criminal justice system incarcerates a wide range of low-rate and high-rate offenders by finding that while about half of the offenders committed fewer than 15 crimes per year, 25 per cent committed more than 135 crimes per year, and 10 per cent committed as many as 600 crimes annually.

Taking these findings, in conjuction with the analysis of California's probationers and the inherent weaknesses in sentencing offense statistics, the offender population has been largely demystified. Placing those who should be in prison on probation or inappropriately assigning them to a less restrictive alternative sentence to save the costs of prison construction is a false economy when these less restrictive sentences permit offenders to murder, rape, or rapidly commit property offenses. Society pays for the decision not to imprison. But how much?

Even though calculating the cost of crime remains an inexact science, techniques are improving. The Office of Justice Programs' National Institute of Justice calculated total published expenditures on crime for 1983, including victim losses, criminal justice, commercial security costs, etc., and arrived at a figure of $99.8 billion.

By dividing the number of victimizations for that year, 42.5 million, into the expenditures, the researchers arrived at an average cost per crime of $2,300. Applying this figure to the information on offense rates gleaned from the Rand research (between 187 and 287 offenses per year), they concluded that a "typical inmate" is responsible for $430,000 in crimes costs per year, or 17 times the $25,000 cost of incarceration.

Sentencing just 1,000 more offenders to prison would obligate our correctional systems to an additional $25 million per year, but on the flip side, 107,000 crimes would be prevented with a net saving to society of $405 million. Not a bad investment return.

The decade of the 1960s and early 1970s brought about a shift in the dominant value of self-control to self-expression and with it the notion that community health and safety must take a back seat to the claims of individuals to do whatever they please, whenever they please, without regard to the social consequences. The zealous defenders of the supremacy of rights over obligations helped to cause our nation's crime rate to more than triple between 1963 and 1981.

Punish the Guilty

To embrace the facile liberal nostrum that community disintegration is the root cause of crime and that sending criminals to prison tends only to worsen their already anti-social behavior is to ignore the most basic of our Judeo-Christian values—that we each possess the God-given free will to make our own decisions about right or wrong, and that in turn each of us is responsible and accountable for our actions. In line with this most basic tenet, President George Bush pledged that, "If you do the crime, you're going to do the time."

The establishment of justice is the highest duty of government, and fairness and predictability are preeminent goals of a society that adheres to the rule of law. The first goal of our criminal justice system must be to protect the innocent; the second, to punish the guilty. If we wish to secure these intrinsic social priorities we must restore the equilibrium to our criminal justice system by building more prisons.

"The phenomenal growth in imprisonment has not reduced crime in our society."

Imprisoning More Criminals Would Not Reduce Violence

John Irwin and James Austin

Critics of the U.S. prison system often argue that only the Soviet Union and South Africa put more people in prison than does the U.S. John Irwin and James Austin, the authors of the following viewpoint, contend that imprisoning more criminals would be ineffective and costly. They write that many prison inmates are first-time offenders who become hardened criminals because of brutal conditions in prisons. They support imprisoning fewer people, and giving them shorter sentences as a way to reduce violence.

As you read, consider the following questions:

1. According to Irwin and Austin, why have prison populations skyrocketed?
2. Why do the authors believe the costs of imprisoning people are underestimated?
3. What are the benefits of shorter prisons terms, in the authors' opinion?

John Irwin and James Austin. *It's About Time: Solving America's Prison Crowding Crisis.* San Francisco: The National Council on Crime and Delinquency, 1987. Reprinted by permission.

Since 1880, the year criminologists began keeping track of prison populations, the number of people locked up in America's jails and prisons has steadily increased. A century ago, the daily imprisonment rate (i.e., the number of persons imprisoned on any given day) was about 120 per 100,000 citizens. Today it is more than 300 per 100,000—*almost a threefold increase.*

In absolute numbers, there are almost 530,000 people in state and federal prisons, 235,000 people in jail, and another 85,000 children in juvenile facilities. The total number of people confined, 850,000, would comprise a city larger than most of the nation's major cities including San Francisco, Cleveland, Denver, San Diego, and St. Louis. There are another 2.5 million adults and juveniles on probation or parole. On any given day, therefore, the criminal justice system supervises 3.2 million people. . . .

What is causing these recent phenomenal increases? It is not increases in the nation's population, which has grown by about 10 percent since 1975, nor crime rates, which have been fairly constant since 1977. Prison populations have more than doubled in the same period.

The evidence suggests that *sentencing legislation,* approved by elected officials, has resulted in courts sending a higher percentage of persons convicted of felonies to prison and for longer terms of imprisonment. . . .

The Million Dollar Cell

Most people are aware that prisons are expensive to build and operate, but few understand just how expensive. Indeed, previous estimates routinely cited by public officials have dramatically underestimated the amounts of money spent on housing prisoners and building new prisons.

Prison and jail administrators typically calculate operating costs by dividing their annual budget by the average daily prison population. However, this accounting practice is quite misleading and produces patently low estimates of the true costs of imprisonment. For example, agency budgets often exclude contracted services for food, medical care, legal services, and transportation provided by other government agencies. According to two studies conducted in New York, these additional expenses increased the official per diem operating costs by 20 to 25 percent. An independent audit of the Indiana prison system found that actual expenditures were one-third higher than those reported by the agency. Besides these "hidden" direct expenditures, there are other costs which are rarely included in calculations of imprisonment costs. For instance, the state loses taxes that would be paid by many of the imprisoned, pays more welfare to their families, and maintains spacious prison grounds that are exempt from state and local real estate taxation. In the New York study conducted by Coopers and Lybrand in

1977, these costs amounted to over $21,000 per inmate.

While there is considerable variation among the states, on the average, prison officials claim that it costs about $20,000 per year to house, feed, clothe, and supervise a prisoner. Because this estimate does not include indirect costs, the true annual expenditure probably exceeds $30,000 per prisoner.

Scant Benefits

America now operates a huge unwanted welfare state, the prison system itself. Taxpayers shell out an estimated $25,000 to $45,000 a year to house, feed and maintain each state and federal inmate. Each new cell costs upwards of $85,000 a year to build and $1 million over 30 years including debt service. Yet the benefits, namely reducing crime, have been scant. Although the rate of certain felonies—burglary, robbery, murder—has dropped somewhat since 1982, violent crime is far worse today than before the spate of jailings began in the mid 70s. Rape and robbery have increased threefold since the 1960s and murder has rocketed by 60 percent.

William H. Inman, *The Angolite*, May/June 1989.

The other enormous cost is prison construction. Prisons are enclosed, "total" institutions in which prisoners are not only housed, but guarded, fed, clothed, and worked. They also receive schooling and medical and psychological treatment. These needs require—in addition to cellblocks or dormitories—infirmaries, classrooms, laundries, offices, and kitchens. Dividing the total construction costs of one of these institutions by the number of prisoners it houses, produces a cost per "bed" as low as $7,000 for a minimum security prison, to $155,000 for a maximum security prison.

However, instead of using current tax revenues to pay directly for this construction, the state does what most citizens do when buying a house—they borrow the money, which must be paid back over several decades. The borrowing is done by selling bonds or using other financing instruments that may triple the original figure. The costs of prison construction are further increased by "errors" in original bids by contractors and cost overruns due to delays in construction, which seem to be the rule rather than the exception. A survey of 15 states with construction projects revealed that cost overruns averaged *40 percent* of the original budget projections.

Consequently, when a state builds and finances a typical medium security prison it will spend approximately $268,000 per bed for construction alone. However, operating costs will greatly surpass construction costs in a little more than 10 years. Assuming a *conservative* $25,000 yearly operating cost per inmate with a two percent inflation factor, taxpayers will spend over one *million dollars* for each prisoner they incarcerate over a 30-year period. . . .

Just what kind of protection does imprisonment offer? The public is told that the unprecedented increase in the use of imprisonment is necessary to deter crime and to remove a growing number of dangerous criminals from the streets. But neither of these objectives has been or can be acccomplished by expansion of prison populations. The phenomenal growth in imprisonment has not reduced crime in our society.

The U.S. crime rate, as measured by crimes reported to the police, increased significantly between 1960 and 1974—the same time the babyboom generation hit its high crime years—ages 16 to 25. Official crime rates did not change between 1975 and 1980, but a moderate decline began after 1980. However, since 1984, there has been an upturn in most categories of crime—just when the supporters of imprisonment had begun to take credit for the 1980 84 declines. More significantly, violent crime rates have *increased* by almost 20 percent since 1976, despite well-publicized efforts to imprison the dangerous or career criminal.

Just How Dangerous Are They?

Politicians have attempted to justify the increased use of imprisonment claiming there is a growing number of dangerous criminals who must be incarcerated. But their argument is not supported by the facts. Only 30 percent of those now sent to prison have been convicted of crimes of violence—a rate that has actually declined since 1926.

Of those convicted of violent crimes, many are accused of assaults and homicides involving family members, neighbors, and other persons they have known for many years. These are reprehensible acts, but are not the kind of "stranger-on-stranger" crimes that frighten the public. Most of the other violent criminals commit "strong-arm robberies" or "muggings." Again, reprehensible acts, but these crimes, the motivations behind them, and the people committing them, are usually quite different than the image of the "uncontrollable predator" that has been sold to the public.

The majority of prisoners have never been to prison before. In California, 33 percent of those sent to prison have served a prior prison term. And only 3 percent have served prior terms for violent crimes. Seventy-five percent of those admitted to prison in Nevada are serving their first prison sentence. Forty-five percent have no prior felony conviction and 65 percent have never been sentenced to jail before.

While imprisoned, most inmates do not commit crimes or become management problems. More than 80 percent of inmates released from prison have no serious disciplinary record while imprisoned. Most inmates are assigned to minimum- or medium-security prisons. Only a small percentage (usually 10 to 15 percent) require maximum security in those notorious prisons the public reads about and sees on television—San Quentin, Stateville, Folsom, and Marion. And, most inmates do not return to prison once released. For many decades, the average return rate to prison after three years, the time when most ex-convicts are likely to return, has consistently been about 30 to 35 percent.

Despite these facts, the media and aspiring politicians portray most street criminals as men who, in spite of many brushes with the law, numerous "breaks" by lenient judges resulting in probation instead of jail, and even repeated prison and jail terms, refuse to live a law abiding life. According to this stereotype, the greed, maliciousness, unwillingness to work, and perverted desires of criminals cause them repeatedly to commit vicious crimes against the innocent.

Disadvantaged Prisoners

A more factual portrayal of prisoners presents a different reality—most prisoners are poorly educated young men raised in slum neighborhoods by low income parents, often a single mother who is underemployed or unemployed. These young men have virtually no job skills or job experience, and no hope of ever getting a stable and adequate job. Most of them grow up in the streets where they live from day-to-day, engaging in ill-planned and unskilled crimes in order to obtain money for their daily needs. . . .

More Crime

If a tour in prison does anything, it induces more crime. . . . Most people who go to jail for two to five years are not hardened criminals, but once they've been locked up, they tend to get a little worse the next time around.

James Ridgeway, *The Village Voice*, September 18, 1989.

The average loss of a burglary, robbery, or larceny—the major property crimes—is $40. The total loss for all street crimes in a year is estimated to be $11 billion. Significantly, the United States spends more than four times that amount ($45.6 billion) on the criminal justice system to fight property crimes. On the other hand, white collar crime, which is rarely included in political campaigns against crime or in criminal justice appropriation, has been estimated by the U.S. Senate Judiciary Subcommittee to cost between $175 billion and $231 billion annually. . . .

As demonstrated in this paper, the best evidence indicates that our drastically increased use of imprisonment has not made society safer. Even worse, there is increasing evidence that it is making society more dangerous.

In our careless extension of the use of imprisonment, thousands of people, who have no prior prison records and are guilty of relatively minor felonies—petty burglaries, forgeries, minor drug offenses— have been packed into dangerous, crowded prisons. A growing number of prisoners are being subjected to extremely long sentences. These long-termers are not only stacking up in prisons and filling all available space, but their long terms make return to a productive, conventional life extremely difficult, if not impossible. Many marginally-involved petty criminals are converted into hard core "outlaws"; mean, violence-prone convicts who dominate crowded prison wards.

The social cost of imprisonment, that is its tendency to increase ex-prisoners' criminal activity, continues to be confirmed by research. The Rand Corporation compared carefully matched groups of convicted felons sent to prison or granted probation and found those sentenced to prison had significantly higher rates of rearrest after release than those on probation. Between 1982 and 1987 the recidivism rate (the rate of re-imprisonment of inmates released on parole) in California, by far the nation's most overcrowded prison system, has doubled.

Even more tragically, imprisonment is increasingly falling upon blacks, Hispanics, and other people of color. Sixty years ago, almost one-fourth of all prison admissions were non-white. Today, nearly half of all prison admissions are non-white. In many states like Florida and California, the imprisonment rate of blacks is at least 10 times higher than for whites. Hispanics are incarcerated at a rate three times higher than whites. Studies show that if one is born black and male, there is a 50 percent chance of being arrested once by age 29. These tragic figures show that if blacks and Hispanics were imprisoned at the same rate as whites, there would be no national prison crowding crisis. . . .

Shorter Prison Terms Are Necessary

There is only one viable solution that would have an immediate and dramatic impact on prison crowding: *shorter prison terms.* This could be done swiftly and fairly through a number of existing mechanisms such as greater use of existing good-time credit statutes and/or accelerating parole eligibility. And, as demonstrated in several states, there would be no significant impact on crime rates.

In Illinois between 1980 and 1983, the Director of Corrections released more than 21,000 prisoners an average of 90 days early because of severe prison crowding. The impact on the state's crime rate was insignificant yet the program saved almost $50 million in tax dollars. A study of the program found that the amount of crime that could be attributed to early release was less than 1 percent of the total crime of the state. In fact, the state's crime rate actually *declined* while the early release program was in effect.

Another demonstration of how swiftly and easily prison populations can be reduced occurred in California from 1967 to 1970. When Ronald Reagan became governor, he instructed the parole board to reduce the prison population. The board began shortening sentences, which it had the power to do within the indeter-

"IF THERE ARE SO MANY 'SOFT' JUDGES, WHY ARE THERE
SO MANY OF US IN PRISON?"

© Renault/Rothco

minate sentence system, and in two years, lowered the prison population from 28,000 to less than 18,000. Many other states are following these examples. Texas, Oklahoma, Oregon, Tennessee, and Florida are just a few states which have been required by the federal courts to reduce overcrowded prison systems by shortening prison terms.

Fewer Prisoners

For such a policy to work, prison terms would have to be shortened across the board. Any attempt by legislators, judges, or parole boards to select certain categories of prisoners for shorter sentences would compound the already discriminatory sentencing patterns and not produce population reductions. The average prison stay in the U.S. now ranges from two to four years, meaning that even marginal reductions in the length of stay for large categories of inmates would have substantial effects on population size. For example, in 1984, 167,000 people were sentenced to prison. If 80 percent of those people had their sentences reduced by 30 days, the nation's prison population would have declined by 11,000 inmates. A 90-day reduction would have resulted in 33,000 fewer inmates and a 6-month reduction, 66,000 fewer inmates.

A maximum prison population should be determined by officials of each state and policies adopted that marginally reduce prison terms to avoid surpassing the maximum population. Unless such reform is adopted, prison populations will continue to rise indefinitely into the 21st century. Reducing prison terms by the amounts advocated may only slow the rate of expansion. But it can be done with no cost to public safety, no changes in crime rates and with enormous dollar savings. It has been done before.

Establishing Apartheid

We *must* turn away from the excessive use of prisons. The current incarceration binge will eventually consume large amounts of tax money, which will be diverted from essential public services such as education, child care, mental health, and medical services. We will continue to imprison millions of people under intolerably cruel and dangerous conditions. We will accumulate a growing number of ex-convicts who are more or less psychologically and socially crippled, excluded from conventional society—posing a continuing threat to others. We will severely damage some of our more cherished humanitarian values, which are corroded by our excessive focus on vindictiveness. And we will further divide our society into the white affluent classes and a poor non-white underclass, many of them convicts and ex-convicts. In effect, we are putting our own apartheid into place.

"Countries with far more generous social welfare programs than the United States . . . all have sharply lower rates of teenage births and teenage crime."

More Social Programs Would Reduce Violence

Lisbeth B. Schorr with Daniel Schorr

In the following viewpoint, Lisbeth B. Schorr and Daniel Schorr argue that with the help of intensive social service programs, disadvantaged children can be diverted from a life of delinquency and violence. By spending more money on children now, the U.S. could reduce future violence, they contend. Lisbeth B. Schorr is a lecturer in social medicine and health policy at Harvard University in Cambridge, Massachusetts. During the presidential administrations of Lyndon Johnson and Jimmy Carter, she led national efforts to help disadvantaged children. Daniel Schorr, a journalist for more than fifty years, is a frequent commentator on several National Public Radio news programs.

As you read, consider the following questions:

1. What type of programs does Schorr contend work best for the most impoverished and alienated families?
2. Why does the author disagree with Charles Murray's argument that spending on social programs actually increases poverty and crime?
3. What conclusion does Schorr reach from her description of Carrie Eleby?

Many Americans have soured on "throwing money" at human problems that seem only to get worse. They are not hard-hearted, but don't want to be soft-headed either. Even when their compassion is aroused by moving stories of desperate families or neglected children, they feel helpless and are convinced that nothing can be done. Fear of actually doing harm while trying to do good, together with the threat of unmanageable costs, have paralyzed national policy-making.

A Tragic Paradox

It is a strange and tragic paradox that confidence in our collective ability to alter the destinies of vulnerable children has hit bottom just as scientific understanding of the processes of human development and the rich evidence of success in helping such children have reached a new high.

These were my thoughts on July 8, 1981, at the end of a Harvard seminar at which I listened to Mary Jo Bane, of the Kennedy School of Government, urging that we pay more attention to American adolescents who are afflicted with what she called "rotten outcomes"—the youngsters who are having children too soon, leaving school illiterate and unemployable, and committing violent crimes.

Professor Bane explained to our group, the newly created Harvard University Working Group on Early Life and Adolescence, that information just becoming available made it possible to identify what proportion of these young people came from single-parent families, how many were temporarily and how many persistently poor, and what fraction came from minority backgrounds, from urban slums, and even from given census tracts.

My colleagues encouraged Professor Bane's intention to investigate in depth the "epidemiology of adolescent rotten outcomes." I too thought it would be useful to know more about who was destined for serious trouble before the trouble became serious. But what really intrigued me was that we might already know enough to keep many of the "rotten outcomes" from happening.

My hunch was that if we could put together what we already knew about the early precursors of adolescent rotten outcomes and—even more to the point—about interventions that could prevent such damaging outcomes, we would have a solid foundation on which to build a strong network of preventive programs and policies, by governmental as well as private agencies. . . .

I found my original hypothesis repeatedly confirmed: We can significantly change the odds for youngsters growing up in environments that threaten healthy development by building on programs that have already proven successful. I also found myself in the middle of a whole other story: Wherever I looked, in health, social services, family support, or education, the programs that worked for families and children living in concentrated poverty and social dislocation differed in fundamental ways from traditional programs that seemed to work for those in less devastating circumstances.

The programs that work best for children and families in high-risk environments typically offer comprehensive and intensive services. Whether they are part of the health, mental health, social service, or educational systems, they are able to respond flexibly to a wide variety of needs. In their wakes they often pull in other kinds of services, unrelated in narrowly bureaucratic terms but inseparable in the broad framework of human misery. These programs approach children not with bureaucratic or professional blinders, but open-eyed to their needs in a family and community context. Interventions that are successful with high-risk populations all seem to have staffs with the time and skill to establish relationships based on mutual respect and trust. . . .

The Inner City and the American Dream

America's inner cities have become the spawning grounds for adolescents who bear increasingly appalling resemblances to rabid, homicidal maniacs. . . .

Perhaps the black and Latino adolescents in the United States have subconsciously adopted the death wish expressed for them in the historical national attitude of America, which programs them to self-destruct between the ages of 15 and 25 years. . . . Welcome to the inner city's version of the American dream. If they would only do it more discreetly, more quietly, then we could all go back to watching the Bill Cosby and Jesse Jackson shows and reminding ourselves how truly wonderful life is in this glorious land of deadly opportunity.

But of course we can still attempt to apply the solution: Assimilate them into the American dream. It's not too late for the next generation.

Claude Brown, *Los Angeles Times*, May 17, 1988.

Anyone proposing new or expanded social programs today must be prepared to respond to concerns that well-intentioned efforts to make things better could actually make them worse. The specter of investments in human services actually doing harm is given an air of reality because so many people are in fact worse off—after twenty years of vastly increased social spending. More children are poor, more children are growing up without stable families, and more young people are out of work.

Of the many possible explanations, perhaps the most influential—as well as the most irresponsible—was proposed by

Charles Murray in his 1984 book, *Losing Ground*. Murray provided intellectual underpinnings to taxpayer reluctance to invest in social programs by contending that Great Society social policies changed the rewards and penalties that govern human behavior, and thereby brought about increasing rates of joblessness, crime, out-of-wedlock births, female-headed families, and welfare dependency. Murray argues that, faced with the choice between an unattractive job and a welfare check, it is "rational on grounds of dollars and cents" for poor unmarried women to decide to have babies. Only the elimination of support from outside the family would discourage young women from pregnancy and encourage both young men and young women to work for low wages and accept the discipline of the workplace—because the alternative would be so grim.

The evidence does not sustain Murray's contentions. First, countries with far more generous social welfare programs than the United States—Germany, Denmark, France, Sweden, and Great Britain—all have sharply lower rates of teenage births and teenage crime.

Second, if welfare benefits figured in the decision to have a baby, more babies would be born in states with relatively high levels of welfare payments. But careful state-by-state comparisons show no evidence that Aid to Families with Dependent Children (AFDC) influences childbearing decisions; sex and childbearing among teenagers do not seem to be a product of careful economic analysis. . . .

The High Cost of Rotten Outcomes

Adolescents in trouble because they drop out of school, engage in criminal acts, or have children too soon are embarked on a rocky life course. Their troubles are a source of pain for themselves and their families, and often a burden for the rest of us. But much of that private pain and public cost can be prevented. With knowledge now at hand, society could improve the childhood experiences of those at greatest risk, and thereby reduce the incidence of school failure, juvenile crime, and teenage childbearing—and some of their most serious consequences.

As I gathered the information to support this proposition, I visited libraries and experts, and observed successful programs in operation. I also caught occasional glimpses of the faces behind the numbers of adolescents in trouble. It was on a visit to a murder trial in the District of Columbia Superior Court that I became involved in the story of seventeen-year-old Carrie Eleby, eyewitness to a particularly savage killing. Mrs. Catherine Fuller, a diminutive black ninety-nine-pound mother of six, had been attacked while walking home in a poor Washington, D.C., neighborhood. When she resisted attempts to grab her coin purse, a dozen young men

261

mutilated her and beat her to death. One of the accused, later convicted with the help of Carrie Eleby's testimony, was the father of Carrie's second child, Tamika.

Carrie sat in the witness stand, responding in barely audible tones to questions about her activities on the day of the murder. She told of having been hanging out and smoking "loveboat," or PCP, of hearing a scream from the alley, and seeing "they was beating on a lady." She identified several of the defendants, including her former boyfriend. Suddenly, in the midst of her listless recital, she erupted in anger. The defense lawyer had asked her to read from the transcript of her previous testimony. The reason for the outburst, the Assistant U.S. Attorney explained to me later, was that Carrie had trouble reading.

In Carrie Eleby I could see a textbook case of the clustering and intertwining of rotten outcomes I was probing in my research. She was a school-age mother of two children, a high school dropout, barely literate, and lived surrounded by violent crime.

The story that began for me that day in the courtroom continued seven months later. Carrie Eleby, still seventeen, had just had her third child. A visitor who saw her soon after she came home from the hospital with the new baby said that Carrie seemed to be bored by the infant and never touched or held her while he was there. Carrie said she was scared to pick up the baby, because "when you pick it up, it's grunting all the time." Both Carrie and her mother seemed relieved that the baby lay quietly in the crib and exasperated by the constant activity of the two toddlers, whom they tried periodically to control with cries of "Shut up!" and "You hateful!"

The Needs of Disadvantaged Children

Serious changes will take place when the community begins to comprehend fully that crime and other evidence of social failure are rooted in the public's refusal to address adequately the needs of disadvantaged children.

Seymour Gelber, *Hard-Core Delinquents*, 1988.

The first time Carrie became pregnant, she was an eighth-grader. She made a brief attempt to return to school after her first child was born, but it didn't work out; she had had trouble with her schoolwork since early in elementary school. Then, in quick succession, two more children. Throughout each of her pregnancies she smoked PCP. During her last pregnancy she made only one prenatal care visit. Leaving her mother and sister to care for her three children, she was now spending most of her time at her new boyfriend's house. Her mother said she didn't understand why

Carrie didn't either go back to school or stay home with her children. Mrs. Eleby thought her daughter needed psychiatric care or at least "mother training."

Mrs. Eleby said things had not really gone right for Carrie ever since she had been hit by a car when she was six. Her legs ached constantly, and she couldn't sleep. But Mrs. Eleby had not taken Carrie back to the doctor since they had been told, immediately after the accident, that nothing was wrong.

As I thought about Carrie, it seemed clear that the adult world had already failed her, and was in the process of failing her children. We can choose to attribute the failure to a weak economy or to weak individual character, to an unjust society or to a society lacking the political will to apply its accumulated wisdom. But whatever causal theories our ideological preferences lead us to, we can agree that life's cards are stacked against Carrie and her children and that they, and the rest of us, will likely pay a heavy price. . . .

Adolescent Violent Crime

Americans murder, assault, rape, and rob one another at a greater rate than citizens of any other industrialized country. Fear pervades American cities, especially after dark. Fear of violent crime (homicide, rape, assault, and robbery) has changed the way we think and the way we live. According to a *USA Today* poll, most American adults consider personal safety the single greatest factor in determining their "quality of life." Their physical safety looms more important than job satisfaction, financial security, marriage, or health. Crime, say 49 percent of New Yorkers, is the single worst thing about living in the city. . . .

Blacks and the poor remain the most frequent victims of crime, but since World War II, the geographical spread of serious crime has made it harder for everyone to avoid. It is no longer confined to a few parts of a city where "gangsters" and others with "evil reputations" hang out, or where the poor and minorities live. Jan and Marcia Chaiken, experts on crime for the Rand Corporation, write, "Crime, like television, has come into the living room—and into the church, the lobbies of public buildings, the parks, the shopping malls, the bus stations, the airport parking lots, the subways, the schools. . . . Crime and the fear of crime have spread from 'traditional' high crime areas into once-serene urban neighborhoods, from the central city to outlying suburbs and towns, and into summer resorts and college campuses."

Still, the victims of murder remain disproportionately black. Homicide is the leading cause of death among young black men. While blacks have the highest rates of committing violent crimes of all kinds, rapes and assaults by strangers are most frequently committed by lone white males.

But age is a more consistent factor in street crime than race.

263

"Crime is a young man's game," says Welsley Skogan, North-western University sociologist. So much so that the peak age for arrests for property crimes is sixteen, and for violent crime, eighteen.

Violent juvenile offenders not only wreak a lot of damage while young, but they are likely soon to become career criminals. The typical violent adult criminal has committed his first crime before age sixteen, and most have spent considerable time in state juvenile institutions. Although most juvenile delinquents do not become adult criminals, virtually all adult chronic offenders were once juvenile offenders. . . .

Responding to the Whole Person

How do we set up the chain of events that ends with young people in jobs and employers being supplied with the human material they need? Essentially, it is a process that responds to the whole person, attempting to fill in gaps, restoring trust in family, law, and societal values, changing feelings and attitudes—in short, developing the self-esteem and new identities and responsible behavior that can open doors. . . .

We can create and maintain drug-free and crime-free environments where growth, motivation, and learning can take place. We can act as launching pads for a broader, brighter future for numbers of people.

Elizabeth Lyttleton Sturz and Mary Taylor, *The Annals of the American Academy of Political and Social Science*, November 1987.

Recent minor fluctuations and even declines in crime rates pale into insignificance in the face of the starkly consistent high level of violent crime in the United States. The risk of being the victim of a violent crime is higher for an American than the risk of being divorced, being injured in a car accident, or dying of cancer. The risk of being robbed is 208 times greater in the United States than in Japan. Homicide rates among young adults in the United States are 36 times as high as in Great Britain and 29 times as high as in Japan. . . .

In Detroit, emergency room physicians say they cannot take all the gunshot victims on the busiest nights. In 1986 Detroit had 646 homicides. Forty-three of the victims were less than seventeen years old. "Sometimes it seems all I do is children's funerals," said Detroit florist Denise Robinson. . . .

The widespread availability of street drugs and a much more pervasive sense of hostility seem to distinguish the present from earlier times. Wanton violence, says writer Claude Brown, is the biggest difference between the Harlem of today and that of the generation in which he came of age and about which he wrote in *Manchild in the Promised Land*. Brown returned to the neighborhood where he had grown up, trying to understand the "senseless, often maniacal, rampant killings of mugging and robbery victims." A sixteen-year-old explained to him, "That's what they do now. . . . You know, you take their stuff and you pop 'em." Brown wrote it was too ghastly to understand, but what he was hearing from the young teenagers he talked to was that "murder is in style now." . . .

Some of the adolescents who leave school early and have babies too soon—and even some who commit serious crimes—will ultimately become self-supporting, responsible, and productive adults. But many will be trapped by the interwoven strands of men without jobs, women without husbands, children without fathers, and families without money, hope, skills, opportunities—or effective supports and services that might help them escape. These young people will become the long-term welfare dependent, the unemployed and unemployable, and the parents who are unable to form stable families of their own.

In the absence of a means of breaking the grim cycle, many of their children will grow up in poverty and in isolated single-parent families. Many will join the ranks of the hungry and homeless. Surrounded by despair, neglect, and violence, these children are unlikely to be given—from inside or outside the family—any vision of the future which would inspire present sacrifice. They are unlikely to get the extra boost of nurturance and encouragement that the children of disadvantage especially need to succeed. They will lack, as many of their parents did, the kind of schools, health care, and social services that might protect them from the worst consequences of their living conditions.

And ultimately, as these children themselves grow into adolescence, many will have their own turn at perpetuating the cycle by leaving school unskilled, having children as teenagers, or becoming delinquent. Disconnected from the mainstream of American society, unable to make the transition to productive adulthood, they too will be stuck in what has come to be callled the "underclass." . . .

Society Can Help

The evidence I have compiled demonstrates decisively that intensive societal efforts can reach and help even those stuck at the bottom—and that the rest of us have a high stake in seeing to it that they are reached and helped. The successful programs are not aimed exclusively at an underclass, however defined. But these programs can prevent some of the disasters that ultimately ensnare people in deep and lasting poverty and despair. They have the capacity to reach those who are not only poor, but who also live in neighborhoods which lack the supports essential to children's healthy growth.

"Crime can never be eliminated. . . . But it can
be controlled, if criminals are regarded as
volitional entities, fully responsible for the
consequences of their actions."

Swifter Punishment Would Reduce Violence

Robert James Bidinotto

In the following viewpoint, Robert James Bidinotto objects to
arguments that violent crimes occur because of poverty. He
believes that there is a criminal personality that causes some people to turn to crime because of their character. To reduce violence,
he argues that society must send a strong message: that crime will
not be tolerated. Bidinotto advocates strengthening the criminal
justice system so that more violent offenders are caught, punished,
and imprisoned. Bidinotto is a writer and lecturer whose articles
often appear in the monthly magazine, *The Freeman.* He is also
the former editor of the monthly magazine, *On Principle.*

As you read, consider the following questions:

1. What proportion of people who commit felonies are
   imprisoned, according to the author?
2. What does the author mean by the "Excuse-Making
   Industry?"
3. What steps would Bidinotto take to make the criminal
   justice system more effective?

Robert James Bidinotto, "Crime and Consequences, Part I: Criminal Responsibility," *The
Freeman*, July 1989. Robert James Bidinotto, "Crime and Consequences, Part III: '. . . To
Insure Domestic Tranquility . . .,'" *The Freeman*, September 1989.

Willie Horton was a habitual criminal, sentenced in Massachusetts to "life with no possibility of parole" for the savage, unprovoked knife slaying of a teen-age boy. However, like many other alleged "lifers" in that state, after only 10 years in prison he was transferred to an unwalled, minimum-security facility. There, he became eligible for daily work release, as well as unescorted weekend furloughs, from prison.

Following the example of 10 other "life-without-parole" killers over the years, Horton decided not to return from one of his furloughs. Instead, months later, he invaded the home of a young Maryland couple, where for nearly 12 hours he viciously tortured the man and raped the woman. . . .

Justice Is the Exception

The Horton episode was not an isolated exception. In today's criminal justice system, justice is the exception. . . .

Of the eight felons per 100 serious crimes who are arrested, one or two are teenagers who are routed to the juvenile justice system (which is far more lenient than the adult system). This leaves only six or seven adults apprehended for every 100 serious crimes committed. Of these, many are released for lack of sufficient evidence or on technicalities; a few are acquitted after standing trial. Of the tiny number remaining who plead guilty or are convicted, most receive dramatically reduced sentences, or are allowed simply to "walk" on probation, thanks to "plea-bargain" arrangements.

The results? According to the federal government, for every 100 serious crimes *reported* in 1986, only 4.3 criminals went to prison. But adjusting once again to account for *unreported* crimes, we find that in 1986, only 1.7 percent of the most serious crimes were punished by imprisonment. In other words, only 17 perpetrators were put behind bars for every 1,000 major felonies.

In calculating his chances of being punished, then, any would-be criminal would logically conclude that the odds are definitely on his side—that today in America, crime *does* pay.

Hence the phenomenon of the career criminal. Most crimes are committed by repeat offenders, often arrested but rarely imprisoned. For example, in 1986, Massachusetts state prison inmates each had an average of 12.6 prior court appearances. Since, as we have seen, the typical criminal gets away with 12.5 felonies for his every arrest, simple multiplication (12.6 X 12.5) suggests that, on average, many of the Massachusetts inmates had committed well over 100 crimes. Few of these inmates were teenagers: their average age was 31. Yet despite their status as career criminals, 47 percent of them had never before been incarcerated as adults. . . .

As every criminal knows, the "criminal justice system" is a sham. The consequences are undermining the motivation and integrity of those who man the institutions of the law. Worst of all, millions of victims, who hope for justice, find that some of the worst crimes against them are perpetrated *after* they go to court.

Irrationality of this magnitude doesn't "just happen." Nor would it long be tolerated, without a complicated framework of abstract rationalizations to soothe, confuse, and dismiss critics. Like most compromised institutions, today's criminal justice system is the handiwork of what I call the "Excuse-Making Industry."

This industry consists primarily of intellectuals in the social-science establishment: the philosophers, psychological theorists, political scientists, legal scholars, sociologists, criminologists, economists, and historians whose theories have shaped our modern legal system. It also consists of an activist wing of fellow-travelers: social workers, counselors, therapists, legal-aid and civil-liberties lawyers, "inmate rights" advocates, "progressive" politicians and activists, and so on.

It was this industry which, in the 1960s and 1970s, initiated a quiet revolution in the criminal justice system. Its proponents managed to rout the last of those who believed that the system's purpose was to apprehend and punish criminals. Instead, the Excuse-Making Industry was able finally to institutionalize its long-cherished dream: not the punishment, but the *rehabilitation* of criminals. . . .

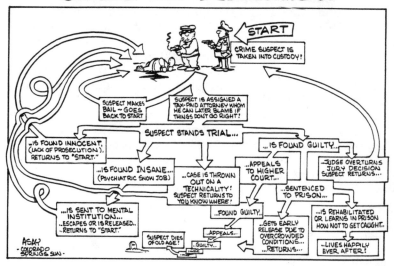

Reprinted by permission of *Colorado Springs Sun.*

Summing up the unintended consequences of these efforts, Charles Murray has written: "The changes in welfare *and* changes in the risks attached to crime *and* changes in the educational environment reinforced each other. Together, they radically altered the [social] incentive structure." This became especially evident in the area of crime: crime rates began to take off while penalties for crime lessened. Soon, "a thoughtful person watching the world around him . . . was accurately perceiving a considerably reduced risk of getting caught. . . . It was not just that we had more people to put in jails than we had jails to hold them . . .; we also deliberately stopped putting people in jail as often. From 1961 through 1969, the number of prisoners in federal and state facilities—the absolute number, not just a proportion of arrestees—dropped every year, despite a doubling of crime during the same period."

Clearly, it wasn't the intention of the social-science establishment that crime rates soar. The Excuse-Making Industry is no diabolical, centrally directed conspiracy, harboring some warped, unfathomable desire to foster criminality. Rather, it's a sprawling intellectual consensus, consisting of many diverse, competing, and often conflicting elements—but united in a single premise: that the criminal isn't responsible for his behavior.

The Criminal Is Not Responsible

There are many variations on the theme that binds the Excuse-Making Industry.

There are sociologists, who hold that environmental, racial, social, and economic factors have "driven" the criminal to his antisocial behavior—a view echoed by economists, usually of a Marxist inclination, who argue that criminals are formed by their membership in an "exploited" economic class.

There are Freudian psychologists, who contend that criminals are helpless pawns of emotional drives rooted in childhood; and behavioral psychologists, who believe criminals are clay, shaped by "negative reinforcers" in their families and neighborhoods.

There are biologists, who cite the alleged correlation between criminal behavior and possession of a so-called "mesomorphic body type"; other biologists and geneticists, who think criminality is caused by genetic, physiological, or biochemical deficiencies; still others, who believe there may be a racial or ethnic "propensity" to criminality.

There are eclectics, who think a combination of such "causes" can "explain" crime.

But whatever the variation, the theme is a constant. The criminal is not responsible for his actions, because man is not a causal agent in any primary sense. Forces and circumstances outside his control "cause" him to behave as he does. He should be forgiven, or treated therapeutically, or placed in a better environment, or counseled to "cope" with his uncontrollable inner demons. But he must not be held accountable for his actions—and, under *no* circumstances, punished for what he "couldn't help.". . .

In the musical *West Side Story*, one juvenile delinquent incisively satirizes the sociological theory of crime, telling the local cop, Officer Krupke: "We're depraved on accounta we're deprived."

Former U.S. Attorney General Ramsey Clark offered a more formal summary of the view that crime is "caused" by external social and economic factors:

> If we are to deal meaningfully with crime, what must be seen is the dehumanizing effect on the individual of slums, racism, ignorance and violence, of corruption and impotence to fulfill rights, of poverty and unemployment and idleness, of generations of malnutrition, of congenital brain damage and prenatal neglect, of sickness and disease, of pollution, of decrepit, dirty, ugly, unsafe, overcrowded housing, of alcoholism and narcotics addiction, of avarice, anxiety, fear, hatred, hopelessness and injustice. These are the fountainheads of crime. They can be controlled. As imprecise, distorted and prejudiced as our learning is, these sources of crime and their controllability clearly emerge to any who would see.

This is probably the most widely held view of criminal causation—and probably the easiest to refute. Whatever might be said of the prevalence of unsavory social conditions today, surely they were even more prevalent in decades and centuries past, and are more prevalent today in Third World nations. Yet despite the fact that conditions and circumstances have been constantly improving for the vast majority of people, crime today is *increasing*; and it is increasing faster in America and other developed countries than in most poorer parts of the world.

Flaws in the System

There are flaws in our present criminal justice system. Two-thirds of the crimes committed are not reported to the authorities. Barely one-fifth of all crimes result in arrest. And of those arrested, some cases are not prosecuted. Other defendants jump bail. And when a case ends in a guilty plea or conviction, still more criminals are placed on probation. . . .

It is time to raise the costs of crime and reduce its rewards.

Jack Kemp, in *Crime and Punishment in Modern America*, 1986.

The sociological excuse (of which Marxist "class warfare" theory is a subset) flies in the face of common sense and empirical evidence. Even within the same poor, inner-city families, some youngsters become criminals, while the majority do not. . . .

Numerous empirical studies demonstrate that criminals simply don't *think* like non-criminals.

A representative study in Colorado found that, even at an early age, future delinquents had "less regard for the rights and feelings of their peers; less awareness of the need to accept responsibility for their obligations . . . and poorer attitudes toward authority, including failure to understand the need for rules and regulations in any well-ordered social group. . . . They were significantly less likely than their nondelinquent [peers] to be viewed as dependable, friendly, pleasant, considerate, and fair." Many other studies have echoed these findings. Stanton Samenow describes the criminal mind thusly: "Despite a multitude of differences in their backgrounds and crime patterns, criminals are alike in one way: *how they think* . . . [all] regard the world as a chessboard over which they have total control, and they perceive people as pawns to be pushed around at will. Trust, love, loyalty, and teamwork are incompatible with their way of life. They scorn and exploit most people who are kind, trusting, hardworking, and honest. Toward a few they are sentimental but rarely considerate. Some of their most altruistic acts have sinister motives.". . .

The criminal welcomes anything that would assist him in his predatory behavior. And here, the Excuse-Making Industry is invaluable to him. Its overall ethical thrust has been to excuse malicious behavior and thus deaden the pangs of conscience. By concocting theories, policies, and programs which excuse irresponsibility, Excuse-Makers have fostered a general social climate of moral relativism—thus undermining any guilt feelings which might act as inner constraints on criminal behavior. . . .

If *justice* is truly to become the central focus of the criminal justice system, then the following reforms—some controversial—must be seriously considered.

Truth in the Courtroom

No facts should *ever* be banished from criminal proceedings. All exclusionary rules concerning evidence and confessions should be eliminated. If police obtain evidence by improper or illegal methods, that should be the subject of *separate* disciplinary or even criminal proceedings against the offending officers. But *evidence is evidence.*

Additionally, it's usually absurd to exclude an individual's past record from court deliberations. Career criminals often operate in unique patterns, which can serve as virtual signatures at certain crime scenes. Yet past records are often excluded as "prejudicial." Admitting these in evidence, to show a pattern consistent with the charged crime, only makes sense. Also, consideration of an individual's past record should be a routine element in all sentencing.

271

Juvenile offense records are often sealed, allegedly to prevent "early mistakes" from "pursuing the child into adulthood." Today, many teenagers are engaging, not in mistakes, but in serious, sadistic crimes. Sealing or expunging their records when they reach adulthood is another perversion of the fact-finding process. They should be admissible into adult sentencing proceedings, as evidence of career criminality.

Career criminals—and anyone with a history of escapes or failures to show in court—should *never* get bail consideration.

Holding People Accountable

When we ask what kind of society the American people deserve, our goal must be a nation in which law-abiding citizens are safe and feel safe.

To achieve this goal, people must be held accountable for their actions. That's common sense. Most Americans are law-abiding, and most believe that there is such a thing as right and wrong—good and evil. . . . A common sense approach to crime means that if we're going to affect people's behavior, we must have a criminal justice system in which there is an expectation that if you commit a crime, you will be caught; and if caught, you will be prosecuted; and if convicted, you will do time.

George Bush, remarks at National Peace Officers Memorial Day Service, May 15, 1989.

As for probation, every crime, no matter how petty, should merit *some* level of punishment, if only to show that *crime has inescapable consequences.* Probationary "sentences" teach offenders—*especially* impressionable young offenders—that "the law" is a paper tiger, that they can get away with crime. A young offender's first brush with the law shouldn't be brutal; but it should definitely be something he'd not wish to experience again.

Plea bargaining should be abolished. Neither necessary nor ethical, it corrupts the entire court process and everyone involved. The cooperation of some criminals should not be bought with the bribe of a reduced sentence: the prize never equals the price. Going easy on lower-level crooks in order to buy their testimony against their bosses merely shuffles the underworld hierarchy: the boss is replaced by the lower-level crook who bought his freedom, and crime marches on.

Even if tough, determinate sentencing laws are passed, they will be undermined and bypassed if plea bargaining is permitted: charges will be reduced to evade the harsher penalties. Ending plea bargaining is the key to making tougher sentences stick. . . .

All convicted felons should serve fixed, determinate sentences for their crimes. Early release being out of the question, there's no reason for parole boards (more savings for taxpayers). This will reduce arbitrariness and the unfairness of inmates serving different sentences for the same crime.

Pre-sentencing defense testimony concerning mitigating circumstances should be admissible only in the case of a *guilty plea*. If a defendant pleads innocent, but is later found guilty, he shouldn't be allowed to abruptly concede his guilt after the verdict, then plead mitigating circumstances before sentencing—not after putting everyone through the trouble and expense of a trial. In all cases, mitigating testimony should be balanced by testimony from crime victims. These statements should be gauged on some fixed point system for altering the usual sentence—but only within a very limited range.

Criminal penalties should increase in severity upon subsequent convictions of other felonies. Borrowing terminology from the Excuse-Makers, I propose "progressive sentencing": the term of imprisonment for repeat offenders should increase in multiples— say, two years for a first burglary conviction; four for a second; eight for a third; and so on. I also propose that this "progressive" feature be transferable among different sorts of crimes, thus preventing criminals from simply varying their crimes in hope of avoiding serious punishment.

Capital punishment never should be applied in cases where a murder conviction depended largely on circumstantial evidence. But in cases of pre-meditated murder in which there is no question of guilt, it should be the *standard* sentence. There also should be a time limit on the appeals process. . . .

Crime and Consequences

The United States was founded on the premise that each individual is an end in himself, and that he is morally and legally self-responsible. Self-responsibility means being accountable for the full consequences of one's actions, for good or ill. Thus the rewards and profits of life, in justice, should go to those responsible for making the world better; the penalties and losses should accrue to those who make it worse. . . .

Crime can never be eliminated, not if we have the power to choose evil. But it *can* be controlled, if criminals are regarded as volitional entities, fully responsible for the consequences of their actions. The answer is to reform the entire criminal justice system, from its basic premises to its routine procedures, with a single goal in mind: to reassert the responsibility of the individual.

273

a critical thinking activity

Evaluating Sources of Information

A critical thinker must always question sources of information. Historians, for example, distinguish between *primary sources* (eyewitness accounts) and *secondary sources* (writings or statements based on primary sources). The account of a parole officer describing how people on parole and in his charge continue to break the law is an example of a primary source. A sociologist writing a report about this trend and suggesting reasons why some people are repeat offenders is an example of a secondary source.

To read and think critically, one must be able to recognize primary sources. This is not enough, however, because eyewitness accounts do not always provide accurate descriptions. Two innocent observers of a murder scene, one who will testify on behalf of the defendant and the other on behalf of the prosecutor, may give different accounts of what happened when they are called to the witness stand at the trial. The historian must decide which account seems most accurate, keeping in mind the potential biases of the eyewitnesses.

Test your skill in evaluating sources of information by completing the following exercise. Imagine you are writing a report evaluating the possible measures the U.S. government can take to reduce crime. You decide to include an equal number of primary and secondary sources. Listed are a number of sources which may be useful for your research. *Place a P next to those descriptions you believe are primary sources.* Second, *rank the primary sources* assigning the number 1 to what appears to be the most accurate and fair primary source, the number 2 to the next most accurate, and so on until the ranking is finished. *Next, place an S next to those descriptions you believe are secondary sources and rank them also, using the same criteria.*

If you are doing this activity as a member of a class or group, discuss and compare your evaluations with other members of the group. Others may come to different conclusions than you. Listening to their reasons may give you valuable insights in evaluating sources of information.

P = *primary*
S = *secondary*

_____ 1. A magazine editorial written by a New
York City policeman stating that gun
control will reduce violence. _____

_____ 2. An American historian's account of
violence in America called *The Roots of
Violent Crime.* _____

_____ 3. A brochure published by the National
Rifle Association providing statistics to
show that gun control will not reduce
crime. _____

_____ 4. Police department reports indicating
the race, age, and education levels of
victims and criminals. _____

_____ 5. TV documentary that explores the
different types of crimes committed in
different areas of the country. _____

_____ 6. An article in *Time* magazine comparing
the criminal justice systems and crime
rates of the United States and Japan. _____

_____ 7. The testimony of a 16-year-old murderer
of how he killed his victim and why. _____

_____ 8. An FBI report linking increasing urban
crime to increasing drug use. _____

_____ 9. The transcript of a radio talk show in
which a suburban man calls in and
describes why he needs a gun to protect
his family. _____

_____ 10. A congresswoman's speech to her con-
stituents explaining that harsher prison
sentences will reduce crime in their
state. _____

_____ 11. A *New York Times* news story giving an
overview on the state of U.S. prisons. _____

_____ 12. A *Psychology Today* article written by a
prominent psychologist and entitled
"Why Stiff Prison Sentences Won't Cut
Crime." _____

Periodical Bibliography

The following articles have been selected to supplement the diverse views presented in this chapter.

Richard B. Abell — "Beyond Willie Horton," *Policy Review*, Winter 1989.

Commonweal — "Carnage Control," April 7, 1989.

Congressional Digest — "The Gun Control Controversy," May 1986.

John J. DiIulio Jr. — "The Impact of Inner-City Crime," *The Public Interest*, Summer 1989.

Ted Gest — "What Should Be Done," *U.S. News & World Report*, August 22, 1988.

Meg Greenfield — "Scandal in the Courts," *Newsweek*, August 21, 1989.

Hendrik Hertzberg — "Gub Control," *The New Republic*, April 10, 1989.

Don B. Kates Jr. — "Why Gun Laws Won't Stop Shootings," *The New York Times*, February 4, 1989.

Jonathan Kozol — "The New Untouchables," *Newsweek*, special issue, Winter/Spring 1990.

Richard Lacayo — "Our Bulging Prisons," *Time*, May 29, 1989.

Robert W. Lee — "Targeting Firearms," *The New American*, August 15, 1988.

John Leo — "A Criminal Lack of Common Sense," *U.S. News & World Report*, August 21, 1989.

Andrew H. Malcolm — "Federal War on Crime Seems to See No End," *The New York Times*, May 28, 1989.

Charles Murray — "Crime in America," *National Review*, June 10, 1988.

Kent W. Perry — "Cops: We're Losing the War," *Newsweek*, March 13, 1989.

Sherry Sylvester — "Wasting Tax Dollars on Jails," *The New York Times*, July 7, 1988.

Susan Champlin Taylor — "A Promise at Risk," *Modern Maturity*, August/September 1989.

Organizations to Contact

The editors have compiled the following list of organizations that are concerned with the issues debated in this book. All of them have publications available for interested readers. The descriptions are derived from materials provided by the organizations. This list was compiled upon the date of publication. Names and phone numbers of organizations are subject to change.

American Civil Liberties Union (ACLU)
132 W. 43rd St.
New York, NY 10036
(212) 944-4064

The ACLU champions the rights set forth in the Declaration of Independence and the Constitution. It works to protect freedom of inquiry and expression and opposes suppression of individual rights, including the rights of those accused of crimes. The ACLU publishes *Civil Liberties* quarterly and *Civil Liberties Alert* monthly as well as policy statements and reports.

American Correctional Association (ACA)
8025 Laurel Lakes Court
Laurel, MD 20707
(301) 206-5100

The ACA is an organization of practitioners and academicians in the corrections field. It works to improve prison standards and supports efforts to rehabilitate criminals. The Association publishes books and the periodical *Corrections Today*.

American Rape Prevention Association (ARPA)
50 Muth Dr.
Orinda, CA 94563
(415) 254-0963

ARPA is specifically not a rape crisis center. It is an organization of men, women, and children dedicated to preventing all forms of sexual violence. It trains women and girls to use weapons against attackers and opposes the philosophy of rape crisis centers that, it believes, encourage victims to depend on law enforcement and social agencies for protection. Its publications include the monthly *ARPA Newsletter* and the quarterly *Journal of the American Rape Prevention Association*.

Cato Institute
224 Second St. SE
Washington, DC 20003
(202) 546-0200

The Institute sponsors programs designed to assist scholars and laypersons in analyzing public policy questions. It is dedicated to extending the social and economic freedoms of the capitalist system and conducts research on issues of violence, drugs, and criminal justice. In addition to the monthly publications *Policy Report* and the *Cato Journal*, the Institute has published a policy analysis paper entitled "Thinking About Drug Legalization," which maintains that drug-related crime is the result of drug prohibition.

Center to Prevent Handgun Violence
1225 Eye St. NW, Suite 1100
Washington, DC 20005
(202) 289-7319

The Center supports gun control as a way of reducing violence in America. It works to educate Americans about the responsibilities of handgun ownership. Its Legal Action Project advocates laws that would make it more difficult for mentally unstable people and criminals to own guns. It publishes fact sheets, pamphlets, and reports such as *The Killing Season: A Study of When Unintentional Handgun Shootings Among Children Occur.*

Center for Women Policy Studies (CWPS)
2000 P St. NW, Suite 508
Washington, DC 20036
(202) 872-1770

CWPS is a nonprofit corporation established in 1972 as a feminist policy research center. It believes that the economic, legal, and social status of women must be improved. It conducts research and provides information about family violence and sexual assault in which women are the victims, among other issues. The Center publishes the quarterly journal *RESPONSE to the Victimization of Women and Children.*

Committees of Correspondence, Inc.
57 Conant St.
Danvers, MA 01923
(508) 774-2641

The Committees' members include individuals and organizations that work to educate students and the community about the harms of drug use. It publishes a handbook of recommended materials to prevent drug abuse as well as the montly *Drug Abuse Newsletter.*

Crime Stoppers International (CSI)
3736 Eubank NE, Suite B4
Albuquerque, NM 87111
(505) 294-2300

CSI works to increase citizen action in crime prevention. It assists in organizing programs that offer anonymous rewards for information leading to the resolution of serious crimes. It has produced a documentary video and publishes *The Caller,* a monthly magazine.

Delancey Street Foundation
2563 Divisadero St.
San Francisco, CA 94115
(415) 563-5326

The Foundation is a residential treatment center renowned for its success in rehabilitating criminals. It distributes a variety of informational materials, including reprints of articles from *The Washington Post, San Francisco Chronicle,* and other publications.

Emerge: A Men's Counseling Service on Domestic Violence
280 Green St.
Cambridge, MA 02139
(617) 547-9870

The Emerge staff is composed of volunteers who have completed a training program on domestic violence. Emerge seeks to end male violence against women by counseling men who batter and helping them explore the causes of their violence and find alternatives. It also offers workshops and classes to educate the community on the abuse of women from a male perspective. Emerge distributes articles on abusive men and the pamphlet "What You Should Know About Your Violent Husband."

The Heritage Foundation
214 Massachusetts Ave. NE
Washington, DC 20002
(202) 546-4400

The Heritage Foundation is a conservative public policy research institute dedicated to the principles of free competitive enterprise, limited government individual liberty, and a strong national defense. It publishes the monthly *Policy Review*, the *Backgrounder* series of occasional papers, and the *Heritage Lecture* series, all of which sometimes address issues of violence and criminal justice.

National Center on Institutions and Alternatives
635 Slaters Lane, Suite G-100
Alexandria, VA 22314
(703) 684-0373

The Center is a private, nonprofit agency that promotes alternatives to prisons. It sponsors the Client Specific Planning Program, which develops alternative sentences for criminals. The Center publishes books, pamphlets, and *Augustus*, a monthly journal.

National Center for Juvenile Justice (NCJJ)
701 Forbes Ave.
Pittsburgh, PA 15219
(412) 227-6950

As the research division of the National Council of Juvenile and Family Court Judges, NCJJ collects court statistics and assesses juvenile justice services, among other duties. In addition to reports and studies, the NCJJ publishes *Today's Delinquent* and *Delinquency: U.S. Estimates of Cases Processed with Juvenile Jurisdiction*, both annually, as well as the semiannual *KINDEX: An Index to Periodical Literature Concerning Children*.

National Coalition Against Censorship (NCAC)
2 W. 64th St.
New York, NY 10023
(212) 724-1500

A coalition of forty-two religious, educational, professional, and civil rights groups, NCAC strives to promote and preserve freedom of thought and expression. It believes censorship of violent materials is dangerous because it represses intellectual and artistic freedom. NCAC maintains a library of information dealing with First Amendment issues and publishes the quarterly *Censorship News*.

National Coalition Against Domestic Violence (NCADV)
PO Box 15127
Washington, DC 20003-0127
(202) 293-8860

The Coalition is a membership organization that offers help to battered women and children. It works with federal legislators to ensure funding for battered women's shelters and programs, develops its own model programs to address these victims' needs, and operates a toll-free hot line for battered women (1-800-333-7233). In addition to its quarterly newsletter, *The Voice*, NCADV publishes a national directory of services for battered women and children and other publications, including a handbook entitled *Manual for Economic Self-Sufficiency*.

National Coalition on Television Violence (NCTV)
PO Box 2157
Champaign, IL 61825
(217) 384-1920

This educational and research organization works to decrease the amount of violence that appears on TV, in movies, and in other forms of entertainment. It sponsors seminars, maintains a speakers' bureau, and publishes educational materials. NCTV publishes *NCTV News* bimonthly.

National Council on Crime and Delinquency (NCCD)
77 Maiden Lane, Fourth Floor
San Francisco, CA 94108
(415) 956-5651

NCCD consists of criminologists and others interested in crime prevention. It conducts research and initiates policies to reduce crime and delinquency in minors. The Council supports community-based programs for crime prevention and citizen involvement in crime-control efforts. It publishes the quarterly journal *Crime and Delinquency* and reports such as *The Juvenile Court: Reclaiming the Vision* and *It's About Time: Solving America's Prison Crowding Crisis.*

National Crime Prevention Council (NCPC)
1700 K St. NW, Second Floor
Washington, DC 20006
(202) 466-NCPC

NCPC is an alliance of government agencies; businesses; and national, state, and local organizations whose goal is to promote citizens' involvement in developing safer communities and reducing crime. It sponsors an extensive advertising campaign to educate the public on crime-prevention issues, maintains a resource center and computerized information center, and conducts crime-prevention seminars. NCPC publishes a variety of pamphlets that provide tips on crime prevention; books include *Making a Difference: Young People in Community Crime Prevention* and *Preventing Crime in Urban Communities.*

National Institute of Justice (NIJ)
PO Box 6000
Rockville, MD 20850
(800) 851-3420

The NIJ is the principal research agency for the U.S. Department of Justice. The Institute serves as a clearinghouse for information on the causes, prevention, and control of crime. Among the publications available are *Alcohol Use and Criminal Behavior* and *Probing the Links Between Drugs and Crime.*

National Rifle Association of America (NRA)
Institute for Legislative Action
1600 Rhode Island Ave. NW
Washington, DC 20036
(202) 828-6330

The NRA is an organization of target shooters, hunters, gun collectors, and others interested in firearms. It has lobbied against gun-control laws and has published *A Question of Self-Defense* as well as numerous other pamphlets, position papers, and articles on gun control. Its monthly magazine is *American Rifleman.*

Parents of Murdered Children (POMC)
100 E. Eighth St., B-41
Cincinnati, OH 45202
(513) 721-5683

POMC is a self-help group of parents and other survivors seeking to help each other live through the grief of having a loved one murdered. POMC also provides information to professionals who want to know more about the problems survivors face. It publishes a newletter three times a year for members.

VERA Institute of Justice
30 E. 39th St.
New York, NY 10016
(212) 986-6910

VERA conducts research projects in criminal justice reform and takes action through various projects. The Victim/Witness Project, for example, provides services to crime victims and police prosecution witnesses. Its publications include *Further Work in Criminal Justice Reform: 1971-1976*.

Victims of Child Abuse Laws (VOCAL)
PO Box 17306
Colorado Springs, CO 80935
(800) 84-VOCAL

This support group offers advice and help for parents and others who feel they have unjustly suffered under existing child abuse laws. VOCAL works to reform these laws and to promote the prosecution of filers of false child abuse reports. It works to educate the community by providing relevant information on child abuse and victimization issues.

Victims of Crime and Leniency (VOCAL)
Box 4449
Montgomery, AL 36103
(205) 262-7197

VOCAL members believe criminals' rights are often protected at the victim's expense. It therefore works to ensure and protect victims' rights and to discourage parole and the early release of prisoners. It publishes the quarterly newsletter *VOCAL Voice*.

Bibliography of Books

Eugene Aronowitz and Robert Sussman, eds.	*Mental Health and Violence.* Canton, MA: Watson Publishing International, 1985.
Georgette Bennett	*Crimewarps: The Future of Crime in America,* 2d ed. New York: Anchor Books/Doubleday, 1989.
Douglas Besharov, ed.	*Protecting Children from Abuse and Neglect.* Springfield, IL: Charles C. Thomas Publisher, 1988.
Arnold Binder, Gilbert Geis, and Dickson Bruce	*Juvenile Delinquency: Historical, Cultural, Legal Perspectives.* New York: Macmillan Publishing Company, 1988.
Frank G. Bolton, Larry Morris, and Ann E. MacEachron	*Males at Risk: The Other Side of Child Sexual Abuse.* Newbury Park, CA: Sage Publications, 1989.
John A. Calhoun	*Violence, Youth, and a Way Out.* Washington, DC: National Crime Prevention Council, 1989.
Robert S. Clark	*Deadly Force: The Lure of Violence.* Springfield, IL: Charles C. Thomas Publisher, 1988.
Gary Collins	*Counseling for Family Violence and Abuse.* Irving, TX: Word Inc., 1987.
John Crewdson	*By Silence Betrayed: Sexual Abuse of Children in America.* Boston: Little, Brown and Company, 1988.
Lynn A. Curtis, ed.	*American Violence & Public Policy.* New Haven, CT: Yale University Press, 1985.
William DeJong	*Arresting the Demand for Drugs.* Washington, DC: National Institute of Justice, 1987.
John Demos	*Past, Present, and Personal: The Family and the Life Course in American History.* New York: Oxford University Press, 1986.
Ralph Adam Fine	*Escape of the Guilty.* New York: Dodd, Mead & Company, 1986.
Mark S. Fleisher	*Warehousing Violence.* Newbury Park, CA: Sage Publications, 1989.
Seymour Gelber	*Hard-Core Delinquents.* Tuscaloosa, AL: The University of Alabama Press, 1988.
Richard J. Gelles and Murray A. Straus	*Intimate Violence.* New York: Simon & Schuster, 1988.
Joseph Goldstein, Anna Freud, and Albert Solnit	*Before the Best Interests of the Child.* New York: The Free Press, 1979.
Linda Gordon	*Heroes of Their Own Lives: The Politics and History of Family Violence.* New York: Viking Press, 1988.
Margaret T. Gordon and Stephanie Riger	*The Female Fear.* New York: The Free Press, 1989.
Guy Gugliotta and Jeff Leen	*Kings of Cocaine.* New York: Simon & Schuster, 1989.

Ted Robert Gurr, ed.	*Violence in America,* vols. 1 and 2. Newbury Park, CA: Sage Publications, 1989.
Ronald Hamowy, ed.	*Dealing with Drugs: Consequences of Government Control.* Lexington, MA: Lexington Books, 1988.
Jalna Hanmer and Mary Maynard	*Women, Violence, and Social Control.* Atlantic Highlands, NJ: Humanities Press, 1987.
Richard A. Hawley	*Think About Drugs and Society.* New York: Walker and Company, 1988.
Ronald M. Holmes and James DeBurger	*Serial Murder.* Newbury Park, CA: Sage Publications, 1988.
Gerald T. Hotaling, David Finkelhor, John T. Kirkpatrick, and Murray A. Straus, eds.	*Family Abuse and Its Consequences.* Newbury Park, CA: Sage Publications, 1988.
James A. Inciardi	*The War on Drugs: Heroin, Cocaine, Crime, and Public Policy.* Palo Alto, CA: Mayfield Publishing Co., 1986.
Don B. Kates Jr., ed.	*Firearms and Violence.* Cambridge, MA: Ballinger Publishing Company, 1984.
Jack Katz	*Seductions of Crime: Moral and Sensual Attractions in Doing Evil.* New York: Basic Books, 1988.
Rita Kramer	*At a Tender Age: Violent Youth and Juvenile Justice.* New York: Henry Holt and Company, 1988.
Jack Levin and James Alan Fox	*Mass Murder: America's Growing Menace.* New York: Plenum Press, 1985.
Elliott Leyton	*Compulsive Killers: The Story of Modern Multiple Murder.* Washington Square, NY: New York University Press, 1986.
Mary Lystad, ed.	*Violence in the Home.* New York: Brunner/Mazel, 1986.
Roger D. McGrath	*Gunfighters, Highwaymen & Vigilantes: Violence on the Frontier.* Berkeley: University of California Press, 1984.
Patrick B. McGuigan and Jon S. Pascale, eds.	*Crime and Punishment in Modern America.* Washington, DC: The Free Congress Foundation, 1986.
Ken Magid and Carole A. McKelvey	*High Risk.* New York: Bantam Books, 1987.
Charles Manson, as told to Nuel Emmons	*Manson in His Own Words.* New York: Grove Press, 1986.
Martin Mawyer	*Silent Shame.* Westchester, IL: Crossway/Good News Publisher, 1987.
Stephen G. Michaud	*The Only Living Witness.* New York: New American Library, 1989.
Alice Miller	*For Your Own Good: Hidden Cruelty in Child-Rearing and the Roots of Violence.* New York: Farrar Straus Giroux, 1983.
Ginny NiCarthy	*Getting Free: A Handbook for Women in Abusive Relationships,* 2d ed. Seattle: Seal Press, 1986.

Joel Norris	*Serial Killers.* New York: Anchor Books/Doubleday, 1988.
Robert K. Ressler, Ann W. Burgess, and John E. Douglas	*Sexual Homicide: Patterns and Motives.* Lexington, MA: Lexington Books, 1988.
Stanton E. Samenow	*Before It's Too Late: Why Some Kids Get in Trouble and What Parents Can Do About It.* New York: Times Books, 1989.
Stanton E. Samenow	*Inside the Criminal Mind.* New York: Times Books, 1984.
Parviz Saney	*Crime and Culture in America.* Westport, CT: Greenwood Press, 1986.
Susan Schechter	*Women and Male Violence.* Boston: South End Press, 1982.
Ira M. Schwartz	*(In) Justice for Juveniles.* Lexington, MA: Lexington Books, 1989.
Charles H. Shireman and Frederic G. Reamer	*Rehabilitating Juvenile Justice.* New York: Columbia University Press, 1986.
Margaret C. Simms and Samuel L. Myers Jr., eds.	*The Economics of Race and Crime.* New Brunswick, NJ: Transaction Books, 1988.
Irving J. Sloan	*Our Violent Past: An American Chronicle.* New York: Random House, 1970.
Kay Marshall Strom	*In the Name of Submission: A Painful Look at Wife Battering.* Portland, OR: Multnomah Press, 1986.
Maury Terry	*The Ultimate Evil: An Investigation into America's Most Dangerous Satanic Cult.* Garden City, NY: A Dolphin Book/Doubleday, 1987.
Lenore E. Walker	*Terrifying Love.* New York: Harper & Row, 1989.
Thomas W. Wedge with Robert L. Powers	*The Satan Hunter.* Canton, OH: Daring Books, 1988.
Neil Alan Weiner and Marvin E. Wolfgang, eds.	*Pathways to Criminal Violence.* Newbury Park, CA: Sage Publications, 1989.
Neil Alan Weiner and Marvin E. Wolfgang, eds.	*Violent Crime, Violent Criminals.* Newbury Park, CA: Sage Publications, 1989.
Terry Williams	*The Cocaine Kids: An Inside Story of a Teenage Drug Ring.* Reading, MA: Addison-Wesley Publishing Company, 1989.
Earl D. Wilson	*A Silence to Be Broken: Hope for Those Caught in the Web of Incest.* Portland, OR: Multnomah Press, 1986.
Marvin E. Wolfgang, R.M. Figlio, and T. Sellin	*Delinquency in a Birth Cohort.* Chicago: University of Chicago Press, 1972.
James D. Wright and Peter H. Rossi	*Armed and Considered Dangerous.* Hawthorne, NY: Aldine Publishing Co., 1986.
Kersti Yllö and Michele Bograd	*Feminist Perspectives on Wife Abuse.* Newbury Park, CA: Sage Publications, 1988.
Franklin E. Zimring and Gordon Hawkins	*The Citizen's Guide to Gun Control.* New York: Macmillan Publishing Company, 1987.

Index

288